The Amalgamation Waltz

The Amalgamation Waltz

Race, Performance, and the Ruses of Memory

Tavia Nyong'o

University of Minnesota Press   Minneapolis / London

The University of Minnesota Press gratefully acknowledges the work of Roderick A. Ferguson, editorial consultant, on this project.

Published by the University of Minnesota Press
111 Third Avenue South, Suite 290
Minneapolis, MN 55401-2520
http://www.upress.umn.edu

Library of Congress Cataloging-in-Publication Data

Nyong'o, Tavia Amolo Ochieng'.
    The amalgamation waltz : race, performance, and the ruses of memory / Tavia Nyong'o.
        p.   cm.
    Includes bibliographical references and index.
    ISBN 978-0-8166-5612-7 (hc : alk. paper) — ISBN 978-0-8166-5613-4 (pb : alk. paper)
    1. United States—Race relations.   2. Miscegenation—United States—History.   3. African Americans—History.   4. Racially mixed people—United States—History.   5. Racism—United States—History.   6. Performative (Philosophy).   7. Collective memory—United States—History.   8. United States—Race relations—Political aspects.   9. Nationalism—United States—History.   10. National characteristics, American—History.   I. Title.
    E184.A1O25 2009
    305.800973—dc22
                                                                    2009001191

Printed in the United States of America on acid-free paper

The University of Minnesota is an equal-opportunity educator and employer.

15 14 13 12 11 10 09   10 9 8 7 6 5 4 3 2 1

Contents

Introduction: Antebellum Genealogies of the Hybrid Future

In the notorious 1802 exposé of Thomas Jefferson's sexual relationship with his wife's enslaved half-sister, Sally Hemings, James Callender derisively referred to Hemings's son Tom as "our little mulatto president."[1] For much of subsequent American history, the idea of a black president has remained a premise for similarly ribald jokes. As national surrogate and leader of the free world, the U.S. president has traditionally stood for everything that blackness was not: commanding, legitimate, virtuous, white. But as the nation entered the new millennium, an inarticulate desire to see the color line subside along with the twentieth century created an opening for the upstart presidential aspirations of the son of a Kenyan goatherder. Widely admired in the wake of "The Audacity of Hope," his keynote address to the Democratic Party's national convention in 2004, Senator Barack Obama of Illinois attracted widespread interest and support when he declared his presidential intentions two years later. In a departure from previous minority candidates, Obama was not dismissed as running a symbolic, shadow campaign. A black politician who could arouse enthusiasm among white voters, Obama promised to turn a page by making blackness secondary to Americanness. In the spiritual idiom of American politics, Obama was a candidate who would *transcend* race. The most famous line from his convention speech, echoed in the historic victory speech he gave four years later, put it well. In a canny update of the national motto, *E pluribus unum,* Obama intoned, "There is not a Black America and a White America and Latino America and Asian America—there's the United States of America."[2]

The rapturous embrace of a black politician who would loudly proclaim a sentiment many whites furtively harbored—that a robust sense of minority or racial identity was not fully compatible with being a proud American—met a range of responses from the ranks of the established black intelligentsia. Perhaps the most surprising came from black conservatives, a group who might have been expected to champion Obama's formula for race-transcending patriotism. In separate editorials, Stanley Crouch and Debra Dickerson both opined against Obama's blackness, derisively pointing out his mixed-race heritage, his white familial connections, his East rather then West African looks, and most of all, the absence of any slavery in his family history. "Black," Dickerson flatly declared, "in our political and social reality, means those descended from West African slaves." If Obama's appeal could transcend race, it was not because of the content of his character, but because of his hybrid background. "Other than color," Crouch argued, "Obama did not—does not—share a heritage with the majority of black Americans, who are descendants of plantation slaves."[3]

Obama's actual racial heritage, these critics charged, was obscured by a neologism that had been championed by the race's previous major presidential aspirant, Rev. Jesse Jackson. In the 1980s, Jackson had led a campaign for the term *African American* to replace *black, Negro,* and *colored* in the long line of names chosen to slough off the stigma that prior ones had accumulated. *African American* was intended to express a hyphenated Americanness fully equal to the others that had been recuperated since the ethnic revival of the 1970s. But *African American* did not fully anticipate the resonance that newcomers with a different stake in African ancestry might also hear in that symmetry. Obama clearly was one. Indeed, what designation could be more appropriate for him, the child of an African and an American? But while technically African American, to his naysayers Obama was so only through linguistic sleight of hand, one that permitted him to steal a designation from those to whom it properly belonged. Dickerson described him to a television presenter as "an *African* African American," with the problematic word anxiously repeated.[4] For his part, Crouch attacked "naive ideas coming out of Pan-Africanism" as "the root of the confusion" over Obama. Read in light of a proper reverence for American heritage and ancestry, Obama was not, he assured his readers, "black like me." "If we then end up with him as our first black President," Crouch concluded, "he will have come into the White House through a side door."[5]

So cavalier a usurpation of the word *black* for the United States—a nation whose "political and social reality" was peremptorily deemed the only one that mattered—is typical of an attachment displayed by Americans of varied race, ethnicity, and political stripe to our "national Thing." More than just a love of country, the national Thing is a powerful force shaping the nation as the source of our enjoyment. The national Thing "appears as what gives plenitude and vivacity to our life," Slavoj Žižek writes, "and yet the only way we can determine it is by resorting to different versions of the same empty tautology." The black Canadian scholar Rinaldo Walcott has cited Žižek in his account of the tendency to assign global applicability to analyses derived from the specifics of the U.S. racial formation.[6] Although U.S. born, Obama was trapped in such a tautological exclusion from African Americanness. He just was not what was meant by the term, according to some, and all the reasons they offered for this exclusion seemed circular. Such rejection illustrates how enjoyment of the national Thing can lead to the paranoid suspicion of the "other" who might steal that enjoyment from us, cuckolding us by sneaking in "through a side door." And it also reflects a libidinal attachment to the nation subtending what are ordinarily understood to be clearly articulated ideological and political differences.

Such suspicious possessiveness of national enjoyment can extend even to slavery. Paradoxically transmuted from a crime against humanity into the heritage of black Americans, in the language of these critics, slavery became a legacy to be zealously guarded against interlopers. Obama skeptics held to tautological definitions of whose slavery counted—*just* that which occurred within the confines of the present-day United States, *just* that which involved slaves from West Africa, *just* that which occurred on plantations—as a kind of shield against Obama's uncanny presence. And no wonder. Raised in Hawaii and Indonesia, bearing an Islamic first name and a Luo surname, Ivy League educated and a best-selling author, Obama embodied precisely the cosmopolitan hybridity against which an obdurate blackness has so often been invidiously contrasted. To the extent that postnational, postcolonial mulattos like Obama were welcomed by a predominantly white American public, they threatened to displace the authentically black in the national imaginary, gaining in the process not only the rewards accorded other newcomers to the melting pot but the superadded benefit of salving the conscience of white Americans, who would be more committed to racial justice if only it were easier.

By embracing mixed-race African Americans who lack the baggage of slavery, these critics held, white America got off far too easily. But the national Thing is not always disrupted by such a conviction that racial justice crawls crabwise in America. Crouch and Dickerson, as well as those who expressed more polite but no less doubting reservations about Obama's racial bona fides, found themselves tethered to the nation through their rejection of it. Rejecting American assimilation and defending America against arriviste impostors amounted to remarkably the same thing insofar as both took on the exclusionary topology of an imagined community threatened on all sides by infiltration. Ironically, such suspicious protectiveness was also observed by Obama's own campaign rhetoric in its attempts to fit into the national Thing. This rhetoric regularly elided his cosmopolitan background in order to reweave his personal story into a U.S.-specific narrative of slavery, segregation, and civil rights. No less than his conservative critics did Obama present the U.S. nation as a horizon of sacrifice and enjoyment (even to the extent of implying that his America was also endangered by unnamed others from whom, as the subtitle of his best seller suggests, the American dream must be "reclaimed"). The national Thing, and the fear of the other who might deprive us of it, underlay the disagreement over the interpretation of Obama's heritage, which was read by both sides always in relation to the U.S. nation-state.

A legitimate and much-belated discussion of the fate of the color line in the twenty-first century thus found itself immediately derailed into the biopolitical question of who counts as black in America. Both sides reasserted the United States as the moral and political horizon of its representative bodies. But a final irony unsettled both Obama's mantling of himself in the "race man" effigy and his conservative critics' riposte that slavery was their exclusive legacy. That irony was the genealogical discovery, announced in early 2007, that Obama indeed possessed a historical connection to the U.S. south: on the slave*holding* side. The discovery of Obama's white slaveholding ancestors in antebellum Kentucky provided the sought-for link to American memory, suggesting that he was indeed "of one blood" with other African Americans who, like the descendants of Sally

Hemings, share an admixture of European ancestry courtesy of the peculiar institution. So whiteness supplied the subterranean link between blackness "East" and "West." Via the unlikely bridge of so-called miscegenation, Obama was finally located in relation to the primal scene of American racism.[7]

Even more startling than this discovery, however, was how Obama's campaign officially responded to it. In a classic ruse, his handlers heralded racial mixture as the alchemy through which the storm and stress of the American racial melodrama was to be brilliantly transmuted into bright dreams for the future. Obama's biracial heritage was, after all, what made him "representative of America." As a spokesman told the press: "It is a true measure of progress that the descendant of a slave owner would come to marry a student from Kenya and produce a son who would grow up to be a candidate for president of the United States."[8] In a single sound bite, the long history of sex across the color line—a history utterly commingled with the history of Africans in America, one that structured the slave relation from its very beginnings, one that shaped the subsequent, torturous logic of Jim Crow, one that underpins the vexed and enduring dynamic of color consciousness within the black population—was magically transmogrified into a simple story of redemption in which a single marriage across the color line redeemed a heritage of slavery. Racism was spellbound before the floating, public proscenium of marriage.[9] Through that proscenium, the nation could transform its sordid and messy heritage into an ever-more robust version of its foundational myth.

Under such circumstances, can it ever be said that racial hybridity subverts the national Thing? Does miscegenation in fact corrode white supremacy? Or does the conjugal union of the races work as a depoliticizing catchall, preempting a more critical engagement with the traumas of the American past? The rising multiracial movement, as well as its academic interlocutor, critical mixed-race studies, has tended to split the difference on these questions, claiming hybridity both as the biopolitical overcoming of centuries of racial domination in the United States and, simultaneously, as the culmination of American integrationist values. Americanism, that is to say, becomes its own remedy. But such a position is helplessly in thrall to the empty tautologies of the national Thing. It accommodates hybridity to an official teleology that is forever reducing the many to the one. Such a politics hardly inspires hope for hybridity's subversive potential.

Critics of the multiracial movement have pointed out how dreams of "biological integration" collude with a status quo structured in racial dominance. This is especially clear when seen in hemispheric perspective, what with tropes of *mestizaje* and *blanqueamiento* prevailing elsewhere in the Americas, tropes that often depoliticize blackness through official denials of its enduring presence. Critics also remain concerned with a slippage multiracial discourse effects between race and racism. Barbara Fields has called this substitution "the great evasion of American historical literature, as of American history itself."[10] And Jennifer Brody, at the end of a review essay on the interconnections of race, mixture, and memory, quotes a slogan from "a moving Washington, DC, bus": "Race is a fiction. Racism is real."[11] Racism is the writing on the wall, such critics argue, but colorblind America is also illiterate.

The anxiety over how easily hybridity causes us to slip between race and racism is often articulated as a concern with historical memory. Skeptics worry that a yearning for a racial transcendence will lead us to neglect the inequalities that form our historical inheritance. If the "audacity of hope" is thus routinely countered with the "burden of history" in contemporary debates over the significance of racial mixture, then these debates suggest the need to pursue much more rigorously than has yet been attempted the underlying relationships among hybridity, heritage, and history.

A clean distinction between race and racism, whether sought through appeals to historical memory or some other means, usually proves evasive. If race is an evasion and a fiction, it is an eminently political one; that is, it is collectively experienced and enacted. We must do far more than expose race's lack of scientific basis to interrupt its efficacy. And we must attend to the ways in which the dream of getting beyond race is, ironically, embedded in the genealogy of the race concept in ways that are not always immediately apparent. The election of Barack Obama certainly stoked a national fantasy of transcending race, or at least, with escaping the divisive and bad feelings that dwelling on racial injustice seems to cause. But rather than use this observation to scapegoat hybridity, we should turn our interrogatory energies toward the national Thing itself. It is the desire for the vindication of national enjoyment, I contend, much more than a desire for hybridity per se, that we need to remain critically vigilant of. Žižek notes that due to its tautological nature and its absence of any specific positive content, the national Thing cannot be directly rebutted. Under certain conditions, however, the very absence and void it occupies can become momentarily visible, temporarily destabilizing the processes by which subjects participate in imagined community. Against hybridity's appropriation by this imagined community, I argue that it can produce such uncanny moments that subvert the national Thing. Under what circumstances it may do so is my concern throughout this book.

   If hybridity is persistently figured in terms of what Lee Edelman has called "reproductive futurity," it is also figured through the trope of a mongrel past.[12] Throughout the book, I unpack the relation between the hybrid future and this mongrel past. If the former selects hybridity as a panacea, the latter presents hybridity as a historical alternative to the overly burdened racial identities bequeathed us by slavery, segregation, and ghettoization. Rather than being in contrast or opposed, the two figures often work in tandem insofar as past and future equally leverage a critique of the present. It is in order to address this supplementarity between history and futurity that I have adopted the specific structure of this book. It moves chronologically through four sequential historical flashpoints. At the same time, my argument is recursive in structure, insisting upon the performativity of each of those moments, by which I mean their ongoing purchase upon the indexical present, their continuous "presenting [of] the past," as historian Greg Dening puts it.[13] My method employs the archive as a practice of "countermemory" but without the pretense of using it to build a complete or coherent historical narrative.[14] The form of hybrid and performative historiography I have adopted is intended to subvert the expected hermeneutic circle of traditional archival research, interpretation, and explication. I seek to both assert and show the performative effects of history rather than simply to add to the weight of history's pedagogy.

Chapter 1, "The Mirror of Liberty: Constituent Power and the American Mongrel," considers the archive of visual and performance culture surrounding the protorevolutionary uprising leading to the Boston Massacre of 1770 and the figure of Crispus Attucks at its center. Drawing on the critical scholarship of constituent power, I investigate the representational capture of Attucks's racial embodiment. I show how performative instatements of his body as black or mulatto, patriot or insurrectionary, native American or circum-Atlantic, alike reflect a fundamental tension between an established state of affairs and the revolutionary process out of which that state is established and upon which its continuance is founded. Integrationist historians have seen Attucks as a black patriot of the American Revolution. Historians of the mongrel past have seen Attucks as representing the kind of mixed subject that has become lost to modern memory as racial categories have hardened. I suggest rather that the hybridity Attucks instates interrupts the temporality of the nation precisely by continuously raising the contested terms of its founding.

Chapter 2, "In Night's Eye: Amalgamation, Respectability, and Shame," turns to the emergence of black abolitionism into public visibility in the 1830s. I focus on the intersection between black protest culture in the north and the white moral panic over the prospective "amalgamation" of the races that rose up in reaction. Most historians have read this moral panic in straightforwardly ideological terms, considering it a deliberate ruse to distract from questions of equality.[15] They have mostly assumed that black activists shared this straightforward understanding of the scare. While not rejecting this explanation entirely, I show how partial it is by exploring the affective consequences of the sexual rhetoric of the amalgamation panic, consequences I link, through Foucault's concept of biopolitics, to racial governmentality. Whereas historians of black respectability tend to emphasize the real social conditions out of which respectability as a strategy emerged, this chapter highlights the virtual preconditions out of which an antebellum black public sphere was imagined, precisely in terms policed by the honor, shame, and continence that responding to the amalgamation panic required. I close the chapter by dwelling on one particularly suggestive case in which negotiating the social conditions of antiblack racism demanded tactics that embraced rather than rejected shame as a transformational resource for attaining respect and dignity.

Chapter 3, "Minstrel Trouble: Racial Travesty in the Circum-Atlantic Fold," takes up another response to the emergence into popular consciousness of the contradictions between slavery and freedom: blackface minstrelsy. Shifting forward into the antebellum decade, I problematize the increasingly orthodox division of minstrelsy into an early radical phase followed by its co-optation by commercial and middle-class interests by the 1850s. I argue that this periodization merely transposes the desire for mongrel authenticity onto the mythic origins of a popular style. It misses the complex responses that black activists and abolitionists had to the genre, almost from its beginning, responses that mirror but also extend the concerns over respectability that animate black responses to the amalgamation panic. Focusing in particular on Frederick Douglass, who is often quoted as a straightforward critic of blackface minstrels, I show how his response to the form must be set within the context of his own circum-Atlantic identifications with the poetry and songs of Robert Burns and with the romantic notion of a national culture more generally. Douglass's engagement with the hybridity of minstrelsy as a cultural form, I argue, was itself split by an ambivalent reaction against U.S. nationalism. Rather than decide the question of whether or not minstrelsy offers U.S. popular culture a usable past, I look to Douglass's response as a historical resource that redirects our attention to a critique of the national popular.

Chapter 4, "Carnivalizing Time: Decoding the Racial Past in Art and Installation," moves into the present to consider efforts in contemporary art and museum installation to pedagogize the antebellum and civil war periods. Taking up the popular pedagogical tropes of historical and embodied memory, I invert the traditional distinction between textual archives and embodied memories by examining collective memory as a "texted" or encoded structure, one prone to the same glitches and errors of transmission as the fallible, falsifiable archive. I link these glitches and mistakes of memory with the conviction of antebellum black activists that justice would come within a racist society only "by mistake," that is, as an unintended, uncaused event rather than an organic and predictable development, thereby moving beyond a corrective or perfectible construction of the nation in which justice is perpetually and pedagogically deferred. By investigating how this black archive presents the past countermnemonically, I thicken my engagement with the temporal dimensions of imagined community, which is what I ultimately consider the discourses of the hybrid future and the mongrel past to engage.

Performance and the Miscegenation of Time

While it is conventional to distinguish the United States from the rest of the hemisphere in terms of its more vigorous rejection of race mixing, I depend upon different axioms in *The Amalgamation Waltz*. American national fantasy, I argue, does not so much dismiss as *defer* racial hybridity, endowing it with the peculiar privilege and power of a horizon, one at which we never quite arrive. This faith in a national transcendence of race is actually quite venerable, not just the effect of recent pre- and postmillennial effusions. It was already visible, for instance, during the antebellum struggle to abolish slavery. Because of this venerable historical provenance, I spend the bulk of this book in a period where, it might be imagined initially, no discourse of racial transcendence at all could have existed. Our belief in the novelty of our contemporary moment is only a repression of our awareness of the history of such deferrals. Insofar as race has successfully been naturalized as a category, so will the story of racial transcendence, as its secret sharer, be necessarily obscure. Bringing this dynamic to light requires a sensitivity to the philosophy of history insofar as temporality is not simply the neutral medium within which structures like "heritage" and "race" appear but an effect that their deployment in thought and action produces.[16]

Race as a human attribute was originally posited to demarcate the pure blood of elites from their lessers. Over the course of time, however, race came to be seen in many cases as the property of those against whom the idea was originally employed to discriminate. It was seized and refigured but never under easy or equal conditions and always with ambiguous consequences.[17] The nineteenth-century "white race" around which U.S. democracy was erected became the twentieth century's "race problem" or "race question," the problematic object of which was rarely in doubt. As is well known, groups now thought of as white—Jews, Irish, Italians—were described in the nineteenth century as races. Other groups—Chicanos most prominently—have historically been granted an official whiteness firmly denied them by their fellow "whites."[18] The attempt to distinguish race from ethnicity in order to retain the empirical validity of the latter has fallen into ruins, and most thoughtful scholars now recognize that there is no positivist refuge from the obligation to think both terms critically. Critical race studies, like critical American studies, is continually engaged in the critique of its own object of analysis.

A critical approach to race should encompass both the history of racial ideas and the forms of historicity and temporality embedded in those ideas and practices. While race as a pseudoscientific ideology proposes to telescope history into biological destiny, its efficacy has always depended on obscuring its own mixed lineage, entanglements, and reversals.[19] Race-thinking may serve as the great American evasion, but it has also at times proved dissonant to national memory. The American intellectual contribution to scientific racism, for instance, is well documented but usually ignored. Nazi

Germany is our idea of a racial state; our preferred self-image is of a nation founded in liberty but unfortunately burdened with a peculiar institution it has been our genius to destroy. As Stuart Hall notes, heritage is "bound into the meaning of the nation through a double inscription," seen as at once the "distilled essence" of the nation which "emerged at the very moment of its origin" and the "ongoing project" of a "constant reconstruction" of that mythic origin.[20] Heritage, with its positive and patriarchal overtones, has been seen as incompatible with a robust recognition of either the crimes committed in the name of race or the crimes of race itself as an invidious difference, luring those it disadvantages with the ruse of recognition. For this reason, extending the concept of heritage to race has always had unpredictable effects. Baseless in terms of the very dimension it claims to endow with destiny and meaning, race is exposed anew in its inability to adequately resolve such apparently basic questions as that of Obama's "racial heritage." In that pat phrase, a number of contradictions are neatly evaded.

Race is a theory of history, so exposing its historicity will trouble its foundations and foreground its assumptions regarding time and temporality. The "miscegenation of time" is the evocative name James Kinney gives to the style of William Faulkner's fragmented novel of crossed southern bloodlines, *Go Down, Moses*.[21] This phrase suggests that the complexity of the relation between hybridity and memory defies representation within the "homogenous, empty time" that Walter Benjamin associates with history, time that Benedict Anderson and Homi Bhabha further associate with the nation.[22] Given Bhabha's contributions to postcolonial and critical race studies, his work has also served as a lightning rod for debates about hybridity.[23] The implication in some of these debates that his work represents an uncritical celebration of hybridity mistakes, I believe, the radical edge that reading it in relation to Benjamin's melancholic historicism might give it. Benjamin's break with the homogenous, empty time of nineteenth-century historiography and his conviction that every document of civilization is also a document of barbarism are registered, I warrant, in Bhabha's account of the disjunctive temporality of hybridity. I draw upon both Bhabha's and Anderson's ideas quite extensively in thinking further about the miscegenation of time.

Anderson describes how, during the nineteenth century, the daily newspaper and the realist novel helped imagine the simultaneity of lives lived in national community. This linear and cumulative time, Bhabha responds, was a time divided against itself. "It must be stressed," Bhabha wrote, "that the narrative of the imagined community is constructed from two incommensurable temporalities of meaning that threaten its coherence."[24] Bhabha accounts for this disjunctive temporality through the interplay of the "pedagogic" and the "performative." The pedagogic, realist form upon which both the nation-state and its fantasy of homogenous, empty time rest is unsettled by performative tactics that seize upon national narratives with a disruptive immediacy, tactics that are filled with the presence of the now and that thereby call the bluff of the ruse of postponement. Pedagogic time is a time of training, waiting, and indefinite deferral. It is life lived in the antechamber of history. The performative moment, by contrast, is characterized by what Bhabha specifies as a "repetitious, recursive strategy," one that refuses gradualism and the reproduction of docile, useful bodies.

Bhabha associates with hybridity both this latter, performative moment and the doubled temporality within which it is embedded. His use of this term, as commentators such as Robert Young have noted, signifies and at the same time signifies *upon* hybridity's racial prehistory. Confronting the question of how hybridity challenges "the social ordering of symbols," Bhabha identifies "the historical movement of hybridity as camouflage, as a contesting, antagonistic agency functioning in the time-lag of sign/symbol, which is a space in-between the rules of engagement."[25] Through imagery of both war and performance, Bhabha associates hybridity with motion and movement, at the same time locating its agency in the friction between the pedagogic and performative, in the no-man's land between warring camps. At the same time as it is located in this nonlocation, hybridity is less a socially instantiated thing than a process, less a noun than a verb.

Hybridity haunts the dreams of racial purity, then, but not solely as its structural foil. Certainly the existence of racial "hybrids" infuriates racists, as demonstrated by the efforts of nineteenth-century scientists to prove that mulattos were infertile and would naturally die out. But hybridity also interrupts the ability of race to narrativize time. I find a suggestive emblem of such disjunctive or hybrid temporality in "the miscegenation of time," a phrase from which the stain of racialist thinking can never be fully removed. The hybridization of genre implied in the miscegenation of time entails not simply the splicing together of different forms but the encounter of genre with its law and therein its indeterminacy. Exposing fictions of race and progress, hybridity unsettles collective and corporeal memory.

Reading Kinney's formulation in both directions—the miscegenation of time, the time of miscegenation—generates new and provocative questions. When is the time, or *event,* of miscegenation? Jared Sexton suggests we invert the usual order in which we imagine the sociogenesis of racial categories and "posit miscegenation as something theoretically prior" to the racialization it is typically seen to unsettle. What if there is first, he asks, "the event of miscegenation, and then, in a moment of retroactivity or capture, there is racialised difference?"[26] If this is the case, then how can we identify and expose the form that miscegenation gives to time, the form, precisely, of bloodlines, interfertility, sexuality, and kinship? These questions suggest that we seek not to abandon hybridity but to historicize it.

Bhabha's use of performativity draws upon the speech-act theory developed by J. L. Austin, Jacques Derrida, Shoshana Felman, Judith Butler, and Eve Kosofsky Sedgwick.[27] This literature exploits the slippage between reality and artifice, between saying and doing, which the word *performance* keeps perpetually and productively in play. Performance, in its most generic sense of an actual as opposed to a potential doing, animates my own inquiry into hybridity and memory. I consider the feedback between the performed and the potential to be a historical matter, as mattering to history whenever it is taken up in and as memory—that is to say, whenever the performed–potential dyad folds back upon itself in acts of cultural recall. I treat memory here not simply as an individual experience but as a collective and participatory phenomenon occurring within "the social frameworks of memory." These frameworks enable a process by which, in Maurice Halbwachs's illuminating turn of phrase, memories "are recalled to me externally."[28] The external, intersubjective, and embodied aspects of social remembering are critical to the ways in which I make use of performance and performativity in this study.

Performance is crucial to any accounting for the antinomies of race and slavery in American heritage, of the ironies and complicities of mixtures ethnoracial and otherwise, and of the chances and hazards of critical American studies in the twenty-first century. Performance—as restored or "twice behaved" behavior—mediates between collective memory and the new, potential, and virtual.[29] Its importance to politics cannot be ignored insofar as social action is organized around symbols, gestures, effigies, and dramatic narratives.[30] At the same time as the new masks the old, the inverse, in which the old masks the new, is also a critical component of historical memory. Marx recognized as much when he observed that "tradition from all the dead generations weighs like a nightmare upon the brain of the living."[31] Performance attunes us to this dramaturgy of newness draped in hallowed tradition and tradition masquerading as novelty. In the work of performance historians like Greg Dening and Joseph Roach, these complex acts of historical substitution and surrogation in performance come to the fore.[32] They help us track the time lag of hybrid agency.

Anxiety has become a bit of an explanatory catchall in certain historical circles, but a robust usage of the term, drawing upon Freud's theory of anxiety as signal, is helpful in accounting for the social effects of hybrid agency.[33] Insofar as hybridity's potential, what it *might* do, has been a longstanding object of concern and fascination, performance was a means of concretizing it. In the jargon of the nineteenth century, for this reason, race mixing was often referred to by its critics as *practical* amalgamation. This insistence on the *practice* of race mixing reflected a conviction that egalitarian possibilities entertained in thought would prove unendurable when actually experienced. A double bind followed, however, from such a concurrent need to assert undesirability through demonstration. Ideology demanded the continuous staging of the officially prohibited, as scholars such as Elise Lemire, Karen Woods Weierman, and Eva Saks have shown.[34] The result was a constant reenactment of the impossible, a loquacious speaking of the unspeakable, and a continual reduction to practice of the impractical heresy of amalgamation.

Consider just one antebellum example, the pseudonymously published *A Sojourn in the City of Amalgamation*.[35] Pathologically fearful of both abolition and amalgamation, this obscene novel obsessively detailed the dystopic contours of a racially egalitarian society to come, one in which mixed marriages are forced upon helpless whites, who must employ a variety of sci-fi prostheses to withstand the abominable odor of their black spouses. Its author, Jerome B. Holgate, as Elise Lemire has discovered, was also a founding figure in American family genealogy (an archival find almost too good to be true).[36] Holgate helped launch the obsessive pursuit of family roots as the temporally displaced management of the racially hybrid future. And he somatized both pursuits in ways that were both depressingly uncreative (black people smell, are loud, etc.) and fascinatingly baroque. His scatological depictions of hybridity as a future made manageable only by an extensible technological array of waste management services provides confirmation, as Jennifer Brody has reminded us, that the word *purity* is etymologically linked to shit.[37] In his fictional and factual pursuits, we see how the event of miscegenation, even when displaced into a dystopic future, logically precedes the anxious pursuit of racial whiteness, as Sexton suggests it might.

Emphasizing the service of performance as ambivalent actualization of a troubling potential provides an important link to the extensive ethnographic literature on inversion, carnival, and masking. Anthropologists have long observed the paradoxical powers of transgression and inversion in performance. Hybridity is both an overabundant and undertheorized keyword in this literature, at once a zoomorphic signifier and a critical, antihumanistic sign. Pnina Werbner states the problem succinctly in the introduction to the edited volume *Debating Cultural Hybridity*. Dismissing as "inadequate" the "old modernist insights into the nature of liminality, the place and time of betwixt-and-between, of carnival, rituals of rebellion and rites of cosmic renewal, or of boundary-crossing pangolins, ritual clowns, witches and abominable swine," Werbner calls for "a broader theoretical framework which aims to resolve the puzzle of how cultural hybridity manages to be both transgressive and normal, and why it is experienced as dangerous, difficult or revitalising despite its quotidian normalcy."[38] This query goes to the heart of the dynamic fostered by the rise of Barack Obama and a whole host other of millennial hybrids. How is it that hybridity evokes the simultaneous suspicion that it is entirely new and just more of the same? That it is what has always already been going on, and that it represents the apocalyptic collapse of a social order structured in racial dominance? These questions suggest that the broader theoretical framework Werbner calls for must include an exploration of history, memory, and what Fredric Jameson calls the political unconscious.[39]

Werbner's work foregrounds both affect and collective memory as key determinants in shaping social responses to hybridity, drawing on Mikhail Bakhtin's distinction between conscious (or "intentional") and unconscious ("organic") hybridization in order to do so.[40] The unconscious/conscious distinction she borrows from Bakhtin potentially opens out questions of history, memory, and subjectivity in productive ways. Filling out ethnographic time with a historiographic supplement does not simply resolve the antinomies Werbner observes. But it does at least help locate them within the chains of signification that give rise to hybridity's time lag. Historical approaches to hybridity, in other words, enable us to explore the acting out of memory not simply in conscious recall and continuous transmission but also in the disjunctive temporality of the unconscious and the archive.

If an important aspect of hybridity must be understood in terms of the unconscious and pertains to a memory transmitted through the signifying chain rather than through conscious recall, then its relationship to heritage and collective memory will be understandably problematic. But this problem can be turned to critical advantage once it is realized what an opportunity it presents to those who would resist the incorporation of hybridity into the national narrative. Identifying hybridity with our national Thing normalizes its transgressions, putting its inversions to work for the project of a national enjoyment. The various appropriations of blackface minstrelsy I discuss in chapter 3 stand out as salient examples of this national incorporation of cultural hybridity. Taking off from Eric Lott's influential critique of the reception of minstrelsy as American national culture, I direct our attention in that chapter to the little noted commentary on minstrelsy by nineteenth-century black Americans. These responses, I conclude, problematize the move to recuperate minstrelsy's fusions as unclaimed national heritage. Such a narrativizing neglects the power of hybridity to corrode rather than support our confidence in the national Thing.

The tension between hybridity and memory I wish to articulate here differs from that drawn by scholars who have critiqued the postmodern celebration of all things diverse and hybrid, which they assert depends upon an elision of both history and affect. This concern extends beyond African American studies to incorporate a range of voices within contemporary racial and ethnic studies. David Palumbo-Liu, for example, deplores "the fetishization of the present," in which "ignorance of the historical past" from which the term *hybrid* springs has "specific political effects." While "the current use of the word 'hybrid' is taken precisely to reclaim and rehabilitate the notion of mixedness," Palumbo-Liu argues, "this revisionist act seems to me to be facilitated much too smoothly, as if material history provided no point of resistance or counterpressure."[41] Jeffrey Santa Ana concurs, arguing "racial minority identity today is largely an affective process of articulating and resolving the contradictions between historically painful emotions and the euphoria of commercialized human feeling in consumer postmodernism."[42] Both critics draw a telling equivalence between history and painful affect. I want here to distinguish my project from such criticism of hybridity in the name of historical memory. Hybridity discourse can be presentist, I concur, but it need not be. And historical emotion, as a number of queer historians are now arguing, is much more various than its reduction to trauma and pain would allow.[43] I actually argue that the divergence between collective memory and hybridity can be a good thing insofar as it produces a jolting or jarring reminder of the political unconscious and disrupts the seamless progression of the national pageantry.

Borrowing compromised terms like *miscegenation* and *hybridity*, as I do, is certainly risky. To speak of the miscegenation of time, when *miscegenation* is a historically specific term that emerged within its particular time, is necessarily to speak in catachresis. I am always mindful of the historical baggage of "amalgamation," "hybridity," and "miscegenation," as well as "blood" and "mixture." Nineteenth-century racial science was obsessed with hybridity as an index of interfertility among population groups. Fears of racial degeneracy motivated a powerful political reaction against racial equality and stymied gender equality as well. With the rise of modern science's attempt to hypostatize race, tracking the intergenerational consequences of racial mixture became key to the deployment of eugenic arguments for racial hygiene, justifying separate but equal and the disenfranchisement of blacks, and new forms of restricting coverture for white womanhood. None of this history is easily abandoned. Or rather, all of this history is far too easily abandoned, making the account-keeping I attempt an exercise in "countermemory." *Countermemory* is Foucault's term for "a use of history that severs its connection to memory . . . a transformation of history into a totally different form of time."[44] Countermemory interrupts heritage's normalizing imperatives, the manner in which it "highlights and foregrounds, imposes beginnings, middles and ends on the random and contingent," as Hall puts it.[45] Countermemory produces a negative heritage and is for Foucault itself a form of participation in the hybrid and transgressive spirit of the carnivalesque:

> The good historian, the genealogist, will know what to make of this masquerade. He will not be too serious to enjoy it; on the contrary, he will push the masquerade to its limit and prepare the great carnival of time where masks are constantly reappearing.[46]

Race and Racism in the Circum-Atlantic Fold

If Foucault inspires my approach to historiography as dramaturgy, he also offers an important motif I will put to use, that of the fold. In *The Order of Things,* the fold captures the "empirico-critical reduplication by means of which an attempt is made to make [humanity] serve as the foundation of [its] own finitude." This fold, as reduplication, is both an operation of discourse and a historical event. It thus pertains to both space and temporality. And, like Bhabha's notions of disjunctive temporality and time lag, the fold connects the discursive and performative forms through which we bring both into coherence. For Foucault, the modern discourse of the human is a fold. With the rise of the human sciences, "philosophy falling asleep once more in the hollow of this Fold; this time not the sleep of Dogmatism, but that of Anthropology."[47] Eve Kosofsky Sedgwick has thought of the fold in terms of the feedback process that so fascinated twentieth-century cybernetic theory.[48] It conveys a nonteleological and complexly affective relationship to an imminent future that the present is already caught up in. As an alternative to rigid anxiety, it spills out suggestive associations with texture and textiles that I will also exploit. I draw on both Foucault and Sedgwick in theorizing the fold within which modern conceptualizations of the human found a hollow in which the concomitant dilemmas of slavery, race, and hybridity appear.

The circum-Atlantic fold for me simply names the period and the problematic that appears between the potential and the performance of emancipation.[49] Rather than an exact historical period, it marks spatial and temporal zones punctuated by a series of key dates—1792, 1804, 1834, 1865, 1888—that take on a recursive as well as sequential relationship through "a moment of retroactivity or capture," as Sexton suggests. Between the potential and the performance of black freedom, I argue, there lies the hollow of a fold within which many of our conceptualizations of race, inheritance, and hybridity were formulated. This period saw the discourses of race appear most insistently, as Paul Gilroy and Saidiya Hartman argue in different ways, precisely in terms of an empirico-critical reduplication of the human as infrahuman.[50] Black people became both subjects and objects of freedom, reduplicating an abstract discourse of human equality. They took on a catalytic role for the potential and the performance of freedom, partaking of a mimesis that proved menacing to a dominating power that found, in that ostensibly flattering reflection, the outlines of its own prospective dissolution.

My specification of this fold as circum-Atlantic decenters national chronology in favor of the disjunctive temporalities introduced, for instance, by the Haitian Revolution (1804) as well as the compensated emancipation in the British West Indies (1834). As augurs of a potential freedom, free people of color in the antebellum north provided the most potent and uncanny image of national hybridity, belonging to a nation that enslaved their people and aspiring to an equality whose substance would necessarily be transformed by their arrival. Following the work of Ira Berlin and Patrick Rael, I seek to understand the history of the antebellum black community in the U.S. north in Atlanticist terms.[51] Their very marginality in terms of the greater socioeconomic forces shaping the Atlantic, Rael has pointed out, was key to their ability to encompass and formulate their critique of the status quo.[52] Marginality was in this particular case a tactical advantage, permitting them to leave an archival record in treatises, pamphlets, newspapers, and correspondence that form a countermemory to the nation's imagined consensus. I read this black archive both with and against its grain, interested in both its articulation of a black presence and its moves to discipline and regulate that presence in an intraracial deployment of governmentality. Above all, I look in it for the traces of the double negation that I will associate with hybridity, with negative heritage, and with performance itself.

Time, space, and mobility all lie in the hollow of the circum-Atlantic fold. Hosea Easton, one of the earliest of these theorists of the black Atlantic, in his 1837 work *A Treatise on the Intellectual Character, and the Civil and Political Condition of the Colored People of the United States,* expressed as much when he described the relationship between enslaved and free people of color "as though a body composed of parts, and systematized by the laws of nature, were capable of continuing its regular configurative movements after it has been decomposed."[53] Coming from a Native-African-American family of New England activists and malcontents, Easton's unforgettably gothic image of racial formation is but one of many with which early black abolitionists, activists, and intellectuals theorized life within the circum-Atlantic fold. Their awareness of regular configurative movement across chasms of time, space, and status, of movement in but not of the laws of nature, powerfully prefigures Foucault's carnivalesque imagery.

Easton's double entendre on the word *decomposition*—meaning disconnection but also death, decay—records the process of history's destruction of the body even as it folds this destruction back into a broader dynamic of potential mobility. In so doing, Easton provides one of the earliest definitions on record for what we now call black performance. His *Treatise* goes on to expound upon the pernicious travesty of insults, reduplicating them within his jeremiad against American racism in order to circulate and, in the same move, to dispel their enervating power:

> Children at infancy receive oral instruction from the nurse. The first lessons given are . . . go to sleep, if you don't the old *nigger* will carry you off; don't you cry—Hark; the old *nigger*'s coming . . . if they do thus and so, they will be poor or ignorant as a *nigger;* or that they will be black as a *nigger;* or have no more credit than a *nigger.*[54]

More than a century before Fanon, Easton vividly theorized the lived experience of black people in white supremacist societies, where the pedagogies of racial stereotyping began at birth:

> Nigger lips, nigger shins, and nigger heels, are phrases universally common among the juvenile class of society . . . Hark; the old *nigger*'s coming—how ugly you are, you are worse than a little *nigger* . . . that slick looking nigger—nigger, where you get so much coat?—that's a nigger priest—are sounds emanating from little urchins of Christian villagers.[55]

Taunts echo in Easton's ear as the pastoral power of his clerical role is mocked by an aggressive bawdry that takes the black body, in whole or in part, as its punch line. The menace of mimesis, as displayed in the incongruities of a "slick" nigger with "so much coat," a preacher no less, punctuates this repetitious aggression with an unmistakable anxiety. No less than Fanon did Easton seek to account for the intense psychic and social consequences of this degradation of the black body. But he also initiated a doubled negation through which the ruses of race could be exposed. In this he was joined by activists like David Walker, Paul Cuffe, Maria Stewart, Samuel Cornish, David Ruggles, Frederick Douglass, James McCune Smith, Sarah and Charles Remond, William Wells Brown, and William Cooper Nell, all of whom articulated a sustained protest and a profound interrogation of that racial condition.

If we can look to this period for early stirrings in antiracist praxis, we can also witness in it the first reservations regarding the ostensible neutral ground of "race" itself. In an 1841 address to an African

American literary society, the recently graduated medical doctor James McCune Smith warned of the coming storm of scientific racism, which as a man of science he was in a privileged position to recognize:

> Learned men, in their rage for classification, and from a reprehensible spirit to bend science to pamper popular prejudice, have brought the human species under the yoke of classification, and having shown to their own satisfaction a diversity in the races, have placed us in the very lowest tank.[56]

In a single phrase, Smith recognized the links between power and knowledge, suggesting that the bigotry Easton experienced as he walked to his Hartford church was not innate or instinctual but represented an education in desire and aversion that took place in the precincts of science as well as, as Easton noted, in the intimacy of the home. Writing in the pages of his comrade Frederick Douglass's Rochester-based newspaper, Smith put the point vividly in what one historian calls "arguably the most concentrated, astute antiracist statement of the entire antebellum era":[57]

> The negro "with us" is not an actual physical being of flesh and bones and blood, but a hideous monster of the mind, ugly beyond all physical portraying, so utterly and ineffably monstrous as to frighten reason from its throne. . . . *It is a constructive negro—a negro by implication*—a John Roe and Richard Doe negro, that haunts with grim presence the precincts of this republic, shaking his gory looks over legislative halls and family prayers.[58]

As his phrase "a constructive negro" shows, Smith posited what we would now think of as the social construction of race. He understood how race was being mobilized in both scientific and popular registers to frighten reason from its throne and to bring humanity under the biopolitical yoke of racial classification. And thus was laid the groundwork for an analysis of racism as springing not simply from the degradations of slavery but, more particularly, in resentful reaction against the attempts to end it. It was the potential of black freedom, and the ruin it brought to the myth of racial purity and white supremacy, that "haunts with grim presence the precincts of this republic."

Smith's characterization of the black image as "a hideous monster of the mind" dovetails in fascinating ways with Easton's comparison of the black population, slave and free, to "a body composed of parts" that were "capable of continuing its regular configurative movements" even when scattered and decomposed. Mobilizing tropes of gothic horror that were similar to those Easton employed, Smith turned the tables on the scientific doubts regarding black intelligence, asserting that it was white people who were deranged from reason by the images of blackness they had constructed. His imagery reflects the generic resources with which black commentary sought to respond to the increasingly romantic imagery of blackness disseminated in such texts as Harriet Beecher Stowe's massively popular, massively influential novel *Uncle Tom's Cabin* (1852). Such instances of the racial gothic countered the prevalent popularity of what George Fredrickson has called the "romantic racialism" of the period, in which black and white races were held to possess complementary but contrasting essences.[59] Such a racial gothic often resurfaces, I posit, whenever idealized images of interracial love and desire are countered with ghastly and traumatic scenes of rape, violence, and intergenerational trauma.

As these short excerpts suggest, the black body was produced within the circum-Atlantic fold as the uncanny remainder of slavery and freedom. Mastering the code of its physiognomic signs—lips, shins, heels—as well as its behavioral predilections—slickness, mimicry, shamelessness—forecast the limits of emancipation, burdening the subject of freedom, in Saidiya Hartman's emotive phrase, with a "travestied liberation."[60] The telling contact this phrase makes among falsification, transgression, and vestment supplies another rationale for a historiographic approach attuned to the folds of the sartorial. As race became the measure of "Man," something as simple as a measure of cloth could either confirm or subvert racial common sense, one in which a supposed black propensity for travesty, burlesque, and malapropism supplied the popular with rich and vernacular fun. Cultural hybridity became the centerpiece of the drama of human liberation as forms of racial and humanistic essentialism were deployed to harness its more irreverent and outrageous consequences. And it is within this context, within this fold, that the discourses of miscegenation and amalgamation proliferated.

Miscegenation: A Spurious Issue?

The legacy of the circum-Atlantic fold, I seek to show throughout this book, remains evident in our fears of and desires for racial mixture and transcendence. Nowhere is this clearer than in the two keywords we have inherited from this period, keywords the discourse of race has yet to transcend: miscegenation and amalgamation. Scholars like Elise Lemire and Betsy Erkkila have shown how crucial the antebellum period remains to our present-day conceptualizations of "miscegenation" and "mixed blood."[61] Yet fewer scholars have emphasized the debt we owe to this period for our ideas regarding the transcendence of race. Insofar as the history of race mixing is told, it has been a history of prohibitions against what a 1691 Virginian law called an "abominable mixture and spurious issue."[62] And it is fair to say that many critics continue to consider miscegenation a "spurious issue" in a more contemporary sense: a red herring that distracts from other more important issues. But what a discourse counts as "false" or "illegitimate" is often an excellent point at which to decipher its operations and ruses, and this is also, I suggest, the case with the discourse of race mixing.

A letter writer to the Civil War–era New York City black newspaper, the *Weekly Anglo-African,* entering into the debate I discuss in greater detail shortly, sought to depict the spuriousness of ethnoracial mixture as an issue, which he associated with a general mania with things progressive, scientific, and utopian in his culture. Satirizing the nineteenth-century interest in the body by playfully anthropomorphizing the century itself, he wrote,

> The nineteenth century, ethnologically considered, is prognathous, having jaw in excess, therefore, addicted to babbling. . . . Nor is it to be wondered at; for although the nineteenth century esteems itself an adumbration of the millenium, and regards preceding ages with a lofty pity, bordering on contempt, yet it is troubled about many things—intricate problems which must be solved before mankind can settle down into millenial beatitude. Hence cerebral excitement, leading men of morbid dispositions to jump from seemingly rational premises to very fantastic conclusions, the illegitimate offspring of illicit processes.[63]

This letter writer posited the fascination with miscegenation as itself incorporating an evolutionary throwback. Each effort to progress toward a millennial horizon exfoliated "illegitimate offspring" and "fantastic conclusions" as the product of its "illicit processes." Rather than take a position for or against race mixing, the writer sought to expose the excessive, affective conundrums of racialized reason itself, satirizing the seriousness with which the supposedly

intricate problems of racial hybridity were being handled by spiritualists, reformers, journalists, and scientists.

The debate he was commenting upon is archived within our critical
terminology by the apparent duplication of the words miscegenation
and amalgamation, and it anticipated by more than a century the
recent attempts to recuperate the latter. Amalgamation and miscegenation are typically held to be synonyms, but that does not capture the complex chronological and connotational relation between
them. It cannot explain, for instance, why a recent advocate for a
new and more positive historiography of ethnoracial mixture should
herald amalgamation as a more accurate and less pejorative name
for what was once called miscegenation.[64] Such a move to reclaim
national hybridity via the old/new word amalgamation belies, ironically enough, the origin of the word miscegenation in precisely the
same scenario a century and half earlier. In an uncanny echo, both
the mid-nineteenth century and the late-twentieth century saw the
outcropping of a theory of racial transcendence tied to the proposed
adoption of a new terminology that might unlock the restorative
power of race.

Hardly any effigy in American history has been more travestied
than the figure of the Great Emancipator himself, Abraham Lincoln.
As a number of historians have shown, all manner of parody and
subterfuge surrounded attempts to tag an unwilling Lincoln with the
advocacy of race mixing, both before and during his presidency.[65] It
is to such partisan efforts that we owe the word *miscegenation*. It
was coined in a pamphlet published during the midterm presidential
election of 1864, *Miscegenation: The Theory of the Blending of the
Races, Applied to the American White Man and Negro*. The word
made an almost instant entry into the lexicon, as it was discussed
everywhere from the partisan press to the hallowed precincts of science to the halls of government, where, in perhaps one of the less
well-thought-out efforts to squelch a new idea that the annals of
our political history record, an incensed representative from Ohio
read portions into the Congressional Record.[66] The *Weekly Anglo-
African* was among the periodicals that noted the first appearance of
the *Miscegenation* pamphlet, about which it commented:

> The view that an admixture of the negro with the other races making
> up the people of these United States would be the final solution of the
> slave question, is neither new nor recent. . . . The word, nay the deed,
> MISCEGENATION [is] the same in substance with the word Amalga-

mation, the terror of our Abolition friends twenty years ago, and of many of them to-day—miscegenation which means intermarriages between white and blacks—"Miscegenation," which means the practical brotherhood and social intermingling of blacks and whites.[67]

While the *Weekly Anglo-African* noted that the "first impressions of several judicious friends of progress" was "that the book was written as a hoax," the paper concluded that it was written "in dead earnest." Although the reviewer objected to the pamphlet's faulty statistics and "doubtful" application of scientific laws, he nonetheless observed "scattered through the pamphlet sudden glimpses of truth, and rare dashes of intuition, which stamps the author as an acute and comprehensive thinker."[68] Largely positive notices of the *Miscegenation* pamphlet continued in the paper for several months, including a reference to it in a speech by the famous black abolitionist William Wells Brown. The proprietors of the *Weekly Anglo-African,* the brothers Robert and Thomas Hamilton, even advertised the pamphlet for sale at their establishment on Beekman Street, along with other reform and abolitionist literature.[69]

Beyond the black press, responses to the pamphlet were less sanguine. With chapter titles such as "Heart-Histories of the Daughters of the South" and "How the Anglo-American May Become More Comely," most whites found it outrageous. Coming in the wake of the deadly New York City draft riots of 1863, in which Irish immigrants and other whites had lynched blacks in the streets and burned down the Colored Orphan's Asylum in protest of a deeply unfair military conscription, the pamphlet's jibes at the Irish (calling them a lower race than blacks who stand to benefit the most from miscegenation) took on the color of fighting words. Yet, despite such incendiary language in such incendiary times, the *Miscegenation* pamphlet was not universally disavowed among whites. As in the pages of the *Weekly Anglo-African,* it initially led to debate and discussion. The pamphlet's sentiments exposed what Raymond Williams called a structure of feeling, a crystallizing but as yet inchoate sense of the world that the new word *miscegenation* seemed to latch onto. The nineteenth century, prognathous of jaw, seized upon this latest opportunity to gnaw upon the great issues of race and nation that so dominated its intellectual and political horizons. While scholars like Lemire rightly point to the *Miscegenation* pamphlet's ideological purpose, I am as interested in the affective resonance, or what Kathleen Stewart might call the "tangle of potential connections" that the word initially summoned.[70] As much as we must understand miscegenation/amalgamation as a trigger for the irruptive, panicked force of mob racism, we must also account for its queasy life in ordinariness, where the "spurious issue" took on the valences of what we too easily, too tellingly, term "fruitless speculation."

In the days after its first appearance, the New York correspondent for the *Philadelphia Inquirer* reported "considerable gossip among Spiritualists, Women's Rights folks and colored people in this city, over a book said to have been written by a highly intelligent educated mulatto girl, on the subject of the mixing of the races." Assuming it to be a black-authored text, the *Inquirer* remarked, "The work has been extensively circulated, in proof, in ultra circles, and is said to be remarkably clever for a negress."[71] Rumor, hearsay, and speculative inquiry accompanied the first appearance of a pamphlet, little of which augured the immense consequence that in retrospect we can accord the appearance of this fateful coinage. Theodore Tilton, the white abolitionist editor of the *New York Independent*, emblematized the guardedly positive response in progressive circles, which tried not to advocate miscegenation without, on the contrary, execrating it. The *National Anti-Slavery Standard* reported that Tilton "expresses the views of most of the intelligent Republicans in Congress" in asserting that "nobody here *advocates* amalgamation," although "doubtless there are very many who believe that in time the two races *will* amalgamate."[72] Mirroring the pamphlet's own recourse to natural law and statistical projection, the compromise position on race mixing was to declare it probable or inevitable but to stop short of welcoming it as desirable.

The distinction between such idle speculations as to the contours of a hybrid future and a prejudicial abreaction against miscegenation is often lost on critics who have stressed the strong aversion to race mixing among even progressive, abolitionist whites. But from the 1830s onward, radical whites followed William Lloyd Garrison and Gerrit Smith in denying that amalgamation was a crime against God or nature. While stopping short of urging it on the public as a matter of policy, as their hysterical foes asserted, they nonetheless depicted marriage as a matter of both personal taste and civil rights. Abolitionists even fought a successful campaign in the 1840s to repeal a Massachusetts ban against mixed marriages.[73] They withstood widespread mockery and baiting with their principled stand against legislated inequality. Although this position was beaten back in the wave of antimiscegenation lawmaking that followed emancipation, it remains an odd emblem of negative heritage, one that mobilizes marriage as an ambiguous image and a "public vow," as Nancy Cott has shown, a political performative and a dramatic reenactment through which both race and gender might be refigured and, possibly, decentered.[74]

No less than their opponents did progressives possess the "rage for classification," deploying discourses of hygiene, demography, statistics, and the rational administration of society to displace political questions onto the supposedly neutral ground of scientific proof. William Leach has traced the rising prestige of social sciences as an empirical bulwark and propaganda tool for American reformers, arising out of the immense social, technical, and political transformations wrought by the Civil War.[75] In this light, we can see how progressives, at least initially, might have believed that they could afford to simply stand their ground when the *Miscegenation* pamphlet appeared, shrugging off its more absurd and satirical sections but embracing its general sense of a hybrid future. Their enemies had said and done worse, and if the fear of miscegenation had really been the trump card many critics now suppose it to have been, Lincoln would not have been reelected.[76] In my view, the lasting effect of the pamphlet lay less in its role as another ritual denunciation of the "taboo" against race mixing and more in the prod it gave to the scientific prestige of race mixing as an American panacea. As the critic in the pages of the *Weekly Anglo-African* noted, it appealed to millennial and progressive yearnings to settle longstanding questions with overly facile scientific presdigitation. It was *Miscegenation*'s positive message of statistical inevitability that to me most warrants comment. Miscegenation and human hybridity, as quasi-scientific discourses, opened out this field in a manner that amalgamation never could. Science, statistics, and natural law became the ground upon which, through appeals to reason, race might be confirmed and validated.

The lure of rationality and its interdependence with speculation, emotion, and irrationality is even evident in the rebuttals of the pamphlet. In its negative review of the *Miscegenation* pamphlet, the *Anthropological Review* of London dismissed the idea that this "form of insanity which is just now affecting the people of Federal America" could be a hoax. Only having found its author in earnest could the learned journal then reassure its readers. "'Miscegenation' will not find a place in future scientific literature," it claimed, "but

it will be most useful as indicating the state of knowledge respect-
ing anthropology in America in the year 1864."[77] That the *Review*
considered the pamphlet bad anthropology is less interesting than its
acceptance of the pamphlet's premise that society ought to be guided
by social scientific principles and that it seized the opportunity to
further champion them. Such an exercise in refutation threatened to
place the outlandish, satirical ideas and images of the *Miscegenation*
pamphlet within the pale of scientific respectability. Science both
warded off and succumbed to its own legitimating aura in playing
this fort-da game with miscegenation. As evidence of this, consider
how the review began with a critique of the pamphlet's poor science
but ended with a poor attempt to match the pamphlet's humor. While
describing the "Heart-Histories" chapter as "too indecent for us to
quote from" (sharing, for opposite reasons, the *Inquirer*'s speculation that "only a Mulatto or a Mulatress could have strung together
such licentious absurdities"), the *Review* closed with a ribald joke of
its own about all the pregnancies contracted among the white "spin-
sters" who had been traveling south to educate the freed people. Race
mixing was apparently only unspeakable when it was being attributed to one's own side of the political fence. The richness of black fun
was to be had even among the learned men, whose rage for order was
in this instance compatible with a lapse into bawdry.[78]

Artfully presenting its neologism as a progressive and scientific
alternative to outmoded amalgamationism, the pamphlet turned prevailing racism on its head, extolling the tremendous benefits of racial
mixture for the future vigor of the nation. However sarcastic, that
gesture exposed the theatricality of the science it sought to lampoon,
unfolding aggressions, doubts, and ambivalences that its authors
could not fully control. Of the many discussions of the *Miscegenation*
pamphlet and its authors—the New York journalists David Croly and
George Wakeman—perhaps the most illuminating remains a small
book published in 1954 by J. M. Bloch.[79] Almost alone among commentators, Bloch has insisted that the parody cannot be read straightforwardly. All parody must evince affection, respect even, for its target, and *Miscegenation* proves no exception.[80] In their effort to enter
into the discourse of radical amalgamationist abolition, Croly and
Wakeman permitted that discourse to enter themselves. The constant
tension of the prose lay in its efforts to represent the consequences
of miscegenation as vividly as possible while containing the very
vividness of that spectacle. The more plausible it made miscegenation

seem to the abolitionist and spiritualist readership it hoped to dupe, the more it risked taking its arguments to heart. As Bloch concludes, "In their travesty on the beliefs of the small groups" of racial egalitarians, Croly and Wakeman "paradoxically held up to ridicule the similar but widely accepted 'reasoning' of the believers in Negro anatomical and physiological inferiority."[81] Donning a literary disguise that readers on both sides of the Atlantic speculated hid a black or mulatto female author, these white male apologists for racism and slavery found themselves caught in the circum-Atlantic fold.

A negative image of our multiracial, hybrid future, I conclude, is embedded in Croly and Wakeman's ribald, satirical pamphlet. And their ambivalence and anxiety regarding race, science, and reform reflect the ambivalence and anxiety of the popular political culture from which their prose sprung. We see this effect in a well-known series of antiabolitionist, antiamalgamationist images produced by the Philadelphia-born political caricaturist Edward Williams Clay several decades before the appearance of the *Miscegenation* pamphlet. Like Croly and Wakeman, Clay sought to both amuse and incense white viewers with shocking imagery of a world turned upside down, a world of emancipation in which whites would serve blacks and black dandies and dandizettes would lord over town. Rather than deploying science, however, Clay's imagery relied on the visual evidences of performance: dance, music, and theater. In addition to *An Amalgamation Waltz* and *Practical Amalgamation (Musical Soiree),* his series included *Practical Amalgamation (The Wedding),* thus linking the public proscenium of marriage to other forms of performance.

Clay's capstone image, titled *The Fruits of Amalgamation,* depicts domestic life of two black–white couples as the apotheosis of abolitionist performativity. In the image, one couple pays a visit upon another found relaxing on the sofa in their comfortable living room. The husband is engrossed in an abolitionist newspaper, while his wife provocatively nurses one of their two mixed-race children. Their domesticity is lived literally under the sign of Othello, as a portrait of Shakespeare's Moor and his wife Desdemona appears directly above them. In their door stand the visitors, the white husband apparently a caricature of William Lloyd Garrison himself. Redoubling the sense of incongruity, a dog and cat play together in the foreground, as if to suggest that affection between the races is as unnatural as that between species.

As an image that dramatically and anxiously depicts the possible "fruits" of emancipation, Clay's print is easily read in terms of political ideology. Just as the *Miscegenation* pamphlet can be read in relation to the Civil War–era draft riots, Lemire persuasively interprets the series in relation to the violent riots against free blacks and the threat of amalgamation that had been sparked several years before the prints appeared in both Philadelphia and New York City.[82] And yet the appearance of these literary and visual goads in the *wake* of violence belies the ordinary sequence of "fighting words." They reflect not the stability of the stereotype but the insecurity that demands it be "anxiously repeated."[83] Croly and Wakeman spent hours reading up on racial science in order to hone the rhetoric of their satire; Clay worked out in repeated and loving detail interracial scenarios he supposedly execrated, producing in the process one of the single largest archives of antebellum imagery of northern black Americans. How much distance can there be between the pen and the hand that holds it? If anxiety is triggered by the feared object, as Hosea Easton recognized, its repetition in insult and imagery could produce fantasy as much as phobia.

This is suggested by an image by Clay that would have fallen out of the historical record if it had not become the subject of a police action when it was offered for sale by a vendor of "obscene, filthy, and indecent prints." In her study of erotic imagery and discourse in nineteenth-century America, Helen Horowitz recounts the prosecution of this particular bawdy etching, "representing a man in the dress of a member of the society of friends in an obscene, impudent and indecent posture with a negro woman." Horowitz's work, which deciphers "obscene, impudent and indecent posture" as a nineteenth-century euphemism for sexual intercourse, leads me to draw a connection between Clay the accused creator of interracial pornography and Clay the antiamalgamationist cartoonist.[84] Making that literally obscene (ob-scene, off scene) connection, the fantasy at the obscene center of Clay's ideology is disclosed.[85]

As documents in the archive of travestied liberation, the *Miscegenation* pamphlet and the antiamalgamation imagery reduplicate the black body within a fold of science and politics, race and sexuality, reason and affect. The clearest evidence that their satirically serious science continues to matter is seen whenever contemporary partisans of multiracialism offer up versions of its arguments. While the word *miscegenation* is dismissed as a racist holdover, the dream of a transracial future that is the pamphlet's actual content remains the horizon of many who are still seeking to reconcile hybridity with the nation.[86] In particular, the pamphlet's mobilization of romance, love, and marriage as augurs and agents of a mixed-race millennium remain as prominent now as then.

This view of marriage enjoyed broad support across the color line. As one letter to the *Weekly Anglo-African* put it,

> Under slavery the two races were becoming rapidly blended. The question is, will this co-mingling continue after freedom is established? There is every reason to believe that it will. . . . There will be this difference, however, between Freedom and Slavery—the intermingling under the latter was not hallowed by the sanction of law or religion while under the former it will be legitimatised by marriage.[87]

Here marriage is mobilized as the legitimating term that will redeem a prior, sordid history of coercive and unfree sex across color lines. Such views are routine today, but it is startling to read such views a century earlier than we might have supposed them uttered. And it is bracing to reflect on how exactly wrong they were about the actual denouement of the war and reconstruction, in which miscegenation transformed into a rallying call for segregating, disenfranchising, castrating, and murdering black bodies. Given the unacknowledged genealogy of our own millennial yearnings in relation to race mixing, can we confidently say we have turned a corner? Or will the event of miscegenation again be a prelude to a recursive and renascent racialization?[88]

Within the discourses of amalgamation and miscegenation there remains the performative–pedagogic split Bhabha identified. The pedagogic deployment of racial hybridity delivered it as a cautionary or promising image of what would be the end result of emancipation and equality. This register appealed to and elicited "race" as a symbolic order, an order that was constantly revised and furiously expanded upon, masking the traces of this patent bricolage as quickly and brutally as possible with every trick in the arsenal of good old American showmanship and hucksterism. But this very process of deception and illusion, as Daphne Brooks's work shows, exposes the performativity of race and race mixing, offering up hints and emblems of a miscegenous body that exceeded the rhetorical conditions that announced and would contain it.[89]

To articulate hybridity, theatricality, and the carnivalesque in such terms is of course not to produce a straightforward apologetic. I am concerned throughout this book with highlighting both the alignment and divergence of hybridity with the national Thing. And I am quite critical of efforts to claim the racial carnivalesque as national heritage. Mine is not a paean to "our mutt culture, bless its shaggy, unruly heart."[90] Nor is it yet another attempt to claim mixed-race America as a utopian future that "will" just happen "in time," as Theodore Tilton held. It is precisely against the passivity entailed by such a romantic racialist scenario, I wager, that the political pugnacity of an untamed hybridity might be mobilized. An attempt to think carefully through both the lures and the loathing of hybridity is key to understanding the complex of reactions a millennial figure like Obama represents for an unfinished democracy such as our own.

1. The Mirror of Liberty: Constituent Power and the American Mongrel

lies a hoax as elaborate in its own way as Croly and Wakeman's *Miscegenation* pamphlet.[1] Attached to a small, leather-bound book is a tag reading, in full, "The Cover of this book is made of *Tanned Skin* of the *Negro* whose *Execution* caused the War of *Independence*—."[2] Although subsequent analysis has determined this ghoulish claim to be untrue, and the leather cannot be identified as human in origin, the powers of fascination this small object holds do not simply end there. Its specious claim literalizes Foucault's description of genealogy's object: "a body totally imprinted by history and the process of history's destruction of the body."[3] In so doing, it also exemplifies Bhabha's claim that the English book is a troubled, hybrid object.[4] For here the book's status as a sign taken for a wonder doubles back upon itself. With a fiction of tanned black skin secreted into the archives of the colonial modern, binding the contents of Western biopolitical authority in its fold, Englishness and Americanness disclose their own fetish of the book as object.

Despite its vagueness, it is not terribly difficult to decipher that the tag refers to the events of March 5, 1770, in Boston, Massachusetts. On that day, five civilians were killed by British troops in what was immediately christened the Boston Massacre. Credited variously with foreshadowing, anticipating, and igniting the American Revolution, the shocking violence of that day was illustrated, declaimed upon, exhibited at trial, and in the subsequent days, years, and decades, repeatedly reenacted. That the "Negro" in question is Crispus Attucks is also easy to surmise (although it is worth remarking that his name

Figure 1. A notebook allegedly covered in human skin, circa 1770–1850. Courtesy of Wellcome Library, London.

is either suppressed or forgotten). Attucks, an Afro-Native sailor and fugitive slave from Framingham, Massachusetts, was felled in the soldiers' first volley. His actions leading up to his death that day became the source of controversy during a subsequent trial and remained controversial over a century later. Efforts to memorialize the Boston Massacre as a protonational anniversary met with the uncanny prospect of a black body on their hands. Martyr or mob leader? Patriot or insurrectionary? Attucks's contested legacy to this day continues to touch upon issues that strike at the heart of American identity and its racial unconscious.[5]

Among the many memorials and mementos of the Boston Massacre, the Wellcome book is surely the most ersatz. Bookbinding with human skin was once notable enough to possess its own term: *anthropodermic bibliopegy*. And while there are plenty of documented cases, the macabre practice, as the Wellcome forgery demonstrates, has also remained in the half-light of legend. Whether real or fictive, much of the power of anthropodermic bibliopegy lay in the shock of the idea itself. It provides a textbook example of Freud's concept of the uncanny in which the familiar is estranged and the strange brought into familiar proximity. The broader practice it indexes—that of preserving relics of the dead—blurs the line between the exalted and the profane. Both saints and highwaymen have found their bodily fragments prized and collected. And various figures, both notorious and obscure, have requested that their memoirs be bound in a fragment from their corporeal vestment. Anthropodermic bibliopegy—another name for "the history of the body"—throws our easy distinction between discourse and bodies into a vertiginous convolute.

And how can we avoid thinking of the horrific traffic in the charred relics of lynchings? Ian Baucom has argued that the Atlantic slave trade inaugurated the capitalization of black bodies, which were endowed with a speculative monetary value that could be gruesomely realized even when, as in the case of the *Zong* massacre, those bodies were casually murdered for the insurance they bore.[6] Isn't the traffic in real or fantastical bodily fragments—whether that of Crispus Attucks or of Jesse Washington, lynched in Waco, Texas, in 1916—the afterlife of this financial revolution, in which the black body can be killed without sanction and therefore acquires in death the grisly aura of a collectible curiosity?[7] If such a fetishism of the part follows upon a literal or figurative castration of the black body, the enduring presence of fragments underscores how even disfiguration can feed a process of accumulation. A performative historiography alive to the presence of the past as traumatic accumulation will therefore not neglect the Wellcome book's evidence merely because it appears under false cover. Rather, it will take up that forgery itself as an object of historical analysis, considering it an attempt to duplicate or mirror the black bodily fragment. And it will ask how such a process might factor into the genealogy of race.

To put things another way, a history concerned only with linear cause and effect will quickly dispose of the Wellcome book as unimportant. A genealogy of performance, by contrast, must examine such anomalies for the historical truths that become visible in the negative space around them, training our attention precisely upon that which an empiricist gaze will overlook. The Wellcome book's reduplication of Attucks's body at both ends of the spatiotemporal continuum I call the circum-Atlantic fold—at its beginning as event/cause and at its culmination as relic/archive—depends upon and reinforces what Michael Sappol calls the "instatement" of the body. In Sappol's history of anatomy and medicine, instatement names the process by which the "anatomical body" was captured by and for "the bourgeois self." Sappol tracks how the body became "if not a microcosm then a mirror or projection, of nation, class, race, gender, species, history, [and] evolution" over the course of the nineteenth century.[8] In the political and cultural vernacular of the nineteenth century, mirrors were routinely evoked simultaneously as representations and criticisms of that which they reflected. Mirroring and mimicry were also preeminent metaphors through which the nineteenth century thought, or failed to think, about racial difference. In this chapter, I take up Sappol's concept of instatement as a mirror of national fantasy, relating it to Bhabha's suggestive application of Lacan's mirror stage. The performance of instatement in the circum-Atlantic fold, I argue, traverses our ordinary divisions of disciplinary objects. It is live and mediated, visual and aural, aesthetic and ordinary. Instatement conveys the fold of materiality and discourse in the deployment of power over and through bodies. At the same time, it reminds us that such a deployment of the body is also a dependence *upon* the body: a dependence upon its labor, its suffering, its capacities, its life.

The presence of the Wellcome book as an uncanny nexus of text and skin, discourse and flesh, thus exemplifies the mirroring and duplicative effect of the social instatements of the hybrid object. Bhabha describes the hybrid object as that which "retains the actual semblance of the authoritative symbol but revalues its presence by resisting it as the signifier of *Entstellung* [displacement or disfiguration]— *after the intervention of difference.*" Bhabha here helps us theorize the presence of the body within the scene of colonial and racial authority as itself taking on an uncanny semblance or mirroring of authority. If colonial and racial power fetishizes difference, hybrid agency disrupts this fetishism with what Bhabha calls an "unpredictable and partial desire," a desire for something that looks like a desire for sameness; almost, but not quite.[9] Hybridity thus restores the real–false distinction I suspended a moment earlier, but only after the intervention of difference—that is, after the appearance of a different standpoint on the Wellcome book, one that relishes Attucks's absence from it as another daring, fugitive escape.

Rereading instatement with Bhabha's account of hybridity thus radicalizes Sappol's mirror metaphor, opening it to a productive engagement with Lacan's mirror stage. The mirror stage describes how a chance gaze upon one's reflection might conjure forth a heretofore undreamt of, if spectral, plenitude and unity of the bodily schema. The mirror stage thus marks the simultaneity and split between seeing and being seen, between the imaginary and the symbolic. The unpredictability and partiality of the desires reflected back by the mirror registers this. As a number of scholars, including Frantz Fanon, Ann Pellegrini, Fred Moten, and Kalpana Seshadri-Crooks, have shown, the mirror stage offers important insight into the process of racial subjectification, insights I further engage in this chapter.[10]

Bhabha helps us see how Lacan's emphasis on the illusory nature of this image of a singular or whole body dovetails with Benedict Anderson's thesis regarding the nation as an imagined community. The rituals, narratives, and technologies of simultaneity (such as the novel and the newspaper) through which the oneness of the nation is conjured mirror the nation's imagined integrity and totality. At the same time, mirroring provides for the semblance of a distancing, apprising perspective upon self and nation, in part through the unsettling awareness it provides of the fictive nature of that totality. For this reason, Lacan and Bhabha help us see how such acts of mirroring are never total or sufficient but always anxious and repeating, part of the process I identified in my introduction with the national Thing.

Taking into account its hybridization of the colonial, racial fetish, the Wellcome book provides an unexpected affirmation of Guy Debord's maxim that "in a world that is *really upside down,* the true is a moment of the false."[11] But to understand that maxim's pertinence within the circum-Atlantic fold, we must take it in a slightly different sense than usual. We must see it as providing the insight that the false book contains a moment of the true, if concealed and traumatic, history of revolution.

The Absent Center of a Potential Nation

In my introduction, I employed the performed–potential dyad to show how performance is wrapped up in the virtual and how parades of horribles are traversed by the very desires they show and denounce. In this chapter, I continue my exposition of the performative by drawing upon the work of Daphne Brooks on illusion, spectacle, and escapology.[12] I circle around the figure of Attucks as a way into the historical and theatrical labors of William Cooper Nell, whose

1855 *Colored Patriots of the American Revolution* helped found one tradition of sly civility. Narrating the nation, John Ernest has shown, was a form of "liberation historiography" for the generation of black activists and radicals who seized upon Attucks like a memory flashing up in a moment of danger.[13] It was also an uncanny act of cultural hybridity, and grasping the full resonance of this claim will entail foregrounding performance's power to make as well as show, to do as well as depict.

Almost all one needs to know about Attucks, and, indeed, almost all anyone actually knows, is that he has served as a kind of black claim upon the promise of the American Revolution. But what kind of claim? And what kind of promise? As with most otherwise ordinary people in history, there is an utter paucity of accurate information about Crispus Attucks, even regarding his name. Where a traditional narrative biography might smooth over the gaps and deceptions of the historical record to create an accessible account of what might have been, I prefer to preserve historical events and identity in palimpsest. Such an approach avoids triumphal and teleological retellings of the national story, locating instead the moments that deconstruct that progressive narrative with their alternative possibilities for historical agency.

Here I pick up on Baucom's productive refusal to distinguish too sharply between history and the philosophy of history. Revolutions are interdisciplinary objects that demand consideration from historical, philosophical, and dramaturgical standpoints, as Marx's later political writings argue and exemplify.[14] Although hardly understudied, the American Revolution has never attracted quite the density of *philosophical* attention that the French Revolution has.[15] Even our patriotic hagiography has tended to focus more on the framing of the Constitution than on the conflict the preceded it, and places its emphasis on the document credited with ushering in modern democratic politics. The *constituted* set of arrangements the revolution bequeathed—arrangements that "strict constructionists" insist must be held to invariantly—has tended to trump a focus on the *constituting* process of the revolution as social drama and world-historical event. As Antonio Negri notes, such a narration of events disciplines both time and revolution. The constituent power that makes the revolution, and which rests upon an entirely different basis than the governmental authority that is made, slips out of the orthodox narrative—slips, or, as Bhabha might argue, splits, with a fragment remaining in the form of the hybrid object, whose menacing resemblance to the authoritative symbol might be seen as constituent power's long historical shadow.[16]

Recent work by Jay Fliegelman and David Waldstreicher in excavating the oratorical and performative context of revolutionary nationalism has begun to redress this imbalance.[17] They have helped redefine "independence as a rhetorical problem as much as a political one," as Fliegelman puts it, with all the oratorical emphasis the concept "rhetoric" obtained in the late eighteenth century. If declaring independence is among the most thrilling of speech-acts, however, then greater attention deserves to be paid to how this illocutionary force was obtained and how revolution selected its representative acts of eloquence in corporeal and racialized terms. This is just to observe with Fliegelman that the "problem of how to speak disguised the larger social problem of who could speak."[18] Fliegelman and Waldstreicher both emphasize how the making of American nationalism silenced black eloquence, the former by showing how revolutionary rhetors defined blackness as the obverse of every virtue deemed valued and necessary for a new republic, and the latter by tracking the depoliticizing parodies of black political speech that emerged in the early national public sphere, parodies that preempted the possibility of a patriotic equation of white and black freedom.[19] Brooks McNamara's *Day of Jubilee* tracks with loving detail the large-scale performances of people in association that characterized life in New York in the early decades of the nineteenth century, illustrating in the process how black people were shunted from parade routes, even as spectators.[20]

Such an approach to the illocutionary context of becoming independent, however innovative in other respects, repeats a standard view of racism in American history as a process of *exclusion*. Crispus Attucks's story, however, carries a more complex lesson than a simple omission or repression. In this chapter, I consequently seek to articulate this difference not through exclusion but through *exception*. The state of exception has been brought to critical attention through the work of Giorgio Agamben. His work foregrounds the exceptional figure of *homo sacer*—the life that can be killed without committing murder, the life that cannot therefore be sacrificed for the good of the community. Homo sacer and the state of exception, Agamben argues, are foundational tropes for modern sovereignty insofar as the ability to decide upon the exception—the ability Foucault glossed as the power to make live and let die—has been modernity's most characteristic signature. The case of Attucks suggests the necessity of theorizing a racial state of exception. Given his prominence in ur-narratives of the nation, Attucks's status as "colored patriot" can be said to corrode the national Thing from within, confronting imagined community with its unimaginable double. To see this, we may draw upon recent historiography of the Atlantic world, signally the work of Peter Linebaugh and Markus Rediker, who have suggested repositioning Crispus Attucks within "a new and different understanding of internationalism as something older, deeper, and more widespread."[21] Tracing the hidden history of an Atlantic revolutionary tradition that preceded that identified by the Enlightenment and associated with the French Revolution, Linebaugh and Rediker seek to restore both the historical dignity of the slaves, sailors, and commoners who built modern capitalism as well as the historical intelligibility of their rebellious worldview, one which as often sought to reclaim a prior plenitude that had been ravaged by wage slavery and chattel slavery.

Although critics have applied the state of exception mostly to conditions of war, the work of Linebaugh and Rediker, in exposing the internecine violence of the process of "primitive accumulation," suggests its applicability to conditions of labor as well. In casting the history of capitalism and internationalism as an internecine struggle between "globalizing powers" and "planetary wanderers," Linebaugh and Rediker write history in the mode Baucom has termed "melancholy realism."[22] In their jointly authored book, and in a subsequent single-authored article by Rediker, Attucks is proposed as a standard-bearer for this motley crew of rebels against the future, "strangers from afar" who "can help change a national story to something transnational, Atlantic, global."[23]

Relocating Attucks's revolt to the peripheries of patriotic historiography discloses the untold trajectory of a circum-Atlantic proletarian whose fugitive acts disrupt our attempts to tell the history of class without race, or vice versa. But his story does not simply change a national story into a transnational one. It also estranges the national story from itself, revealing the absent center of a potential nation. The unseen, circum-Atlantic gaze upon the nation that Rediker claims as Attucks's "affirmative revenge" might also, conversely, be seen as the errant cause of a protonational identity utterly estranged from itself. Although there has been a salutary and corrective emphasis on the transnational, this new emphasis should not lead to a loss of focus on the critique of nationalism and, in particular, on critiques of the national that proceed from scales that are smaller rather than larger than the nation. As I seek to suggest throughout the remainder of this chapter, Attucks's story is not only that of a circum-Atlantic body instated by revolutionary nationalism but also of a hybrid object between red and black moving fugitively across a landscape, one we must approach at a more local level to read its signposts properly.

Making the Boston Massacre, Making the Mongrel

So what is the relationship between a potential nationality and the circum-Atlantic class of slaves, sailors, and commoners of which Attucks is taken to be representative? This question can be taken up most productively through a focus on the iconography of the Boston Massacre. Rediker insists that Attucks was excluded from proto-nationalist iconography, arguing, for instance, that Paul Revere's famous print of the Boston Massacre—a print he claims "may be the most important political work of art in American history"—omitted Attucks.[24] According to Rediker, Revere's print "dramatically falsified its subject by leaving Attucks out of the picture altogether."[25] Repressed at the center of the national ur-narrative, Attucks reappears at its Atlantic margins. Or does he?

I had already been working on Attucks's story and Revere's print for years when I first encountered this claim, and I have to say when I read it, it initially stunned me. I had always "seen" Attucks in Revere's print, so Rediker's claim that he had been left out altogether took me aback. I rushed to look at it again. What I saw surprised me.[26]

Seven visible soldiers are shooting directly into a crowd. Three bodies lie bleeding on the ground, a fourth is borne away, and a fifth, bleeding head just visible, is also being carried. Since the text below the print specifies five dead, six wounded (two mortally), the massacre is presumably still underway at the moment Revere portrays it. In the versions of this print I have seen, the redcoats of the soldiers, the red blood streaming from the wounded, the blue of the sky, and the brown coat of the oddly impassive dog in the foreground are all hand-colored. But the human faces are left mostly uncolored, with a few only very slightly colored in with a tan wash. The absence of color on many faces suggests how presumptively whiteness operates, as white as the cloud of smoke around them, as white as the paper

Figure 2. Paul Revere, *The Bloody Massacre Perpetuated in King Street Boston on March 5th*, 1770. Courtesy of American Antiquarian Society.

on which the image is printed. The visual identity of colored and un-colored white encapsulates in a glance this naturalization.

Revere's print, itself based on an earlier print by Henry Pelham, appeared for sale before the month was out. As an immediate response to the event it records, it sought to inflame its viewers against the British garrison and, by extension, imperial hegemony. Titled *The Bloody Massacre,* the caption of this colorful, action-packed image named the "unhappy Sufferers" and pleaded their case before "a JUDGE who never can be brib'd." Part of a coordinated rhetorical, political, and legal effort, the print defined the events on King Street as a metonymy of the colonies' aggrieved relation to the metropole. While it stopped short of justifying open insurrection, once war did break out, the Boston Massacre was retrospectively seen as one of the fuses that lit the powder keg of revolution. This retrospective redefinition of the event is literally illustrated in Revere's print. The Boston Massacre did not just happen, it was made, and one of the most important sites of this making or performing was this famous print.

Still, the status of Attucks in it is more complicated than the phrase "dramatic falsification" would imply. On all prior occasions I had looked at this image, given what I knew of the historical event, I had presumed that Crispus Attucks was one of the two fallen bodies in the foreground. After reading Rediker and looking again, I realized that my ability to "see" Attucks was due to my having first encountered this image not as Revere's original but in a nineteenth-century variation that served as the frontispiece to William Cooper Nell's 1855 history, *The Colored Patriots of the American Revolution*.[27] This version is loosely based on Revere, but it also mirrors a tradition of battlefield painting, in particular, John Trumbull's *The Death of General Warren at the Battle of Bunker Hill* (1784). In Nell's image, the dying Attucks is being cradled in a pose directly modeled on the dying general, and he is unambiguously depicted with dark skin and curly hair. Because of my familiarity with this later image, I had simply transposed Attucks's body onto Revere's earlier print when I first saw it. Unthinkingly, I had supposed that Revere had indeed represented Attucks; he had simply represented him *as white*.

My supposition was after all not groundless. Crispus Attucks *is* named in the subtitle of Revere's print as one of the event's victims, and no one else is depicted either individually or realistically in the print. Rediker contrasts Revere's treatment of Attucks with another image of the Massacre that clearly represents Attucks as black. In this version, Attucks is standing and raising a stick in open revolt against the soldiers. But Rediker is mistaken in identifying this image as the Pelham print upon which Revere based his. This image of what I call "the insurrectionary Attucks," like Nell's frontispiece (which I call "the deposition of Attucks"), was actually created over a half-century later, by W. L. Champney and J. H. Bufford, most likely for abolitionist purpose. Pelham's print actually looks much closer to Revere's. It does indeed depict a fallen body with a darker

Figure 3. Frontispiece to William Cooper Nell, *The Colored Patriots of the American Revolution,* 1855.

complexion, curlier hair, and "Negroid" features, but the difference is not as dramatic as with either of the 1850s images.

If Revere based his image on Pelham, then he possibly glossed over Pelham's attempt at racial typification, as Rediker claims. But it is truly hard to say, given that Revere's print is just generally cruder than Pelham's. Revere also introduced a number of other changes and simplifications that hardly seem driven by ideological calculation. And it is not as if the figure Pelham depicted as generically nonwhite was therefore any closer to what Crispus Attucks actually looked like.[28] What Rediker saw as dramatic falsification, I argue, was a result of his considering the insurrectionary Attucks to be closer to the actual event, in the double sense of more accurate and sequentially precedent. But the second view is mistaken, and the first is quite ambiguous. That the insurrectionary Attucks is actually a belated image, one that emerged only when a civil war over slavery was seen to be increasingly inevitable and the image of the Massacre was retrospectively revised, is a vivid example of the circuitous time lag between the performative and the pedagogic.

But while Rediker, no less than Revere, saw in Attucks a reflection of his own revolutionary desires, this hardly excuses the latter

Figure 4. Henry Pelham, *The Fruits of Arbitrary Power, or The Bloody Massacre*, 1770. Courtesy of American Antiquarian Society.

Figure 5. Detail of *The Fruits of Arbitrary Power, or The Bloody Massacre*. Note Pelham's attempt to depict Crispus Attucks with distinctive hair and facial features.

Figure 6. W. L. Champney and J. H. Bufford, *Boston Massacre, March 5th, 1770*. Published by Henry Q. Smith, 284 Washington Street, 1856. Courtesy of American Antiquarian Society. This antebellum reimagining of the Boston massacre draws on the image made famous by Revere, even as it departs meaningfully from his print and Pelham's original.

or renders the whiteness of his print politically innocent. Here I take issue with Barbara Lacey's opinion that Revere's print "conveys the important idea that ordinary men, without regard for skin color, are to be honored for the heroism and self-sacrifice that eventually resulted in the creation of a new nation."[29] Sharing my original assumption that Revere "includes" Attucks by depicting him as white, Lacey implies that we treat this as an honorific. Such a reading would only further obscure the politics of whiteness, thus ignoring the stakes behind Revere's visual assertion of racial sameness with the other British subjects in the image, the soldiers, which identity a depiction of the colonial crowd as motley or colored would obviously spoil. Revere's visual politics, pace Lacey, are quintessentially in "regard" for skin color.

Rather than see Attucks either included or excluded by Revere's print, a critical reading of the visual evidence leads me to understand his status as an *exception*. "The exception," Agamben argues, "is what cannot be included in the whole of which it is a member and cannot be a member of the whole in which it is always already included."[30] Such a limit figure is indeed reached in the absent presence of Attucks in Revere's print, within which it is impossible to say finally whether or not he is included or excluded, because he is clearly both.

The simultaneity of inclusion and exclusion is reflected in the ambivalent reaction to the events of March fifth. The riot and shooting on King Street initially divided the populace, a division best illustrated by the fact that the future revolutionary and president, John Adams, defended the soldiers at trial. What is more, he did so successfully. Conversely, the inquest into Attucks's death—signed on March sixth by many of the town's worthies—read like a prosecuting attorney's opening statement, attributing the cause of his death to his being "willfully and feloniously murdered." A biopolitical imperative is disclosed in this interpolation of a legal verdict—"murder"—into a medical inquiry. The inquest was indeed the first instatement of Attucks's body. As Sappol argues, instatement abrogated poor, racialized, and often anonymous bodies for the social performance of bourgeois anatomy and autonomy. Displays of knowledge about the human body were materially occasioned by the asymmetric exposure of certain bodies to the doctor's scalpel. This scientific dynamic, I argue, had a political double in the abrogation of Attucks's body to the patriot's cause.

That the political instatement of Attucks was conducted in quasi-anonymity makes the point all the more forcefully. A grievance of murder was reached before his name had been correctly ascertained, and the inquest actually names him "Michael Johnson," a pseudonym he had apparently been using while working in Boston. By the time Revere's print appeared, this anonymous-sounding Anglo name had been replaced by a more hybrid appellation (a further indication that Revere's efforts to revise away Attucks's presence was, to say the least, confused and self-contradictory). But his anonymity lasted long enough to raise a question: How did a body fall as Michael Johnson on March fifth, only to live in memory as Crispus Attucks?

The answer is found in the advertisement William Brown placed in the *Boston Gazette* on October 2, November 13, and November 20, 1750, twenty years prior:

> Ran-away from his master *William Brown* of *Framingham,* on the 30th of *Sept.* last, a Molatto Fellow, about 27 Years of Age, named *Crispas,* 5 Feet 2 Inches high, short curl'd Hair, his Knees nearer together than common; had on a light colour'd Bear-skin Coat, plain brown Fustian Jacket, or brown all-Wool one, new Buckskin Breeches, blue Yarn Stockings, and a checked woolen Shirt. Whoever shall take up said Run-away, and convey him to his abovesaid Master, shall have ten Pounds, old Tenor Reward, and all necessary Charges paid. And all Masters of Vessels and others, are hereby cautioned against concealing or carrying off said Servant on Penalty of the Law. Boston, October 2, 1750.[31]

The advertisement observes the conventions of its genre, giving a brief physical description, an inventory of clothes, and some indication of the personality and likely actions of the fugitive. It includes the correct prediction that "Crispas" would run off to sea. And while Brown's advertisement appears as matter-of-fact as Revere's print appears ideological, both participate in the production of Attucks's body as an object to be owned, used, and potentially disposed of. Historical awareness of this advertisement first surfaced in the immediate wake of the massacre, and it has remained a key, perhaps the key, piece of archival, biographical evidence about Attucks's otherwise anonymous life ever since. The ironies and accidents of the archive are nowhere more startling than in a runaway slave advertisement confirming the provenance of a newly enshrined protonational patriot. Crispas's stolen vestments, enumerated to expose his crime of self-possession, now enfold a nascent nationality that might find, in that crime, a mirror of its own ambitions.

So, what's in a name? *Crispas* or *Crispus* indexes the coercive substitution of servile identities for African ones insofar as it is an instance of the diminutive use by slaveholders of exalted names from Western antiquity as appellations for slaves. By contrast, as one nineteenth-century source put it, "The name Attucks is certainly an Indian name signifying 'deer.'"[32] Framingham is next to Natick, where a community of "Praying Indians" was established in the 1650s. Displaced during King Phillip's War twenty-five years later, this community was never able to reconstitute itself on the same terms afterward. A "Molatto Fellow" like Crispus Attucks testified to either the survival or the surrogation of the Massachusett Indians of Natick into the eighteenth century.[33] The very fact that he was granted a surname in death is telling: surnames were routinely denied slaves, but as a "patriot" felled by British gunfire, it was critical that such an honorific resurface.

The hybrid name Crispus Attucks thus stands in for a doubled process of racialized erasure and surrogation, indexing black and native pasts that are incompatible with official national memory. The name provides a possible bridge between native survival and slave fugitivity, at the same time proving so deceptively useful to the white colonist's struggle that even John Adams, who justified the soldiers' actions in court, later signed a revolutionary letter "Crispus Attucks" in a daring literary and racial impersonation.[34] Attucks's hybridity was caught in the fold of pedagogic and performative memory, "concealed and carried off" despite the admonitions of his master (and in the face of the contrary recollection of his master's descendants, who had cheerily informed nineteenth-century historian William Cooper Nell that Attucks had eventually returned to faithful service as a slave!).

The logic of halfness, mixture, and blood quantum is the language of law (as is particularly clear in the British colonial equivalent *half-caste*). It thus extends rather than subverts the logic of exception. For this reason, it has been more productive for me to recast the mulatto as a being out of place, unexpected, and anomalous. Such is indeed the context of Attucks's escape, when *Molatto* appeared as part of an identifying personal description, along with clothing, skill set, and knock-knees. Such is also the case in the uneven attentions paid him in national and protonational hagiography. Attucks's escapology may have taken him out of the frying pan into the firing zone. But in so doing, it registered, as Rediker rightly insists, a power belonging to the incongruous and unexpected assemblages of the "motley crew," whose presence in the streets of pre-Revolutionary Boston was registered less by sight than by raucous sound.

At the soldier's trial three years earlier, John Adams had informed the court that

> We have been entertained with a great variety of phrases, to avoid calling this sort of people a mob.—Some call them shavers, some call them genius's.—The plain English is gentlemen, most probably a motley rabble of saucy boys, negroes and molattoes, Irish teagues and out landish jack tarrs . . . shouting and huzzaing, and threatening life, the bells all ringing, the mob whistle screaming and rending like an Indian yell, the people from all quarters throwing every species of rubbish they could pick up in the street.[35]

Adams carefully mobilized all of the worries Boston's elite had over the "many-headed hydra" of subaltern revolt. More than just disorderliness and violent behavior, he emphasized the racial composition of the crowd, or rather, its lack thereof. His words of abuse— boy, negro, molatto, Irish teague, and jack tarr—indexed disorders of age/rank, occupation, race, and nationality. And the sound of their voices enhanced the disorganization of their bodies: they whistled, screamed, and gave an "Indian yell" (or was it a banshee cry?). They not only picked up "every species of rubbish" to throw at the soldiers, they were themselves species of rubbish. Their violence was not the performance of nationality but a performance of waste.[36] And, as Adams concluded, all this disorder fell

> under the command of a stout Molatto fellow, whose very looks, was enough to terrify any person. . . . And it is in this manner, this town has been often treated; a *Carr* from *Ireland*, and an *Attucks* from *Framingham*, happening to be here, shall sally out upon their thoughtless enterprises, at the head of such a rabble of Negroes, &c., as they can collect together, and then there are not wanting, persons to ascribe all their doings to the good people of the town.[37]

In capturing the raucous sounds and social energies of the likes of Attucks for nationalist purposes, the patriots risked being captured in return, by and for the many. An invidious distinction was needed, then, to distinguish the "good people" of Boston from the *multitude* just "happening to be there," the protocitizens from the lumpen substrate of history that could be acted upon but never itself acted except "thoughtlessly."[38] It followed Sappol's pattern of bourgeois instating of the lumpen, anomalous body when Attucks was posthumously conscripted to the role of citizen of Boston. But such uses became vectors for insurgent and undisciplined desires and affiliations, necessitating a rigid policing of the terms of such instatement.

Thus, long after the trial and revolution, a historian of the American Revolution continued to dismiss the King Street crowd as a "multitude" of "rioters," "a band of the populace, led by a mulatto named Attucks." At midcentury, the *Boston Transcript* repeated this description of a "misguided populace" and termed Attucks a "firebrand of disorder and sedition."[39] Such language admitted the force and energy of the rioters but sought to command, describe, and direct it. The controversy over erecting a public monument to the Boston Massacre, which erupted several times during the nineteenth century before a monument was finally dedicated in the 1880s, reflects the residue of unease the Massacre continued to create in American public life. It suggests that the evocation of an exceptional state of affairs, such as the constituent power of a revolution, brings upon its heels a counterreaction seeking to declare that revolutionary process complete and authority reestablished. In the words of Dana Nelson, it seeks to "manage" democracy, rendering it a problem of effective governance rather than a participatory and above all *loud* process.[40]

The ad also brings up another contiguity between Attucks and the discourse of hybridity: his specification as "Molatto Fellow." But using this specification requires a distinction between hybridity thought of as halfness and hybridity thought of as anomaly. Tropes of halfness, mixture, and mixedness denature the more subversive potential that the anomaly might bear in relation to the sovereign decision. In order to excavate the political implication of Attucks as Molatto Fellow, we must suspend our dominant conceptions of multiracialism as a hidden source of redemption in the American past, encapsulated by figures who somehow straddled the color line, and relocate the mulatto in the genealogy of black and native fugitivity. Shifting focus from the scopic drive that figures the mulatto as "neither black nor white" allows what Fred Moten calls a "phonic materiality" to resound.[41]

Before abolitionist sentimentality and minstrel burlesque figured "the mulatto" as a social type—one bearing, as Foucault wrote of another nineteenth-century fabulation, the homosexual, "a morphology, with an indiscreet anatomy and possibly a mystical physiology"—the word represented a vector of interpellation and a loud, social, and illegal cacophony.[42] The juridical legibility of the mulatto first emerged, unlike its later statistical counterpart, not in order to speculate upon the inner meaning of blood quantum but rather to include the exception and thus to preserve the law's authority to decide. The racial state of exception, I conclude, produces situations of legal, racial, and political anomaly that cannot be accurately reproduced in terms of mixedness or halfness. In particular, such situations refuse the discourse of harmonization or "integration" so critical to romantic and, as we shall see, heterosexual deployments of "race mixture."

An alternative provenance thus opens for the mongrel mulatto prior to its attachment to the biopolitics of blood quantum. Here we can pick up on Jack Forbes's suggestions and consider how *mulatto* in the early modern Atlantic world might have served as a catchall term for that which might otherwise escape racial categorization, a tactic still discernible in eighteenth-century U.S. legislation examined by Joanne Melish. Such legislation did not deploy *Molatto* to speculate on the ethnological niceties of Indian versus Negro nor to identify the Molatto as half-white and therefore entitled to special privileges. Instead, efforts to enforce a white–nonwhite distinction—one modeled on master–servant, husband–wife, parent–child distinctions—included the exceptional category of molatto in order to preserve the sovereignty of racial decision within the law.[43]

We can employ this understanding of the exception to approach again the uncanny symmetry of hybrid agency. And we can reconsider Samira Kawash's proposal, in her reading of nineteenth-century black narrative, for a theoretical shift from hybridity to singularity. Kawash's use of singularity appears to be based less on Badiou and more on Deleuze, Spinoza, and Agamben himself (albeit the Agamben of *The Coming Community* rather than the Agamben of *Homo Sacer*).[44] After detailing some limits to hybridity as model, Kawash proposes singularity as an alternative communitarian ethic: "This togetherness is not the community of obligation or communion between subjects; rather, in this togetherness would be a community without rule, in which otherness, or singularity, would occur without being destroyed or incorporated through the imposition of the identity of the same." "Responsibility," she argues elsewhere, "requires the recognition of singularity, the unique, the unrepeatable, the unknowable, the irreducible otherness of the other."[45] In resisting an overly expository account of who Attucks really was, I have sought to be responsible to his irreducible otherness. And yet I have done so in full awareness that the sovereign decision does not exempt the singular, unrepeatable, and unknowable but seeks to enfold it within the exception. Consequently, I argue, the critical uses of mirroring, duplicative, antifetishistic hybridity are not obviated by a fidelity to the singular, as Kawash suggests. If anything, such a fidelity to the singular requires an even greater determination to map hybrid temporality and agency.

If an ethics of singularity is not to descend into pure nominalism, we must remain alive to the repetitions of the strictly unrepeatable, of restorations with a critical difference, of, in a word, performance. As I turn here to antebellum efforts to perform fidelity to the events of 1770 and the legacy of the American Revolution, I do so in full recognition of how much those efforts fall short of the kind of ideal Kawash spells out. Indeed, in an earlier article, I took to task the omissions and exclusions of the forms of community making employed around the effigy of Attucks.[46] But I now think that to dismiss these efforts as rule-bound and obligatory efforts at mimetic patriotism would be to miss their performativity, a performativity established precisely in terms of the time lag between event and iteration. It would be to miss how, for performance, fidelity to the past can never be in terms of "how it really was" but must instead struggle somehow to restore and make new.

But if this in the case, then we must follow Agamben's argument a step further and consider his exegesis of Walter Benjamin's eighth thesis on the philosophy of history:

> The tradition of the oppressed teaches us that the "state of emergency" in which we live is not the exception but the rule. We must attain to a conception of history that accords with this insight. Then we will clearly see that it is our task to bring about the real state of emergency.[47]

Benjamin's distinction between the "state of emergency" (in scare quotes) and the *real* state of emergency is glossed by Agamben in terms of the "attempt by state power to annex anomie through the state of exception" and the countervailing attempt "every time to assure . . . an existence outside of the law."[48] I have been arguing for the presence of this struggle in the making of the Boston Massacre and its attempted instatement of the anomalous, mongrel, molatto body. And although *anomie* and *anomaly* are not etymologically linked, the conceptual work the former does for Agamben inspires my own attempt to specify *anomaly* as that which the law seeks to annex, but whose existence outside the law it is our task to preserve, in part by laboring to bring about a real state of exception. At the very least, it has been seen as the primary task of the tradition of the oppressed. In the remainder of this chapter, I seek to substantiate this claim by considering the commemorative performances of Attucks and the American Revolution within the black abolitionist politics in the period after 1840. Those politics did indeed seek to attain to a concept of history in which the racialized state of exception that annexed Attucks's effigy to the nation might lead to a real state of exception in the struggle against slavery, an existence beyond the law of slavery and the symbolic order of race.

Black Abolition as a Mirror of Liberty

In the famous Silent Parade organized by the NAACP in 1917 in New York City, a man at the head of the procession carried a banner reading "The First Blood for American Independence was Shed by a Negro Crispus Attucks."[49] The parade surrogated antebellum black militia, who also marched under Attucks's blazon. At the 2004 Democratic National Convention in Boston, black presidential contender Al Sharpton invoked Attucks's name. Throughout the nation today, buildings and parks are named after Attucks, and any number of accounts of his life designed for young readers are available in print (although, tellingly, no full-dress biography exists). All this makes Attucks among the more ubiquitous figures of African American history, one of those obligatory "firsts" through which the black experience in America is narrated, along with Phillis Wheatley and Benjamin Banneker.

That Attucks is as well known as he is, and as easily identified with African American history, is largely the fruits of the efforts of a little-known black abolitionist and historian, William Cooper Nell.[50] Nell, a faithful toiler in the vineyards of reform, assisted William Lloyd Garrison in the printing of *The Liberator,* which led a series of campaigns against discrimination and segregation in schools, theaters, and common carriers. Embracing a proto-Duboisian vision of propagandizing the race, Nell's historicist efforts resulted in two publications, *Services of Colored Americans in the Wars of 1776 and 1812* in 1851 and *The Colored Patriots of the American Revolution* in 1855, that emphasized neglected black contributions to a nation that enslaved and excluded them. Before American history was professionalized in the hands of men like George Bancroft and Frederick Jackson Turner in the second half of the nineteenth century, the antebellum histories of black writers like Nell, Henry Highland Garnet, James W. C. Pennington, and R. B. Lewis were a preemptive riposte to the consensual narration of a collective white past that excluded black achievement.[51]

Although often most remembered today as a historian and abolitionist, Nell devoted much of his life to a form of urban social work that, a half century later, might be associated with the settlement house movement.[52] Born into a needy, abused community relieved Nell of the obligation to "settle" into one, but much of his rhetoric and practice anticipated later reformers. He initiated a long list of educational, self-improvement, and amateur theatrical societies in Boston, where he lived out his days, the majority of them spent as a bachelor whose friends fretted over his "single-ness."[53] Among the organizations he initiated, according to Dorothy Porter Wesley, were "the Juvenile Garrison Independent Society, the Boston Minor's Exhibition Society, the Young Men's Literary Society, the Boston Mutual Lyceum, the Histrionic Club, and the Adelphic Union Library Association."[54] Like many a "Socrates in the slums" after him, to borrow Kevin Murphy's telling phrase, Nell initiated local and regional associations that sought to extend a Victorian ideal of genteel Christian culture to impoverished and working-class Americans.

Nell's political activism emerged out of his desire to participate in the educational and social life of the intellectual capital of America. Never forgetting the insults he experienced as a child, Nell worked tirelessly to gain access to Boston schools for black children. When just thirteen, he had been excluded from a dinner at Faneuil Hall honoring student award winners of the Franklin Medal. Nell surreptitiously attended anyway, posing as a waiter. The chair of the school committee spotted him and called him over to shamefacedly admit, "You ought to be here with the other boys."[55] Early on, Nell had mastered the maximal potential of the minimalist gesture. It is typical of his assiduous but unshowy style that among his wartime activities many years later was serving on a state committee charged with going through Massachusetts statutes and removing the word *white*.[56]

An incident in 1853, when Nell, fellow black abolitionist Sarah Remond Parker, and Parker's sister Caroline were all turned away from the Howard Athenaeum Theater, then presenting the opera Don Giovanni, captures their particular mix of social striving and political agitation. Denied the seats for which they had paid, the party was thrown out of the theater when they declined segregated seating. Remond Parker sued for assault, and in the end they returned to gain admission on their own terms.[57] As such incidents reflect, Nell's life encapsulated the strife experienced by free people of color in a period when simply performing the ordinary routines of urban life could be met with insult and incensed outrage. His participation in antiracist histrionics, on and off stage, shed light on the title of a black magazine of the period that Nell supported: *The Mirror of Liberty*.[58] Black women or men enjoying, educating, or simply transporting themselves about town held up an uncanny mirror to the liberties enjoyed by whites, threatening assumptions of white superiority with a sly and hybrid civility. An exception to the law of racial slavery, free blacks thrived in the interstices of a New England society that, by the 1850s, had officially disowned its own (then quite recent) history of slaveowning. In so contradicting the convenient formulation of a "free north" and "slave south," the free people of color in Boston, New York City, Philadelphia, and elsewhere antagonistically cooperated with America's aspirational imperative.

Nell's feminized activism on issues of education, self-improvement, scholarship, and healthy recreation has, however, led to his being assigned a lower historical profile than famous men like Martin Delany and Frederick Douglass. Much of this fate seems to follow from Nell's unwillingness to embrace the role of race leader to which, through their very contrasting styles, both Delany and Douglass eagerly aspired. A gendered discourse of independent manhood underlies the usual political differences drawn between Delany and Douglass, whose early cooperation on their joint venture, *The North Star,* gave way ultimately to the pointedly titled *Frederick Douglass' Paper*.[59] The notorious quip attributed to Douglass, "I thank God for making me a man simply; but Delany always thanks him for making him a *black man*," nonetheless bespeaks a shared and assumed ground of masculine identification.[60] Nell, by contrast, was seen as potentially lacking even that. Douglass impugned Nell's manhood, calling him a "contemptible tool" for daring to side with William Lloyd Garrison at a time Douglass had come into conflict with his former mentor.[61] Douglass's anger that Nell would place his loyalty to Garrison above his loyalty to the race, as personified in Douglass, also reflected the gendered impetus behind Douglass's drive to come out from under Garrison's shadow. The flip side of such a drive toward masculine self-making was the anxiety produced by Nell's apparent willingness to continue indefinitely in a supportive rather than a leadership role. "Nell toiled inconspicuously," one historian aptly concluded, "in the antislavery garden."[62] That in the Howard Athenaeum incident, Nell seems to have understood the appropriateness of Sarah Remond Parker bringing the suit, given the limited advantage black women held in invoking ideologies of bourgeois female respectability, underlines his prioritization of cooperative and cogendered political engagement.[63]

Nell's political style has not, however, been typically read in this generous way. Insofar as antebellum black activists have been divided into integrationists and nationalists, assimilationists and emigrationists, Nell has typically been assigned to the former, less radical, more accomodationist side. But before we accept this historical judgment, we might consider the feminist scholarship that has critiqued the masculinist bias in the narration of black leadership. Hazel Carby has shown how even male leaders who espoused support for woman's rights (as Douglass did) could continue to champion a normative image of the "race man" that implicitly excluded or sidelined both women and other men who could not live up to its requirements.[64] Marlon Ross has built on Carby's insight, refiguring the black male reform tradition as an anxious process of "manning the race."[65] Posing manhood as a desired goal rather than a biological given reveals the stakes in patriarchy for men routinely denied access to it.

Ironically, as Ross shows, manning the race as a task frequently fell to feminized men like Nell, as we can see in the public commemorations he organized as tribute to the militant, manly memory of Crispus Attucks. Sympathetic to the Quaker principles of his friend, the poet John Greenleaf Whittier, Nell assured readers in his first military history that "my predilections are, *least* and *last* for what constitutes the pomp and circumstance of war." His was not, he assured them, "any eulogy upon the shedding of blood" but a corrective to an exclusionary record.[66] Nell continued to take such a nuanced stance even into the Civil War years, a time when most abolitionists, black and white, pacifist and otherwise, embraced a war to end slavery. Martin Delany served in the Union Army; Frederick Douglass sent his sons and served as a military recruiter among black men. Nell, who was of the same generation, joined women like Sarah Remond Parker in writing patriotic pamphlets and organizing morale-boosting events, such as Crispus Attucks Day, on the home front.[67]

Nell's orchestration of a commemorative ceremony for Crispus Attucks in 1859 came on the cusp of war and on the heels of over a decade of work in print culture, social work, and black history. As early as 1845, according to his correspondence, Nell had been working on "the Biography of Attucks," the kernel of a progressively more expansive historiographic project that, by its 1855 incarnation, greatly exceeded its titular task of simply narrating military contributions to the revolution.[68] Indeed, *The Colored Patriots* is such an omnibus, sprawling work—organized geographically rather than chronologically, encompassing the entirety of the period between the Revolution and 1855 and including a mix of history, fiction, and romance—that the apparent narrowing of subject from the earlier *Services of Colored Americans,* which dealt with not one but two wars, is illusory. It is history as assemblage, composed in indirect fulfillment of the task of writing the biography of Attucks.

As John Ernest has observed, Nell endeavored "to create a historical work capable of shaping a community and preparing that community for action," and his shift from demarcating specific, punctual dates ("1776," "1812") in his first work to using the open-ended word *Revolution* suggests to me that Nell was posing the possibility of the American Revolution as unfinished in his own time and inviting his readers, male and female, black and white, to imagine themselves participating in that unfinished revolution.[69] In this sense, all the women and men he described in his book—from Phillis Wheatley to Denmark Vesey to Deborah Samson (the white woman who disguised herself as a man in order to serve in General Washington's army) to Crispus Attucks—were included in an open-ended vision of the "Colored Patriots of the American Revolution." Each term in that title underwent a subtle transformation in Nell's text, mirroring back the key ideologemes of national discourse in what nevertheless amounted to a counterstatement to the constituted power upholding the national interest.

That Nell's activism was not interpreted by dominant American society as desirable "assimilation" is reflected in the response these mimetic gestures gleaned. In 1851, Nell had joined a group of six other signatories—including Charles Remond and Lemuel Burr—in petitioning the Massachusetts Legislature to erect a monument to Crispus Attucks as "the first martyr in the Boston Massacre." Rejecting their petition, the Legislature turned to its own historical council to produce the assertion that Attucks had not, in fact, been the first to die for American liberty. As Nell noted in response to this rebuff, such a splitting of hairs willfully repressed the earlier town tradition that had made the March fifth "famous in our annals as the day which history selects as the dawn of the American Revolution." By building upon an abandoned collective memory, Nell's recovery work had inadvertently revealed the arbitrary and contingent character of historical narration. Recognizing this, Nell had acidly noted, "The rejection of the petition was to be expected, if we accept the axiom that a colored man never gets justice done him in the United States, except by mistake."[70] An unexpected sentiment, to be sure, coming from the mouth of someone who supposedly embraced Americanism and its values!

I will return to Nell's rich and strange maxim in chapter 4, where I suggest that its sarcasm indexes a particularly apt way of practicing history as negative heritage. Here I want to note two aspects of Nell's apparently thoroughgoing pessimism that might otherwise be neglected. The first is the concept of the mistake as a principle of historical determination, and the second is the status of race as axiomatic, that is, as consisting "on the basis of non-defined terms."[71] Arguing that American values can never *intend* to grant the "colored man" justice, Nell implied the presence of an unintended justice at the limit of American law, that is, as its mistake. At the same time, he exposed the rule-bound yet arbitrary status of race as a symbolic status founded on a set of unstated and undefined rules. Rather than being based on the self-evident facts of nature, race as symbolic law is based on circularly defined terms. One need not argue for the philosophical subtlety of Nell's wry observation to appreciate the richness of this vernacular insight into the state of exception. And where legal or petitionary redress failed, as it must fail given the tautological reasoning of American racism, a set of other, subterranean strategies came into play.

These strategies sang the nation in an unexpected and uncanny key. In a remarkable coincidence, the Dred Scott decision disenfranchising blacks and removing any safe harbor within the union for fugitive slaves was handed down March 6, 1857, one day after the anniversary of the Boston Massacre. Nell seized upon this concurrence. In a broadside calling for the observance of Crispus Attucks Day on March 5, 1858, Nell wrote:

> In view of the alarming spread of despotism in these United States—the suppression of Free Speech in one half of the Union—the subjugation of white citizens, and annihilation of the citizenship of Colored Americans by the Dred Scott Decision, the subscriber has, after mature deliberation, concluded, that now is the timely and significant hour for an application of that sentiment in the Constitution of Massachusetts, which declares *"that a frequent recurrence to its fundamental principles is absolutely necessary to preserve the advantages of liberty, and to maintain a free government."*[72]

Nell's citation dramatically evoked constituent power against the spread of despotism, placing the U.S. government of the 1850s in the very position Revere had placed the British monarchy in the 1770s: as a remote, unresponsive, and unjust power. Tellingly citing the state rather than the federal constitution, Nell sought to remember those protonational political energies, to "muster" them in the military sense of gathering for training, exhibition, and display. The pacifist Nell was led to celebrate the legacy of black military service not in the name of the nation but in the terms of a protonational political desire, indexed particularly by Crispus Attucks himself, whose militancy had little to do with military service per se. It reawakened the awareness that the first "colored patriot" was a street fighter, not a soldier.

Nell couched his public call issued in January as a mustering of militancy to reassert local and state social memory against federal authority. The doubled historicity of that occasion—protesting Dred Scott, remembering Attucks—registered multiple and competing temporalities at work in the consecration of Boston and Massachusetts as liberated ground, throwing into question oversimplified dichotomies of black integration or separatism from white society. Crispus Attucks Day, which was then held annually through the war years and up to the one hundredth anniversary of Attucks's death, engaged black and radical Boston in the reenactment of the projective past, interrupting the smooth progress of the nation with the contrapuntal voice of black patriotism.

These historical performances sought to appropriate, to use Walter Benjamin's celebrated phrase, "a memory as it flashes up in a moment of danger."[73] The social memory of insurrection, which was consciously evoked against the tyranny of the nation-state, had multiple determinants. Among the most neglected of those determinants were the minoritarian social desires that reside in the oft-occluded histories of African American and Native American New England and in the even more occluded Afro-Native intersections. Hovering above this complex commemorative practice was the effigy of a fallen Attucks, whose image always graced the publicity literature and who made a regular appearance in the reenactments of the Boston Massacre that were usually a feature of the day. His martial black image, leading a group of men to assault British troops on Boston soil, clearly surrogated the abolitionists' own image of themselves storming jails to free captured fugitives and, in the war years, clamoring to enlist.

Part of this martial black image drew from Attucks's mongrel past. One can detect something of a mongrel, monstrous Attucks in the earlier-mentioned and remarkable revisioning of the Boston Massacre scene drawn in 1856 by William Champney, lithographed by John Bufford, and sold in beautiful full color by Henry Q. Smith of Boston. If the 1770 trial had turned on whether Attucks and the others would be viewed as sacrificed patriots or rowdy insurgents, and if the corresponding clash between Revere's pictorial depiction of a "horrid massacre" and Adams's courtroom indictment of the "motley rabble" mobilized these twin alternatives to politically opposed intent, then a certain overlap became apparent in the 1850s revivals. In this image, the urge to draw Attucks nearer by means of his likeness has also resulted in a much more militant, erect, and angry Attucks than had been depicted previously. He is shown with a club in his hand and thus merging the images produced through Revere's patriotface and Adams's hatchet job. If Champney's depiction is any indication (and its appearance in woodcut form on the war-era Attucks Day broadsides suggests that is), then the Attucks celebrated by black abolitionists might be thought of as a "rowdy molatto" cleverly disguised as a "colored patriot."

Marcus Wood's excellent account of Crispus Attucks Day as commemorative ceremony, while mindful of crediting Nell as its "organizational genius," places too strong an emphasis on the organic connection of this event to what he calls "long-standing performative tradition" in the "African-American community in Boston." Situating Crispus Attucks Day within "an unbroken history of African-American freedom festivals" not only understates the self-conscious novelty of what Nell was attempting, it unwittingly reemphasizes the event's status as a compensatory response to white exclusion.[74] Most problematically, as we shall see further in chapters 2 and 3, it misses the intraracial struggles over race leadership and appropriate forms of festivity in which Nell and others of his generation were engaged.

This is not to assert that black communities in the northern states lacked performance traditions that were both similar and different from those in southern plantations. Scholars have studied these traditions of black communal celebration before and after emancipation in the north.[75] Africans in New England had been celebrating their own annual festivals since "old colony times." The most telling of these early black celebrations was Negro Election Day on which slaves gathered and elected leaders and judges among themselves, ceremonial roles that frequently carried real authority within the slave community. While such a commemoration displayed its mimetic and supplementary nature in its very title, it was by no means a farce enacted for the benefit of slaveholders but a real concession to slave culture and its demands for limited self-organization. White Americans in the colonies must have possessed their own ambivalent relationship to elections, given their status as subjects to a Crown and Parliament not of their choosing and a very limited suffrage even for those positions they could select. The ritual inversion of Negro Election Day, when the least members of society enjoyed a power the greatest lacked—the power to select their own king—spoke to more than just the reaffirmation of white over black: it bespoke the commonness of the disinherited that was indeed routinely evoked in the revolutionary era whenever patriots, conveniently, bemoaned their status as slaves to King George.[76]

With the advent of revolution and independence, Waldstreicher shows, an American nationality enacted through social performance came increasingly to exclude black participation. This racist reaction against black participation in patriotic commemoration drove New England blacks to commemorate an alternative calendrical cycle, especially, after 1833, West Indian emancipation day. The racist attack on black participation in the public performance of nation, however, overdetermined reformist reactions against black popular culture in the late 1820s and 1830s. Black leaders, drawn primarily from the clergy, came to despair of and disparage black public life as rowdiness, associating it with alcohol consumption, immorality, and impiety. Rather than embrace a tradition of public black festivity, these reformers and race leaders sought to harness and redirect that impulse toward forms of participation and display that would prove more respectable, all the time insisting that this was not a quietist gesture but the truest act of fidelity to the interests of the race. In 1839, for example, two separate celebrations of West Indian emancipation—the centerpiece of antebellum black commemorative practices—were held in Boston, because of dispute over temperance. Nell, perhaps predictably, sided with "the Cold Water Festivities."[77]

Rather than a collective black subject summoning forth a Crispus Attucks Day out of the unbroken history of its performative traditions, then, what took place after 1859 was the result of the dramaturgic and reformist initiatives of Nell and his cohort making a public claim upon national, not just racial, memory. The program for the first Attucks day drew upon Hosea Easton's *Treatise,* discussed in my introduction, in making explicit its proclamation of a state of exception.[78] The program excerpted Easton's argument that the American Revolution destroyed slavery by creating an interregnum in which "the colored people . . . were held no longer by any legal power."[79] Because there was then "no efficient law in the land except martial law, and that regarded no one as a slave," the revolutionary state of exception had nullified slavery from then on. While recognizing that the U.S. Constitution tacitly recognized slavery, Nell cited Easton to the effect that this constituted state of the affair was negated by the constituent powers of its own revolutionary formation. Crispus Attucks Day sought to attain to a performed conception of history in which the state of exception proclaimed by the state—that black people had no rights a white person was bound to respect—would be supplanted by a real state of emergency.

Arguments like these were not designed to persuade courts of law: they were meant to inspire in their readers and performers a spirit of insurrection. But the methods used are, to modern readers, surprising. At the event itself, first held at historic Fanueil Hall where Crispus Attucks had lain in state along with other victims of the Massacre, fiery speeches by the likes of Wendell Phillips, Charles

Remond, and Garrison himself were accompanied by a seventy-five-cent coat check, the Attucks Glee Club, tableaux vivant, and scheduled appearances by local celebrities that lent the proceedings an air that was equal parts stage spectacle, parlor soiree, and political rally. Poems by Frances Ellen Watkins and Charlotte Forten were sung by the male Glee Club, and the "Living Mementoes" section of theatrical tableau included scenes of Washington crossing the Delaware. As it became an annual event into the war years, its eclectic aspects grew. By 1862, the day's programming had taken on all the appearances of a genteel variety show:

> a series of exercises, consisting of TABLEAUX—Historical, Mythological, Classical, Humorous, and Domestic: To be represented by a Select Volunteer Company of Young Ladies and Gentlemen, Masters & Misses. The whole interspersed with appropriate Music, and the Vocalising of Operatic gems, by the Boston Quartette Club.

That particular winter evening culminated—in a manner designed to compete with concurrent stagings of *Uncle Tom's Cabin*—with a grand Allegorical Tableau

> in which are deposited Souvenirs of Attucks, viz., his CUP—an original copy of the "Boston Gazette" of November, 1750, containing an Advertisement of Crispus Attucks' runaway from William Brown, of Framingham . . . [and] The MUSE OF HISTORY and the GENIUS OF LIBERTY are on either side—the one invoking a Nation's recognition of the Patriotic Services of Colored Americans—the other proclaiming Freedom to the enslaved—while JUSTICE approves the mission of both.[80]

Authenticating details such as William Brown's ad for the runaway "Crispas" were integrated into this pedagogic, inspiring, and no doubt unsettling spectacle. In 1864, as the Civil War ground on and Lincoln campaigned for reelection, the celebration included a performance by Nell himself, playing Jeremy Diddler in a "Humorous Dramatic scene, entitled HOW TO GET A BREAKFAST."[81] As should be clear from even this incomplete archive, Crispus Attucks Day was not a collective or organic continuation of such colonial-era slave practices as Negro Election Day or even public commemorations of the emancipation in the West Indies. It seems much more specifically an attempt to hybridize bourgeois amateur theatricality—in an era when the theater remained in disrepute among the pious and required a variety of aliases under which to operate—by inserting the incongruous element of black participation and performativity, beginning with the requisite heroicization of Attucks but proceeding much further into areas humorous and dramatic, historical and mythological, commemorative and playful. These performances instated black patriotism and delivered "representative" images meant to correct and potentially chasten other members of the community. Robert Reid-Pharr has shown how the justly celebrated early novels of the African American literary tradition often took on such a domesticating agenda.[82] The much more pervasive and participatory cultures of public performance and magazine and newspaper readership (the medium within which the most read of these novels were first circulated) must be seen in the light of this ongoing effort at reforming the race, however mixed or inconclusive its results.

Crispus Attucks Day would be lost in an overly facile division of early black political culture into nationalist and integrationist, militant and suasionist factions, popular and bourgeois.[83] To reckon with black abolitionist performativity is to challenge the assumption of its mimetic nature, which as I have argued is also to challenge assumptions about mimesis itself. In her study of black politicized performativity in the nineteenth and early twentieth centuries, Daphne Brooks demonstrates the promise of this approach in her consideration of the moving panorama exhibited by the fugitive slave Henry Box Brown, an exhibit he named *The Mirror of Slavery.*[84] Brooks demonstrates how such acts of mimesis and reflection could serve to alienate and estrange the image of America. Mimicry could be menacing insofar as it represented, as in the case of Brown, an absconding with the means of representation. As scholars such as R. J. M. Blackett, Audrey Fisch, and Marcus Wood have shown, the peripatetic mobility of black abolitionists, particularly after the 1840s, helped stoke a cosmopolitan disapproval for the barbarism practiced in the southern U.S. states, at the same time holding up an unflattering mirror to the nation as a whole.[85] Such transnational human rights campaigning did indeed sustain the radical flame lit by eighteenth-century revolutionaries and abolitionists, even as it accommodated itself to the teetotaling, perfectionist, and spiritualist predilections of the American reform tradition.[86] Martin Delany left work at the *North Star* to enroll in medical school, and David Ruggles, the militant New York City abolitionist and publisher of the aforementioned *Mirror of Liberty,* the man who harbored a young fugitive from Maryland named Frederick Bailey during his first few days in freedom, went on to found a successful water cure establishment catering to the transcendental set.[87] R. J. Young makes the obvious point that, with few exceptions, reform politics was a paying career for black abolitionists, and an upwardly mobile one at that. And while Young chooses to emphasize how such ambitions would have purportedly alienated ordinary black folk, it is clear that personal and professional goals could be recognized and embraced as well as castigated and impugned within the black community.[88] The black American public's deep and abiding love for culture heroes drawn from the arena of sports and music, already nascent in the nineteenth century, should serve as a reminder, where reminders are needed, that black authenticity is rarely asserted solely in terms of a static class location.

And if class was a volatile category within these settings, so too was the body. Abolitionist performance culture existed on a direct continuum with its evangelical, temperate, spiritualist, and sentimental environment, with all the ingrained Christian suspicions of bodily excess implied therein and all the wacky unpredictability that the absence of an established religious authority could give free reign to. Black abolitionist uplift politics, insofar as they signaled for the support of white reformers, had to simultaneously emphasize and cultivate the black American body and negotiate its perilous proximity to a slave culture that black abolitionists could neither disavow nor embrace. This negotiation could be seen in Hosea Easton's ginger strides through Hartford's street in "so much suit." And it was equally evident in Nell's politico-theatrical turn as Jeremy Diddler in "How to Get a Breakfast."

When Attucks first surfaced in abolitionist politics as a "colored patriot" in the 1850s, that latter notion served to mediate a contradiction between the patriotic ties to land and liberty that black abolitionists strongly felt and their equally fervent moral revulsion against the nation's upholding of slavery and racism as being fully consonant with democracy and freedom. That is to say, it both evoked and troubled the national Thing. Historians are increasingly willing to speak of the performative dimension of this mediation in nonpejorative terms. Jeffrey Kerr-Ritchie has put forward the thesis that black militia practice in the antebellum north—and other black and brown mustering elsewhere in the Atlantic slave plantation complex— represented a "rehearsal for war" understood as forever imminent so long as slavery survived.[89] I want to call attention to Kerr-Ritchie's telling metaphor of "rehearsal," which brings together military and theatrical connotations within a single alternative and performative temporality. In an environment of constitutionally sanctioned, democratically ratified racial oppression, black abolitionists and their allies turned to revolutionary memories in both determination and despair. In revisiting the period leading up to the colonial war of independence—a period in which performances like the Boston Tea Party and the Boston Massacre played a key role—they consciously reenacted and radicalized the past.

But if the effigy of Attucks is thus not solely motivated by a compensatory correction of the historical record, but also by the inhabitation of the political present by a fugitive and insurrectionary spirit, then we must rethink the customary use of mirroring as stabilizing metaphors, that is, as simply mimicking a static national or racial identity. In the bourgeois conventions at work in "cold water" festivities and sentimental stage spectacles, spectacles like the drawing room version of *Uncle Tom's Cabin* Stowe herself adapted for the staged readings of the elegant black actress Mary Webb, one can see the mirror metaphor taking on other connotations. A split and tension within the race over questions of political radicalism, race pride, gendered propriety, and bourgeois respectability emerges clearly in the scholarship of Carby, Ross, and Reid-Pharr. David Ruggles's magazine title *The Mirror of Liberty* captures many valences of what we might call this politicization of mimesis. We might use it to reread the somewhat outmoded attempts to divide early black politics into camps not simply as ex post facto simplifications but as indirect affirmations of this fundamental split in a black subject constituted in community. This split is already recognized in the well-known shorthand through which black history is so often read—as the agonistic rivalry of a series of exemplary race leaders: Douglass and Delany, W. E. B. Du Bois and Booker T. Washington, Martin Luther King Jr. and Malcolm X. Every effort to stabilize once and for all the ideological content of their exact difference founders on the real complexity and constant evolution of each of these individuals. But what those failures expose, potentially, is the abiding presence of the split itself. Rather than evade it by resolving it back into camps and proscribing one or the other, we might move past the great man theory that wrongly condenses black history into the gestures of admittedly heroic individuals and instead linger "in the cut" as a valid structuring principle of black collective life.[90]

In furthering this examination of the split subject, we may wish also to follow Seshadri-Crooks in drawing a distinction between the subject of the imaginary, with which Lacan associated the mirror stage, and the subject of symbolic racialization, which clearly possesses some relation to mirroring and mimesis, but not on precisely the same terms. The consequence of identifying racial subjectivity with the ego's imaginary formation in the mirror stage, Seshadri-Crooks warns, is that it leads us to "accept race as an a priori fact of human difference." "In other words," she continues, "there is no possibility of interrogating the structure and constitution of the subject of race."[91] In her compelling account of the mirror stage, Seshadri-Crooks argues:

> The difference between the visible body as an ego function, and the visible body as a function of Whiteness or racialization, can be understood as the difference between seeing and being seen. The subject of the imaginary is constituted as *seeing* by the signifier, whereas the subject of race is constituted as *seen,* the subject of the gaze, through a certain logic of the signifier.[92]

Crispus Attucks Day, we may conclude following Seshadri-Crooks, reconstituted the racial subject as seen in the discriminatory gaze. It did so not merely by renegotiating that "seen" but by producing the split through which the possibility of another alternative and participatory seeing might occur.

Within the field of the visible, in other words, there is preserved a fault line between the symbolic law of race and the insurrectionary embodiments of the imaginary, a split or cut Moten associates with the massive undertheorization of black phonic materiality. We can make use Moten and Seshadri-Crooks's reconsiderations of the mirror stage to argue that the symbolic law of race, even in its efforts to decide upon the exception, meets a limit on the other side of a coin that is always turning. Not in spite of but because of the contested nature of the terrain Nell sought to map through his eclectic mimetic performances, the visual reiteration and sonic amplification of a "colored patriotism" provided occasions for a dramatic and unexpected escape.

2. In Night's Eye: Amalgamation, Respectability, and Shame

In the autumn of 1833, a traveling agent for the antislavery journal the *Emancipator and Journal of Public Morals* was traveling northbound by stagecoach from Pittsburgh, Pennsylvania, to Lake Erie, "the beautiful western country," as he called it, having witnessed the successful formation of the Pittsburgh Anti-Slavery Society and built regional contacts and subscribers for his New York City–based newspaper.[1] The stagecoach departed after midnight, and the six passengers, crowded together in an "Egyptian darkness," fell into conversation. The subject turned to the burning issue of abolition. The traveling agent, in his first season as an antislavery worker, reported that his fellow passengers "all declared themselves opposed to slavery, but could not exactly agree upon a plan of removing it." Like many Americans, they were particularly hung upon the question of what to do with free people of color who would not voluntarily return to Africa. If free blacks were permitted to remain, they asked, what would prevent them from marrying into white society and creating a mongrel posterity?

The agent stunned one passenger, the most virulently opposed to both abolition and amalgamation (the agent nicknamed him "the animal"), by openly admitting he would happily marry a black woman in preference to a white. Flummoxed by this dark revelation of abolitionist amalgamationism, the hostile passenger declared to the others:

> Well, to be candid, I did not in reality believe it was a question of amalgamation by intermarrying, but when I discuss the question, I have used the term amalgamation as a scare crow, because it seems

to be the only thing that will reach the prejudices of the public, and prevent them from falling in with their [abolitionist] measures. As much as I have harped upon amalgamation, I never could believe that so many good people would engage in advocating such a doctrine until *now*.[2]

"The animal," under cloak of darkness, disclosed the amalgamation charge to be a "scare crow," or what in rhetorical circles is sometimes called "a parade of horribles." It was put up to "reach the prejudices of the public" in a way rational argumentation seemed unable to, and it usually decided the question. But this particular night he was unable to bait the traveling agent further or convince him to recant the "devilish bad taste" of wanting a black wife. So the passenger lapsed into silence until morning, when, to his astonishment, and the mirth of the other people on board the coach, he discovered that the man he had been talking to "in night's eye" was not as he supposed white, but black. When the coach stopped at an inn, the indignant traveler attempted to exclude his erstwhile interlocutor from the breakfast table. But the other passengers banded together in defense of the rights of David Ruggles, their erstwhile "amalgamator," to at least culinary equity.[3]

Ruggles relished retelling this anecdote not only because it exposed the insincerity of an antiamalgamation rabble-rouser but also because the impromptu debate conducted in night's eye provided a singular occasion in which the "spurious issue" of race mixing could actually be turned to his advantage. In a premonitory version of John Rawls's political parable, darkness drew a veil of ignorance around the specific dispensation that individual participants in this political discussion might be assigned in the future they projected. This threw the biopolitical presumptions of race-thinking into specific, if temporary, disarray. Night, along with the enforced conviviality of the common carrier, afforded Ruggles rare access to the abstract and formal equality of the bourgeois public sphere.[4] Exercising his manhood rights to reason publicly and to marry according to "taste," Ruggles outwitted someone who could not imagine that the hypothetical racial equality under discussion might be happening right under his nose.

At the same time as Ruggles relished this victory, such a wresting of equality by means of subterfuge could not but have had unsettling consequences for his ongoing ruminations on the nature of

American liberty. In his many travels for reform and abolitionist causes, Ruggles would frequently clash with railroad, steamboat, and coach conductors over their enforcement of what he was one of the first to refer to in print as the "Jim Crow car."[5] Ruggles well understood that any given triumph against American racism would be contingent and temporary. In the magazine he published between 1838 and 1841, *The Mirror of Liberty,* he frequently complained about American color-phobia, which he considered the antithesis of the highly vaunted rationality and piety of Americans. If a black person but "happens to occupy a promiscuous seat in a meeting house with whites, the amalgamation lyre is struck—its melodious notes awake the whole council of pandemonium." While the unmarried Ruggles had "rode in the stage coach, breakfasted, dined and supped with some of the best women and men in the nation," and never had "any of the young ladies" he met been taken with "fits of love for us and become bedlamites," yet his fellow Americans insisted:

> Oh, horrible! for black folks to attend the same house of worship and occupy promiscuous seats with white folks! Hear! O spirits of the deep—AWAKE! let the earth quake! Let ANGELS blush until the whole UNIVERSE be crimsoned. QUAKERS and CATHOLICS! SAINTS and SINNERS! be surprised, discomfited and revenged![6]

Mimicking the language of piety through which the scandal of amalgamation was voiced, Ruggles reflected that language back as an indictment of American morality. At the same time, he mocked the notion that he sought a white wife, casting the idea as a "non sequitor."[7] What do we make of this predicament into which black activists found themselves on the threshold of emancipation? Can we read Ruggles's anecdote not only as a parable about the amalgamation panic but also as a broader critical commentary on the corporeal boundaries of the public sphere?

In this chapter, I take up the relation between moral panic and public culture. Historians have long understood how America responded to the advent of "immediatist" abolition in the 1830s with a widespread and violent campaign against the immoral race mixing that abolitionists were taken to advocate and practice.[8] Mob violence followed the collapse of colonization as an imaginary solution to the real contradictions of slavery, and the resultant climate was intense in terms of the hatred felt for abolitionists. But while this period has been read for its ideological content, its implications for the formation of political subjectivity have been less often broached. Within this formation, the role of sexuality and affect has been particularly neglected. That an incitement to speak of sex accompanied the first broad struggle the young democracy had regarding black equality has rarely been understood to have had long-term implications for American democracy. And yet the final laws against marriage across the color line were only struck down in 1967.

There is little doubt that "the amalgamation lyre" was repeatedly and loudly sounded in assemblies both religious and secular. In his history of the organized antiabolitionist rioting that peaked in the summer of 1835, Leonard Richards notes that such riots were often coordinated from the high precincts of society:

> Almost every major city and town in the nation held anti-abolitionist rallies. From Maine to Missouri, from the Atlantic to the Gulf, crowds gathered to hear mayors and aldermen, bankers and lawyers, ministers and priests denounce the abolitionists as amalgamationists, dupes, fanatics, foreign agents, and incendiaries.[9]

Foes of abolition, Richards notes, "repeated no charge with greater pertinacity than that of amalgamation, and none could more effectively stir up the rancor and the brutality of a mob."[10] Their efficacy reflected the power of what sociologist Stanley Cohen called "moral panics," situations in which "moral entrepreneurs" drawn from the ranks of the clergy, media, and the professions respond to a social crisis by identifying a dangerous social contagion against which they can then lead a public campaign.[11] But two factors distinguish the 1830s. The first is the level of lawless violence to which groups led by "gentlemen of property and standing" felt entitled to resort to, their rough reliance on a principle of "lynch law" often associated with the frontier conditions of settler colonies. The second difference lies in the moral status of the scapegoated minority. While contemporary moral panics frequently target groups seen as deviant—homosexuals in the 1950s, youth subcultures in the 1960s and 1970s, and "welfare queens" in the 1980s—antiamalgamation rioting targeted a group that presented itself as righteously political and morally reformist.

As the title of the journal Ruggles sold suggests, *Emancipator and Journal of Public Morals,* black and white abolitionists also saw themselves as "moral entrepreneurs." They sought to restore decency on contrary terms to their racist foes. This dynamic gave the public controversies over amalgamation their specific valence. Abolitionists did not, by and large, accept that they were amalgamationists. Instead, as Ronald Walters has shown, they flung the accusation of sexual incontinence back at slaveholders, constructing a picture of an "Erotic South" in which immoral liaisons between white men and enslaved black women were part and parcel of a society given over to the free exercise of the most boisterous and depraved passions.[12] If the "scare crow" of amalgamation partly articulated, as Richards argues, men's "dread of sinking below their forefathers' station and their nightmare of becoming cogs in a mass society," then the abolitionist depiction of slavery as a Southern Sodom reflected a comparable unease with social and racial fluidity.[13]

As much can be seen in Ruggles's entry into the archive of moral entrepreneurship, *Abrogation of the Seventh Commandment, by the American Churches,* a pamphlet he published in 1835.[14] *Abrogation* sought to persuade northern women that they must break church communion with southern congregations because of the immorality slavery licensed. Leveraging growing concern in northern cities about the rise of prostitution, drunkenness, and unregulated entertainments, *Abrogation* sought to redirect that sense of moral scandal southward. "Not only in taverns, but in boarding houses, and, the dwellings of individuals," the pamphlet claimed, "boys and girls verging on maturity altogether unclothed, wait upon ladies and gentlemen, without exciting even the suffusion of a blush on the face of young females, who thus gradually become habituated to scenes of which delicate and refined northern women cannot adequately conceive."[15] Conjuring a scene of utter sexual, gendered, and generational disorder, Ruggles flung the accusation of promiscuity, understood in its nineteenth-century sense as disordered proximity, back at the slaveholding South. If antiabolitionists feared the general leveling of society that abolition portended, such abolitionist ripostes could equally appeal to fears of untrammeled social disorder.

Abolitionists and their foes agreed that sexual disorder was the problem: and they each attributed it to the other side. This does not in itself confirm the "bourgeois" nature of abolitionism, as some scholars have suggested. Indeed, the breadth of shared assumption across political, sectional, and racial divisions, when seen in the dialogic perspective that the work of Bakhtin and his circle makes possible, can underline what was at stake in terms of social conflict and struggle. All sides of the slavery question deployed a highly charged language of sexual and gender nonconformity and contagion; what

better confirmation of Volosinov's insistence that "differently ori-
ented accents intersect in every ideological sign"?[16] The emphasis that
Volosinov, Bakhtin, and their school placed on the *refraction* rather
than simply the *reflection* of social life "in the ideological sign" has
been furthered in the British cultural studies tradition of Stuart Hall,
Allon White, and Peter Stallybrass.[17] I pick up these suggestive connotations of accent and refraction in my own account of how the
materials of bourgeois culture, including its deployment of sexuality,
became contested ground in abolitionism and early black activism.

But why did "amalgamation" become the fraught vehicle of this
semiotic, social, and as we shall see, affective struggle? The word
amalgamation possesses distinct resonances to otherwise comparable
terms like *mestizaje* and *blanqueamiento.* Typically understood as a
synonym for *miscegenation,* amalgamation must be historicized on
its own terms, given that it was disseminated several decades earlier
and did not originate with a racial meaning. Originally drawn from
metallurgy, amalgamation referred to a process through which a
catalytic agent such as mercury was used to extract a precious metal
from ore. Where miscegenation at the time of its coinage indexed
a progressive, social scientific rationality, amalgamation evoked associations at once more physical, chemical, and mystical. The word
root itself, *amalgam,* likely possesses an Islamic derivation, according to the *Oxford English Dictionary,* adding an orientalist air to the
popularity of its usage in the nineteenth century. Amalgamation as
technical apparatus was a lineal descendant of alchemical processes
that sought a mystical "marriage" of elements. As Sue-Ellen Case
notes in her study of alchemy as a performance of science and the virtual, "metaphor and analogy figure the process of transmutation as
a porous interface among different orders of things, through trans-
mutable and affective relations." Within "alchemical discourses, gender appears as an element of change, assigned across substances."[18]
This older, occult association almost certainly supplied part of the
rationale of applying amalgamation metaphorically to marriages
across the color line. Practical amalgamationists, like medieval alchemists, were accused of meddling in the ordained and regulated
order of things with their heretical doctrines and obscure practices.[19]
For their part, radical abolitionists embraced the idea that their cause
was a spiritual crucible for transforming America, body and soul,
just as alchemists sought in gross matter the mirror of the soul's
transfiguration.[20]

An awareness that amalgamation is simply a different metaphor rather than a potentially more accurate replacement for miscegenation is not, however, widely shared. More common is the presumption that it simply supplies a more neutral alternative to the discredited miscegenation. Recently, historians eager for a new narrative of "ethnoracial mixture" have sought to reclaim amalgamation. One prominent example is David Hollinger, who has argued:

> The national experience with intimacy across ethnoracial lines has been one of amalgamation *interruptus:* irregular, stutter-step, tension-filled, and sometimes violent, and thus quite different from the spontaneous, relatively relaxed intimacy leading to closure so often celebrated under the sign of the melting pot. But it has been amalgamation nevertheless, and on a scale and within a time frame that gives it a strong claim to being one of the central features of the history of the United States when viewed in comparative perspective.[21]

Hollinger rightly rejects miscegenation for its indelibly racist connotations and aptly draws out the implications of dividing American history into a "melting pot" for whites and "miscegenation" for peoples of color, particular those of African descent. But his proposal to replace this state of affairs with amalgamation as somehow more accurately reflecting an underlying reality—sometimes "relaxed" and "leading to closure," sometimes "tension-filled" and leading to "amalgamation *interruptus,*" but always problematically described in incredibly loaded, sexual language—betrays some lack of appreciation for how amalgamation was historically mobilized. Hollinger's rhetoric indeed dovetails with the romantic view that seeks to recover, reconstruct, and relegitimate the interracial as the secret history of America. If Americanism has up until now withheld legitimacy from its spurious issue, scholars like Hollinger suggest a new historiography can retroactively bequeath it. Amalgamation can then be proposed as a successor to Frederick Jackson Turner's "frontier thesis."[22] It is telling that the most vivid image Hollinger can find for the limits of this process of racial and national incorporation is interrupted or unproductive sex that fails to reach "closure."

Amalgamation, I argue in response to such claims, should not simply be taken as the name for a love across color lines that was repressed and punished by the sovereign power of white supremacy. Amalgamation, as David Ruggles recognized, was a political deployment of sexuality through which American subjects were gendered and racialized. Insofar as amalgamation conjured up the body as the site of visibility, responsibility, and a potentially aberrant "taste," amalgamation discourse helped constitute what David Kazanjian has called "racial governmentality."[23] Kazanjian's study of race in early national political culture contributes to a growing literature that seeks to leverage Foucault's insights into biopower, governmentality, and the history of sexuality. In this chapter, I seek to extend this engagement with Foucault by considering the deployment of affect as a technology of the racial self. My emphasis on affect is meant to attend to the consequences of sexual speech in public domains, to highlight the exteriorizations as much as the interiorizations that amalgamation effected. Affects like shame, embarrassment, and outrage were routinely deployed to accentuate and refract the bourgeois semiotics of sexuality and morality, particularly when it came to the issue of amalgamation. Rather than an alternative ground upon which a more inclusive history may be reconstructed, the spurious issue traverses the history we have as a disruptive and destabilizing principle that helped generate the divisions we imagine it will now conquer.

Racial Governmentality in Night's Eye

Governmentality for Foucault begins in the training of docile and useful bodies, a process he tracks across three essential texts: *Discipline and Punish*, *"Society Must Be Defended,"* and *The History of Sexuality, Volume I: An Introduction*. Along the way, Foucault builds an argument that crosses the domains of labor, punishment, nationalism, eugenics, racism, and most famously, sexuality. Among his most notable findings was the claim that "sexuality" was neither a biological given nor solely the object of official repression, but was on the contrary targeted, nominated, and assiduously elicited over the course of the nineteenth century. The body was governed by ascertaining the truth of its sex. Inverting the standard view of Victorian prudery, Foucault insisted upon the volubility of sexuality in this period, and what he calls its "deployment" was much more than simply an array of new prohibitions. It was rather the nexus of prohibition and confession that renders sex and the body knowable and categorizable.

From his own unwitting confession, we can see how Ruggles's interlocutor used the amalgamation charge to name and disseminate sex rather than simply repress it. And performance was a key vehicle for the dissemination of sex through moral panics, in part because of the dialectic of sincerity and artifice noted in the work of Karen Haltunnen. If the deployment of sexuality fostered an uneasy awareness of obscure desires and discreet predilections, this only intensified, on the one hand, the ritualization of the social evidences of purity and, on the other, the facility with which those evidences might be mimicked and thereby falsified.[24] "Confidence men" and "painted ladies" were twin bugbears of urbanizing America, and the abrupt eclipse of the village ideal as effective arbiter of moral discourse propelled, as a number of historians have shown, much of the evangelical fervor of American abolitionists.[25]

In my introduction, I discussed the political caricatures of E. W. Clay, and their work as a visual analogue to the mode of engagement taken by Ruggles's interlocutor. Indeed, Clay directly attacked Ruggles at least once, in an 1838 image *The Disappointed Abolitionists*. In perhaps the first attempt to caricature a black activist with any degree of verisimilitude, Clay portrays Ruggles in abolitionist action, confronting an incensed man who holds a chair ready to throw at an interracial group of abolitionists—Isaac Hopper, Barney Corse, and Ruggles—as he clutches in his other hand a bag of money. As the irate slaveholder exclaims, "Of all the d——d pieces of impudence I ever know, this surpasses!" A bespectacled David Ruggles, flanked by his abolitionist compatriots, worries, "I don't like the looks of this affair. I'm afraid my pickings will not amount to much!" A comment on the so-called "Darg controversy" in which the abolitionists gave refuge to a fugitive slave who had stolen some cash from his Virginian master, along with himself, while the two were visiting New York, Clay's cartoon depicts abolitionism as a confidence game, indicting the likes of Ruggles as slick urban opportunists preying on the pocketbooks of virtuous agrarian gentlemen.

I return to Clay's images here in order to highlight their specific performative and affective qualities, qualities that in turn shaped the way abolitionists and activists like Ruggles reacted and responded to them. As Nancy Davison has noticed, there is a preponderance of depictions of performance in Clay's antiblack, antiabolition, and antiamalgamation cartoons. Images from his earlier *Life in Philadelphia* series (1828–30), she notes, "strongly resemble scenes in a play."[26] And indeed, Clay's transatlantic inspiration for the series depicting

Figure 7. E. W. Clay, *The Disappointed Abolitionists*, 1838. Courtesy of American Antiquarian Society.

black dandies and dandizettes in his hometown of Philadelphia, Pierce Egan's popular picaresque novel, *Life in London* (1821), was adapted for the stage on both sides of the Atlantic. Notable among these productions was an 1823 production mounted by William Brown's African Company of New York, that city's first black theater.[27] The performative context of urban black life is important for reading Clay's stereotypes against their grain. Beneath the surface of Clay's caricatures of black self-fashioning, read by Clay as a transparent and absurd effort to mimic whites, lies a subterranean world of play whose values Clay partly elicits.[28] Visual and performance culture must be read in relation to each other in order to specify how the work of the stereotype is never static but, as Bhabha suggests, must always be anxiously repeated.

Bourgeois sexuality and racial whiteness were both constructed in contradistinction to subaltern, racialized, and proletarian life. Clay's images, like their British inspiration, slummed in the world they also held at arm's length. Egan's narrative, adapted by William Moncrieff as *Tom and Jerry, or Life in London* (first performed 1823, first published 1826) was "among the most popular and influential creations of the early nineteenth century."[29] Popular prints of scenes from the novel by George and Robert Cruikshank displayed in the window of London print seller Rudolf Ackerman attracted the eye of Clay when he took his European tour between 1825 and 1828.[30] And a couple years later, another young American on the make claimed similar inspiration from Egan's characters. "I have merely sought to give a sketch of the lowest classes," a piqued T. D. Rice wrote in to the *New York Mirror,* which had panned his appearance as the original "Jim Crow" at the Bowery Theater, "something in the same style with *Tom and Jerry,* so long the favorite of the stage in England as well as in America."[31] Insofar as amalgamation panic stoked fears of a subterranean city populated by fugitive slaves, bespectacled black abolitionists, and disreputable stage entertainers, it also registered a growing awareness of this new and protean reality.

The fusions of black performance were feared to be becoming ubiquitous in New York, New Orleans, and London. The "African waltz" occurred in locations both real and imagined, north and south, English and American. In the notorious Five Points area of New York stood Almack's, "one of the many black-run dance emporiums then operating" in the district.[32] It was here in 1841 that a visiting Charles

Figure 8. I. R. and G. Cruikshank, *Lowest Life in London*, 1821. Illustration from Pierce Egan, *Life in London* (New York: Appleton, 1904).

Dickens first encountered a performer who was almost certainly William Henry "Juba" Lane. Called Pete Williams's place in its later years, after its proprietor, Almack's was a circum-Atlantic instantiation of Pierce Egan's fictional "All-Max" in London's East End, itself a sly retort to the tony West End club Almack's Assembly Rooms. Where the real English Almack's catered to the toast of society, All-Max welcomed a "group motley indeed;—Lascars, blacks, jack tars, coal-heavers, dustmen, women of colour, old and young." The mongrel bunch, Egan informed his reader in slangy prose "were all *jigging* together, provided the *teaser of the catgut* was not *bilked* of his *duce*."[33] Moncrieff's staging of this dancehall included a "Comic Pas Deux" between "African Sal" and "Dusty Bob."[34] Such scenes of revelry could be elicited on an American stage only within certain boundaries, and the conventions proscribing actual black performers were not enough to prevent fear of the contagiousness of black performance.[35]

As Marvin McAllister has found, American reviewers objected to the staging of this scene, for which one could find "no name" for his reaction to this particular scene "but *disgust*." The provincial's excitement for a play that promised a whirlwind tour of the highs and lows of the exciting metropolitan life was understandably antagonized by an encounter with the black Atlantic lumpenproletariat he knew all too well from his own hometown. One critic was happy to find, in the mainstream Park Theater production of *Tom and Jerry*, "the *waltzing* . . . entirely *cut out*." Brown's version, by contrast, "prominently advertised" the African "waltz" with what McAllister believes must have been a "thoroughly satisfying homoerotic spectacle" of "two twirling, double-shuffling men."[36] Replacing blackface and wool wigs with the "genuine article," Brown's staging nevertheless retained one key element from prior productions: the portrayal of African Sal by a transvested male actor.[37]

In taking Egan's *Tom and Jerry* as a site of semiotic and performative contestation, Brown's production offers an important standpoint from which to reread Clay's notorious images of amalgamation. Clay's images of a fantasized abolitionist amalgamationism participated in an insistence upon the *appearances* of respectability. In *An Amalgamation Waltz*, elegantly dressed black–white couples are gathered in a sumptuous ballroom. As if in parody of integrated abolitionist gatherings, they are dancing the waltz, cheek-to-cheek, breast-to-breast. Arms grasp corseted waists, holding them close; others gesture in broad invitation. Gloved hands rest upon broad shoulders, brushing up against military epaulets, as the whirl carries them across the floor. Those couples that dot the perimeter are talking, smiling, and canoodling. One gentleman has daringly removed his glove to grasp his companion's hand flesh to flesh. European images of the waltz similarly satirized the vulgar aspirations of social climbers and egalitarian-minded women.[38] *An Amalgamation Waltz* can be positioned in an American branch of this genealogy of satire, lampooning the dancers' pretensions to polite bearing. It does so through an obscene discourse that exposes abolitionist egalitarianism as a mask for covert elitism and, through the same gesture, exposes that covert elitism as itself disguising shameful passions. The high-toned dance they perform, the cartoon informs us, is a poorly sublimated expression of a low-down desire.

Social dancing and sexuality were closely associated then as now. What requires historical attention is the embourgeoisiement of specific forms, such that what seems to us today as elite and respectable could contain very different connotations in an earlier era. The waltz was a Germanic peasant dance that scandalized Europe with its sensual physicality as it migrated up the social ladder in the eighteenth century. It signified class in conflicting fashion, bearing the simultaneous trace of elite impatience with the overly rigid social choreography of the court and of bourgeois ambitions desirous of attaining a genteel pose. These black and white nineteenth-century American couples were thus waltzing into a highly fraught performance space, positioned between Old World tensions, on the one hand, and the growing contradictions of a young America on the other.[39] Fear of a spreading sameness, of a general leveling leading to cultural chaos, granted the waltz an enduring symbolic potency in an era of revolution in both Europe and America. The waltz was easy to learn, involved close physical contact between the sexes, and was fast-paced and breathy. It broke with convention, even as some democratic-minded aristocrats scandalously adopted it. Banned in Britain until the early nineteenth century, the waltz was regulated even on the European mainland, its potential dangers comparable only, perhaps, to another revolutionary dance that also emerged in the 1830s, the polka.

As a device to disgust and titillate a white male public, the amalgamation waltz associated abolition with Europhilic decadence and the subversion of the American republican experiment. Other images from Clay's series illustrated a miscegenous musical soiree and an interracial wedding presided over by a black preacher. In each case, racial equality was conflated with sexual intermingling, and imagery of "the world turned upside down" was employed to argue that elevating blacks could only be accomplished by degrading whites. In this zero-sum scenario, egalitarianism among American whites depended upon a collective superiority over blacks, and any disruption of that racial contract would result in either the reassertion of the dreaded Old World class structure or the general leveling of society into one homogenous, chaotic mass.

The cultural logic of amalgamation thus operated as a biopolitical supplement to the democratic imagination. The tendentious complaints against African "waltzing" at the real and fictional Almack's/All-Max dancehall can be compared to the labeling of what we now call blackface minstrelsy as "Ethiopian Opera." African and Afro-Celtic dance forms like the jig and juba could get refracted in hostile reviewers' eyes as distortions of the elegant waltz in the same way as minstrel tunes were likened to black travesties of operatic arias. In all these areas, popular performance forms were instated as national culture through a process rife with class and status anxiety. It is here, I suggest, that amalgamation assumed its historical significance. The concept of amalgamation, as a metaphor of transformation, was wrapped up in the mobility and thrill of the waltz, jig, and juba. As a deployment of sexuality, it was specifically racialized. But to say that is only to beg the question of how, precisely, race was mobilized in this period as itself a mutable and even volatile category.

Amalgamation was not one but an ensemble of metaphors. Amalgamation can describe a process of *mixing,* one of *extracting,* or one of *transforming.* The idea of mixture or blend is the most familiar to us. In the multicultural present, it is almost instinctive. Less familiar is the metaphor of transformation, in which two or more substances are destroyed to produce a new one, or that of extraction, in which a raw material is processed, often with the help of a catalytic agent, to remove its valuable ingredient. The moral lessons derived from mixing, extracting, and transforming are similarly multiple. *Purifying,* for example, attaches itself more easily to extraction than to mixing. *Revolutionizing,* in turn, is more connected to transforming than to either extracting or mixing. The very common moral inference of *debasing* or *mongrelizing* seems better suited to mixing as a metaphor than to either transforming or extracting. All these connotations were immanent within the sign *amalgamation* and could be accented or refracted to a variety of purposes. They overlap with and differ from the subsequent connotations of *miscegenation*. It is important to pay attention to them not simply out of a drive toward greater historical accuracy but also in order to grasp the general principle out of which racial formation constantly revises its terms while repressing acknowledgment of that ongoing process. This may further the difficult task of denaturalizing both sex and race, in an intellectual context where it is still common to rely on either sex or race as the foil against which the social construction of the other is emphasized.

Approaching amalgamation as an American keyword through which the biopolitical implications of a democratic and egalitarian society were performed allows us to demarcate the amalgamation waltz as a real and imagined zone of contestation. Although Foucault's work from the early 1970s contains an underappreciated direct engagement with the genealogy of racism, it is actually his commentary on class that most illuminates my discussion of racial governmentality in the "night's eye" of American democracy. Part of Foucault's argument against the repressive hypothesis is made through the claim that sexuality was not deployed primarily as a mechanism of class warfare but rather operated as a discourse that sought first to clarify and control the boundaries of the bourgeois self. "The living conditions that were dealt to the proletariat," Foucault went so far as to observe, citing Marx, "particularly in the first half of the nineteenth century, show there was anything but concern for its body and sex. . . . Conflicts were necessary (in particular, conflicts over urban space . . .) in order for the proletariat to be granted a body and a sexuality."[40] Although here Foucault appears to be at his most nominalist, his observations drive at an important point requiring further elaboration in the American context:

> Some think they can denounce two symmetrical hypocrisies at the same time: the primary hypocrisy of the bourgeoisie which denies its own sexuality, and the secondary hypocrisy of the proletariat which in turn rejects its sexuality by accepting the dominant ideology. This is to misunderstand the process whereby on the contrary the bourgeoisie endowed itself, in an arrogant political affirmation, with a garrulous sexuality which the proletariat long refused to accept, since it was foisted on them for the purpose of subjugation. . . . We must

return, therefore, to formulations that have long been disparaged; we must say that there is bourgeois sexuality; and that there are class sexualities.[41]

Foucault cautions against our readiness to see sexuality at the site of Pete Williams's dancehall, instead pointing to how it might first have been deployed, as a mode of bourgeois self-policing, in the imaginary spaces of the amalgamation waltz, polka, wedding, and soiree, and only subsequently disseminated across the body politics. Instead of a repressed history of interracial desire, we confront the eliciting of amalgamation as a boundary of the bourgeois self against which, Foucault suggests, we might look for refusals.

In interpreting the responses of moral entrepreneurs like Ruggles to the amalgamation panic, I follow Foucault in arguing that we do indeed need to return to long disparaged formulations and understand the deployment of sexuality as the site of a class struggle. This struggle cannot be reduced to race, and neither can race be reduced to it. But unless we see how class affects and identities became modalities in which race was lived, we will misrecognize the stakes of black abolitionist and activist reflections and refractions of the bourgeois deployment of sexuality.

Shame in the Circum-Atlantic Fold

Of key historical significance here are black activists and abolitionists who served as historical mediators between the bourgeois public sphere and the sentimental culture of reform, on the one hand, and on the other a small but growing population of free African Americans of which they were taken to represent and lead. I have already suggested that this exercise in racial representativeness and leadership must be understood as a process rather than a given. Here I want to consider how the deployment of sexuality figured into their efforts at race leadership, given the apparent obstacles to full equality the moral panic around amalgamation presented.

Critical in this discussion are the enduringly problematic writings of Thomas Jefferson. Like Crispus Attucks, Jefferson repeatedly resurfaced in the decades after 1830 as a contested figure for black collective memory. Alternately a fount of republican inspiration and a shocking source of racial insult, Jefferson's unavoidability is best evidenced in William Wells Brown's fictionalization of the story of his black progeny, *Clotel, or The President's Daughter* (1853). This sense of being the inheritors of Jefferson's America, or, perhaps, its illegitimate scion, resurfaced in the black writing of the 1830s through the 1850s. David Walker devoted long passages in his 1829 *Appeal* to rebutting Jefferson's *Notes on the State of Virginia* (1787), and his biographer notes that "no African American prior to Walker" went after Jefferson "with anywhere near as much vehemence and scope."[42] The responses of Walker and Brown suggest how significant a reckoning with the legacy of Jefferson's racial thought was taken to by the generation of black activists whose public careers began in the decades after his death in 1826.

But to what were these writers responding? David Kazanjian has traced the emergence of racial governmentality in Jefferson's writings, showing how Jefferson's support of colonization schemes articulated elements of "a hybrid, liberal racism" that execrated slavery but insisted that black and white could not peacefully coexist under shared conditions of freedom.[43] Kazanjian draws attention to a particularly telling formulation of Jefferson's: "Nothing is more certainly written in the book of fate than that these people [the slaves] are to be free. Nor it is less certain that the two races, equally free, cannot live in the same government."[44] In a doubled rhetorical movement—from "people" to "races," from "freedom" to "government"—Jefferson charts the lineaments of a separate and unequal future. His support for colonization sought to "persuade" freedpeople that they should colonize and Christianize Africa or some other black nationality.[45] The alternative would be a horrendous mongrelization of the democratic experiment in which Anglo-Saxon liberty would become diluted in a sea of lesser races.

It is telling that Jefferson could convince himself that a people held in chattel slavery could not be governed. Of what, we may ask, did this racial ungovernability consist? For Jefferson, at least, it consisted in part in the inability to blush:

> Are not the fine mixtures of red and white, the expressions of every passion by greater or less suffusions of colour in the one, preferable to that eternal monotony, which reigns in the countenances, that immoveable veil of black which covers all the emotions of the other race? Add to these, flowing hair, a more elegant symmetry of form, their own judgment in favor of whites, declared by their preference of them, as uniformly as is the preference of the Oranootan for the black women over those of his own species.[46]

While this passage is often discussed for its specious species argument, I am more interested in how Jefferson's rhetorical deployment of animality cues a specific affective response among whites. We might note that Jefferson made this speculation in the section of *Notes* devoted to "The Administration of Justice and Description of Laws." And he here evoked a juridico-biological principle of black shamelessness that had already been established in American law. Maryland, for example, punished slaves according to a doctrine first articulated in 1729 that held blacks to "have no Sense of Shame, or Apprehensions of future Rewards or Punishments."[47] Such laws spelled out the difference between slave husbandry and the governance of rational men.

In enumerating the impossibility of interracial conviviality or shared government, Jefferson had issued forth his own parade of horribles: ugly hair, inelegant bodies, black lust for white bodies, and, in the ultimate non sequitur, ape lust for black bodies. It is worth noting how such a parade tethers whiteness, through the great chain of being, to both blackness and animality. Betsy Erkkila notes in passing that Jefferson referred to himself in private correspondence as an "Oran-ootan" at least once.[48] The grotesque body of the racial other, as Stallybrass and White argue, is deployed to ambivalent purpose: it both attracts and repels.[49] Skin and its capacity to blush manage this threshold, and a bodily predilection to affect is instated as the boundary between self and other.

The inevitably partial separation of the bourgeois self from the grotesque body underscores the significance of the rhetorical economy of shame, preference, and embarrassment. It is relevant that Jefferson claimed to be embarrassed to make his arguments against black humanity. What embarrasses him? The structure of his opening question, "Are not the fine mixtures of red and white . . . preferable . . . ?" reflects a somewhat pained appeal to his white, European audience for recognition. Among other objectives, it invites the cosmopolitan reader to picture the whiteness of the postcolonial Creole, to confirm that whiteness as distinct from and preferable to other kinds of bodies circulating in the Atlantic littoral. Part of Jefferson's embarrassment, in the eyes of the Old World, is the wish not to be taken for anything other than as white.[50] And a further embarrassment follows upon this invited gaze of white recognition, which Jefferson's language of preference, symmetry, flowing, and elegance all evoke. Is this not a sexual, desirous gaze, laid indifferently upon bodies both male and female, simply because they are white? Flowing hair and symmetrical form may connote femaleness, but they do not specify it; what is specified rather is race. Gender does not appear in this passage until the final sentence. Jefferson has invited a masculine, scientific gaze upon all New World bodies of European descent, bodies that are thus feminized by virtue of being an object of study and scrutiny. But this gaze is also necessarily homoerotic in that it is he who invites and directs this gaze upon his own body as evidence of a shared, impassioned bond.

If Jefferson thus founded the difference of the races upon an insidious demarcation between those whose susceptibility to shame and embarrassment rendered them governable because they were self-governable, then how did this shape the responses of his black interlocutors seeking to both rebut and transform his conception of a government of republican liberty and virtue? To answer this, we must investigate the politics of affect and in particular of shame in ways that queer theory makes available. Eve Kosofsky Sedgwick helped ignite critical interest in shame with her provocative reassessments of the mid-twentieth-century work of Silvan Tomkins. Although read primarily in the context of queer studies, I find her approach to affect and shame in particular potentially generative to critical race studies. In a well-known essay, Sedgwick argued:

> As best described by Tomkins, shame effaces itself; shame points and projects; shame turns itself skin side out; shame and pride, shame and dignity, shame and self-display, shame and exhibitionism are different interminglings of the same glove. Shame, it might finally be said, transformational shame, *is performance*.[51]

Throughout this chapter, and particularly at its conclusion, I investigate this intermingling of shame and dignity, display, and exhibition. And I consider this transformation of shame as part and parcel of the politics of respectability. According to Sedgwick, the queer subject transforms shame and stigma not by transcending or repressing them but by employing them as resources in the production of new modes of meaning and being. "Queer performativity," Sedgwick summarizes later on, "is the name of a strategy for the production of meaning and being, in relation to the affect shame and to the later and related fact of stigma."[52] Rod Ferguson has suggested that we attend to the putatively nonnormative affect and sexuality of the black subject as a potentially useful site for extending queer theoretical praxis.[53] I pick up this suggestion, keeping in mind Ferguson's admonition not to simply extend a queer theoretical approach to questions of race but to also permit racial formation to transform queer critique.

My argument here differs slightly from the now canonical account of Fanon referenced in my introduction, in which insult and abuse hails the black subject, causing a precipitous and shame-induced fall into a "racial epidermal schema." Shame in the circum-Atlantic fold was not solely by direct insult. It also circulated promiscuously and unpredictably in a public sphere to which blacks were presumed to lack access.[54] Jefferson's discourse on racial governmentality, un-like that of "hate speech," was not intended for a black audience at all. When the black polymath Benjamin Banneker responded to him, Jefferson was again embarrassed. He had intended his views for white eyes only and had used them to produce an exclusionary bour-geois public sphere that Banneker's letter had somehow broached. In this he might be compared to Ruggles's interlocutor, who similarly assumed the whiteness of the public sphere, or to E. W. Clay, whose cartoons presumed a white male subject.

Rather than interpellation, then, a better metaphor here might be that of eavesdropping.[55] Black subjects eavesdropped on an anxious discourse of white superiority, black inferiority, and the dangers of racial contamination. Overhearing this discourse, they replayed and refracted it, precisely in the hopes of shaming whites about it as well as using it as evidence to rouse other blacks out of their acquiescence to the present state of affairs. Consider the recommendation of David Walker, who observed that

> Mr. Jefferson's very severe remarks on us have been so extensively argued upon by men whose attainments in literature, I shall never be able to reach, that I would not have meddled with it, were it not to solicit each of my brethren, who has the spirit of a man, to buy a copy of Mr. Jefferson's "Notes on Virginia," and put it in the hand of his son. For let no one of us suppose that the refutations which have been written by our white friends are enough—they are whites—we are blacks.[56]

Walker asks his black male readers to buy the *Notes* and pedagogically transmit it to their sons as a kind of prophylaxis against American racism. Rather than responding to an insult, he was calling attention to one. "Have they [the whites] not," Walker demanded to know, "held us up as descending originally from the tribes of *Monkeys* or

Orang-Outangs? O! my God! I appeal to every man of feeling—is not this insupportable?"[57] His transcription of his audible moans and exclamations performed the appropriate response to the shameful insult he delivered. It responds to Jefferson's denial of black capacity for affect with a vivid textual enactment of that very thing.

David Walker's "man of feeling," who circulates shame as a technique of the self, leads me to posit that race emerges in its modern form only when it becomes possible to be ashamed of it. Walker invited black readers and auditors to eavesdrop upon a circum-Atlantic conversation among enlightenment philosophes. The insults of Jefferson were refracted by black men in hopes of shaming black men and their sons into vindicating their race. Such an attempt at subjectification must be read in light of Saidiya Hartman's powerful critique of the "burdened individuality of freedom."[58] Hartman's bold claim is that the extension of humanity across racial boundaries, in the form of empathy and a reparative emphasis on shared susceptibility to pain, shame, and joy, cannot be read straightforwardly. Instead, she reads this humanization as at the same time a responsibilization, highlighting with Foucault the double-edged connotation of the word *subject.*

Women as well as men could deploy the gendered logic of shaming. They also could interpellate black men as docile and degraded precisely in order to goad their audiences into proving them wrong.[59] "Had our men the requisite force and energy," Maria Stewart told a disgruntled audience of Freemasons in 1833,

> they would soon convince them [whites] by their efforts both in public and private, that they were men, or things in the shape of men. Well may the colonizationists laugh us to scorn for our negligence; well may they cry, "Shame to the sons of Africa."[60]

Like Parker, Stewart publicly shamed black men to instigate racial self-recognition and solidarity. Stewart's speech reflects the gendering of shame insofar as female modesty was viewed as desirable, while men in particular were intended to respond militantly to insults.

Degraded, shameless men were feminized and queered. We see this in an 1848 article entitled "Sambo's Mistakes" that the famous white abolitionist John Brown published, under a pseudonym, in the black newspaper the *Ram's Horn.* John Stauffer economically summarizes this strange document in which Brown "posed as a black man and chided himself for tamely submitting to white laws and authority."[61] While Stauffer directly contrasts the authentic cross-racial identifications of antislavery men like Brown and Gerrit Smith with "parodies or caricatures such as blackface minstrelsy," I see these performances as implicated in each other.[62] As he recites Sambo's "mistakes," Brown's remonstrance is clearly a mixture of self-criticism and carping about the behavior of black people he knew in abolitionist contexts and beyond. "Sambo" reproaches himself for reading "novels & other miserable trash," for believing that "chewing & smoking tobacco would make a man of me but little inferior to some of the whites," for attending political meetings "so eager to display my spouting talents & so tenacious of some trifling theory or other that I have adopted that I have generally lost all sight of the business at hand," and for have never having brought himself

> to practise any present self denials although my theories have been excellent. For instance I have bought expensive gay clothing, nice Canes, Watches, Safety Chains, Finger-rings, Breast Pins & many things of a like nature, thinking I might by that means distinguish myself from the vulgar, as some of the better class of whites do.[63]

Brown's alter ego displays an incapacity at self-government that is reflected in his wasteful consumerism and reckless dandyism. Instead of husbanding his resources, Sambo dresses up in gay clothing and enjoys life in Philadelphia, New York, or wherever. While Brown is clearly disapproving of this image, he paints it as vividly as a Clay cartoon or a T. D. Rice song.

The use of images of degraded, vain, and ridiculous behavior to correct and chastise could also be the subject of an ironic defense of the convivial pleasures of the mongrel city. To see this, we might compare "Sambo's Mistakes" to the letter T. D. Rice signed "Jim Crow" when he sent it to the *New York Mirror* fifteen years earlier. No doubt sarcastically, Rice justified his "nigger affectation of white manners" as a negative example for others to follow. Addressing the standard bourgeois assault on the disreputable promiscuity and race mixing his performance condoned, Rice argued,

> I do not see why [you] should be so anxious to warn New York Desdemonas against Gumbo Cuff, by repeating to them, over and over again, that neither Gumbo Cuff nor Jim Crow are equal to Othello . . . and if dandyism is rendered contemptible in their eyes by

its copying the blacks, may not the copy render a service to society by inducing the ladies to discourage its original in the whites?[64]

Both Rice and Brown, at roughly the same historical moment, deploy the figure of the dandy as a corrective mirror against which to measure more proper deployment. That Brown does so sincerely, while Rice's irony is seemingly bottomless, is of less import than their shared investment in impersonating blackness in order to produce the appearance of respectability.

How a staging of racialized shame and anguish on the bodies of oneself or others might serve the project of governmentality is suggested in another specimen of antislavery pedagogy, an anonymous playscript published in the 1830s. *The Kidnapped Clergyman: or Experience the Best Teacher* vividly imagines the shaming of a typical, pious antiabolitionist. In the play, the Clergyman is portrayed as an effete and pompous intellectual who returns from preaching an antiabolitionist sermon to a stream of distinguished visitors flattering and bestowing rich gifts on him. Abruptly, however, kidnappers enter the room, strip and whip him, and carry him off. Their leader orders his cronies to "Gag the noisy rascal" and then to "strip him and give him twenty lashes, well laid on." Uncomprehending as to how he might end his agony, one persecutor whispers in his ear to "Say, Dont master, dont; O God Almighty, master, don't." The Clergyman obeys, and although he is knocked down, kicked, and whipped numerous times, survives.[65]

The bulk of the not very dramatic play consists of scenes in which the legality and morality of slavery is exhaustively debated, and includes one in which the Clergyman and a slave woman named Dinah alternately entreat their owner for freedom, he on the grounds that he is white and she on the grounds that any reason the Clergyman can give for why he should be free applies to her as well. In this vicious parody of the public sphere, the Clergyman learns that the axioms of raciology exclude all too well the reasoning remonstrance of the enslaved.

> DINAH: Massa, great changes in dis world. . . . White man preach in de pulpit, slavery right; now, he feel de change too; he made a slave himself. He say de negro degraded race. White man a little degraded himself now. . . .
>
> CLERGYMAN: My indignation chokes me. Is it not enough, that I am obliged to humble myself, and entreat for my release . . . but I

must be obliged to speak alternately with this—? for shame sir, for shame.

PLANTER: If your indignation chokes you, I am glad of it, as it will save me the trouble.[66]

The scene distills in miniature the performance scenario in which shame and shaming circulate in the circum-Atlantic fold. Dinah, speaking in dialect, evokes great changes in the world. Where the Clergyman tries asserting his rights as a white man, Dinah shrewdly observes that his sermonizing in defense of slavery has set the stage for his own degradation. In response, the Clergyman acts as if the only thing worse than being enslaved is the shame of being forced to speak in turn with Dinah, to have his elevated discourse placed in the same frame as her deficient speech. Willing to humble himself to another white man, he experiences as utterly paralyzing the experience of being equated with a black woman. His feeble attempt to shame the slaveholder is a desperate attempt to restore an imagined fraternity of white men. The play is remorseless in its satirizing of this particular deployment of affect.

The shared capacity for pain, suffering, and humiliation, which was at the core of the abolitionist humanitarian appeal, paved the way for the scenes of subjection that Hartman has anatomized. But it could also counter its own humanistic appeals. In one chilling scene in *The Kidnapped Clergyman,* evidence is read out in court to specify that the cleric's white body is in fact that of a Negro slave:

With regard to the identity of the person, there can be no doubt. He is described as five feet nine and a half inches tall; having three of his front teeth knocked out, his back very much whaled with the lash, and one ear half cut off. . . . I have witnesses here, to swear they have heard him preach to the blacks.[67]

Like a fugitive in a slave advertisement, the kidnapped cleric is here reduced to the identifying marks of trauma upon his body and to hearsay regarding his speech-acts in a subterranean slave counter-public.[68] The play's dramatization of the process of racialization remains pertinent insofar as race is produced within the circum-Atlantic fold as freedom's remainder. Having one's body racially delineated in court, the dramatic text warned, could be extended to whites. At the same time, the aggressive display, stripping, abuse, shaming, and torture of the clergyman's body worked as a revenge fantasy, expressible by black and white abolitionists alike. Whatever else it may be, the *Kidnapped Clergyman,* like "Sambo's Mistakes," also worked as an aggressive, interracial bawdy joke—"Oh! Oh! Oh!" says the Clergyman—one that elicits shock, horror, as well as vivid gratifications of witnessing a hated person humiliated.

Performing Respectability

If shame and shaming were critical ingredients in black and white antislavery theatricality, they also operate as a quiet historiographic principle in selecting certain representative stories to reproduce as heritage. Respectability played a prominent role in early black political culture. And it remains important today, where among its many gestures is the frequently expressed injunction against airing dirty laundry in public. The domestic principle embedded in this bit of common sense is the subject of Robert Reid-Pharr's sustained examination of the protocols of desire at work in antebellum black fiction. Reid-Pharr characterizes the emergence of the black American novel as a literal and figurative cleaning house, one that he argues rejected the promiscuous interraciality indelibly associated with the southern plantation household and projected the ideal of a progressive, bourgeois, and respectably autonomous black household in its stead.[69] But within this domestic economy, he reminds us, the black body remained a problem in at least two senses. First, its extradomestic proclivities required constant policing, cleansing, and correction. And second, embodiment itself remained a sticking point in the pursuit of the disembodied privileges of the bourgeois self.

Reid-Pharr here inverts the traditional wisdom that holds that "the production and reproduction of the American slave state necessitated the development of forms of racial distinctiveness with which we are now familiar," suggesting that it was, to the contrary, the free black political culture that emerged after the 1830s that embraced "a process of racial modernization in which notions of racelessness and indeterminacy become untenable."[70] This enables him to produce a convincingly revisionist account of the critical role mulattas and mulattos play in much nineteenth-century black fiction, as discomfiting indexes of a "sticky southernness" with which the northern black community "has been plagued."[71] Taking Frank Webb's 1857 novel, *The Garies and Their Friends,* as a case study, Reid-Pharr shows how the titular family's trajectory from the messy intimacies and oppressions of the south to freedom in Philadelphia is trailed by "slaves, servants, runaways, and amalgamationists" who "people" Webb's romance in a manner "necessitating a great, unmerciful cleansing." This is how Reid-Pharr interprets the race riot that climaxes the novel, killing off a number of the more unwieldy characters.[72] The traumatic riot nevertheless is productive, in Webb's narrative, of a modernized blackness now cleansed of past, problematic attachments, transformed via the triumph of a particularistic instantiation of bourgeois principles. If violence thus proves a crucible within which modern black subjectivity is forged, it leaves open the question Reid-Pharr seeks to foreground throughout: the continued evasiveness of the body.

We can compare Reid-Pharr's reading of Webb's fictional account of a race riot with David Walker's incensed response to bans against marriages across the color line. In listing the various injuries visited upon black manhood by white supremacy, Walker asks:

> Do they not institute laws to prohibit us from marrying among the whites? I would wish, candidly, however, before the Lord, to be understood, that I would not give a pinch of snuff to be married to any white person I ever saw in all the days of my life. And I do say it, that the black man, or man of colour, who will leave his own colour (provided he can get one, who is good for any thing) and marry a white woman, to be a double slave to her, just because she is white, ought to be treated by her as he surely will be, viz: as a NIGER!!!![73]

Walker's "double slavery" reflects the rhetoric of his day surrounding potential enslavement to one's passions and desires, the obverse of being an upstanding and sentimental "man of feeling." Walker's gratuitous insult to black women underscores the misogyny at work in these deployments of shame, which produces an imagined fraternity of black men by protesting the intrusion and pollution of women. Respectability is won at the cost of a demonstrated self-government forever thrown into doubt by the potentially shameless acts and desires of other men.

But the deployment of shame as means to the uplifting of the race does not exhaust the implications of a queer theoretical affinity for the transformations and interminglings of shame. Instead of seeing shame as producing only a single and predictable outcome, we might follow Kathryn Bond Stockton's suggestion that shame might contain multiple registers and forms of affinity. Her suggestive readings across black and queer literary and cultural forms are shaped by a determination "to ask of my texts what they imagine debasement produces, at certain moments, for those people who actually undergo it, who, in a manner of speaking, practice it."[74] This notion of a practice of shame may productively refigure our grasp of the antebellum politics of respectability if we also keep in mind Sedgwick's twinning of shame and dignity, exhibitionism, and self-display. Shame and shamelessness, ultimately, are thrown into a complex relation by these thinkers, and in my final example, I want to grasp how this transformation of affect might be read in the specific historical moment of the amalgamation panic.

In the summer of 1836, two summers after vicious antiabolitionist, antiamalgamationist riots had ripped through New York, a white master mason named Robert Haslem casually solicited Mary Jones, a black prostitute, in the streets of lower Manhattan. Jones led Haslem into an alley, and whether or not Haslem offered payment, Jones nonetheless accepted it, as Haslem learned to his dismay shortly thereafter, when he discovered that his wallet had been lifted and replaced with that of another man. Tracking down the owner of the wallet, Haslem persuaded him to admit to a prior liaison with Jones, and the two men set off to report a crime. Locating a police officer, Bowyer, the three men devised a complicated scenario for entrapping Jones, one in which officer Bowyer's brother was also involved. Under this complex scenario, Bowyer would pose as a john while his brother played look out, and the group trolled Manhattan until they spotted Jones. When Bowyer propositioned and subsequently arrested Jones, he found in the process several men's wallets on her person, as well as the surprising discovery of her male genital anatomy.

Peter Sewally, alias Mary Jones, became a minor figure in New York City's rogues gallery after his trial and conviction the next day in the Court of General Sessions. Induced to appear in court in the women's clothing he was wearing when apprehended, Sewally was roundly mocked and prodded by a gawking and contemptuous crowd in the court as he defiantly entered a plea of not guilty to the official charge of grand larceny. With two johns and a police officer testifying against him, Sewally was quickly convicted and sentenced to several years at Sing Sing. A portrait of Sewally titled *The Man-Monster* quickly appeared in New York lithography shop windows, and the sensational nature of his guise ensured Sewally's enduring notoriety beyond the pages of the police blotters.[75]

THE MAN-MONSTER,

Peter Sewally, alias Mary Jones &c&c

Sentenced 18th June 1836, to 5 years imprisonment at hard labor at Sing Sing for Grand Larceny

Published by H.R. Robinson, 48. Courtlandt St. N.Y.

Figure 9. *The Man-Monster, Peter Sewally, alias Mary Jones.* Published by H. R. Robinson, 1836. Collection of The New-York Historical Society, negative 40697.

The penny press that circulated the story of the Man-Monster could not contain its prurient interest in a phenomenon that to this day still fascinates people about queer and transgender bodies: how did Sewally *do* it? In particular, antebellum New York wanted to know, how did he do it with a series of apparently unsuspecting red-blooded men, at least some of whom paid for the privilege? Although one article veiled its explanation in garbled Latin, word quickly got out that Sewally had worn a strategically placed slab of beef. This sexual innovation circulated as lore for decades in New York City, and Sewally was long known as "Beefsteak Pete."[76] Having persuaded men through guile to imagine and enjoy a surrogate vagina, he was obliged to "wear" this exposed fiction publicly as a sobriquet, notoriety ensuring that even in a city of strangers, his anatomical reputation would proceed him.

The antebellum American concern with confidence men and painted women expressed a worry regarding deceitful and deceiving figures who exploited the absence of personal history and tight community oversight that were among the city's urban advantages, presenting themselves as sincere and honorable when in fact they were dastardly and plotting. Sewally's monstrousness lay both in his evident race and in the shocking conflation of the gender binary around which the dynamics of middle-class propriety pivoted. Here was the confidence man *as* a painted lady, and both of these gender performances were of interest to a hostile public. The *New York World* described him as a "great he negro by the name of Peter Sewally" who "has for a long time past been doing a fair business, both in moneymaking, and *practical* amalgamation." The paper described his courtroom appearance "attired *a la mode de New York,* elegantly, and in perfect style. Her or his dingy ears were decked with a pair of snow white ear rings, his head was ornamented with a wig of beautiful curly locks, and on it was a gilt comb, which was half hid amid the luxuriant crop of wool." Sarcasm was evident in the disconnection between Sewally's attempted elegance and the abject reality of his "dingy" skin and wooly hair.

As with E. W. Clay's satirical attacks on Philadelphia dandies, the caricature here cuts both ways: certainly against Sewally but also against well-to-do ladies and gentlemen attempting French pretensions along Broadway. The ridiculous sight of Sewally's attempted style was an indictment on style as such, as the paper went on to note: "His waist was squeezed into a size that would have put to blush the veriest dandy in the city, and his or her toute ensemble was engaging in the extreme—at least so thought Mr. Robert Haslem." The recurrent mock indecision as to Sewally's gender here reinforces the equation drawn between his feminine waistline and that of male dandies, implying something deviant and effeminate about the dandy as such and casting impolite doubts as to whether or not "Mr. Robert Haslem" was in fact deceived as to Sewally's gender or whether indeed gender had not become stylized beyond recognition within the flux of urban life.[77]

Most worthy of notice was the paper's insistence that Sewally's enterprise was equal parts "moneymaking" and "*practical* amalgamation." What are we to make of this telling alignment? Both are sarcasms, but the modifier "practical" redoubles the satire insofar as it indexes the standard antiabolitionist charge that equality *in theory* meant amalgamation *in practice*. Sewally's activities were thus obliquely produced as evidence against the claims of abolitionists, as indexing the social chaos that would accompany the overthrow of slavery and racial domination. Insofar as amalgamation functioned primarily as an index of this impending chaos, and not as literal reproduction across the color line, it can be said that Sewally indeed represented the practical amalgamation as antebellum New Yorkers both feared and, it must be said, were titillated by.

Keeping in mind that bag of money Mr. Varg held away from the avaricious David Ruggles in E. W. Clay's cartoon, we might also weigh Michael O'Malley's suggestive comparison of nineteenth-century discourses of species and specie. Insofar as whiteness worked as a kind of gold standard for virtue and governability, black citizenship could be figured as a kind of counterfeit currency, a fake masquerading as and depreciating the real thing.[78] While men like Ruggles valiantly endeavored to remonstrate with, shame, and cajole other black men into a state of collective dignity, their own successes at self-improvement and moral entrepreneurship could be seized upon as diluting and discrediting those values and thus as much a masquerade and deception as Sewally's street walking.

Sewally's story has been told in relation to the history of prostitution in New York City, and it has also been told in relation to the history of same-sex desire and acts between men. He has not been written about, however, in relation to African American history, despite the numerous fine-grained histories of early black New York we now have. Leslie Harris's *In the Shadow of Slavery* (2003) does not mention Sewally, despite her focus on the lives of everyday black New Yorkers and their interactions and struggles with the white working class. Shane White's *Stories of Freedom in Black New York* (2002) similarly omits mention of Sewally, despite its focus on the multiracial sporting life of theater, dancehalls, painted ladies, and confidence men. Since Sewally's story is fairly well known, one cannot assume that these well-researched histories have simply missed his presence. Rather, it seems, his story has simply been left out as too sensational to merit sustained analysis and integration into the social history of everyday black life in New York. Like other queer subjects, Sewally's excessive visibility in his own time has ironically helped ensure his invisibility to a posterity that has considered him too strange to be true.

That Sewally's story should be seen as too sensational for black history is doubly ironic in that the sole record we have of his own words testifies to his own conviction that he was accepted in the black community of his own day. Sewally told the police at the time of his first arrest that his cross-dressing persona had been accepted at balls thrown by African Americans in both New York City, where he was born and raised, and New Orleans, which he had visited. His public claims must be read carefully in their context of interrogation and ridicule, in which acceptance by his own people was perhaps the one refuge from scorn he could easily claim without fear of contradiction. And yet, it is indeed the case that he continued to circulate in black New York for many years after being exposed in the press and imprisoned, and studies of subsequent periods confirm the presence and popularity of drag balls in urban black centers into the early twentieth century.[79]

Clearly, a historiographical preference for depicting the black community as unified in struggle, normative in sexuality, and steadfastly pursuing the social respectability unfairly denied them by white racism has made little space for stories like Sewally's. In suggesting the importance of such an apparently marginal person, I am seeking to reopen the fraught relation between race and sexuality in the African American past. Drawing unawares on a long tradition of abolitionist polemic, the contemporary literature on this historical intersection has emphasized sexuality primarily as a vector of white male domination and violation of black women. It therefore categorizes sexuality in the African American experience as a historical trauma attached to the messy southern household. The emphasis on sexuality as trauma, as Reid-Pharr suggests, unwittingly feeds into the ideology of respectability insofar as the recurrent "solution" to this historical violation of women has been a militant, masculinist redemption of the race.

My purpose, like Reid-Pharr's, has not so much been to minimize this historiography of coerced sex and reproduction—which was a real and significant aspect of historical experience—as to resituate it. The narration of trauma has overwritten the historical mapping of black bodies and pleasures that might not simply confess the truth of their sex but, when placed on the stand, might refuse the imperatives of shame and transfigure their spectacularization into a dignified shamelessness.

A rhetoric of violated, feminized blackness served the abolitionist movement at a moment when it was crucial to respond to and resignify the moral panic around practical amalgamation. As a humanitarian discourse, abolitionism was led ineluctably into a "pornography of pain," increasingly dependent on the depiction of ever-more grievous assaults in ever-more colorful language so as to overcome the psychic defenses of white audiences to admitting black humanity.[80] Excluding the possibility of same-sex or cross-racial desire, this attempted education of black desire was built on the basis of a verbose discourse of violated black femininity and outraged black male honor. In founding racial identity upon trauma, however, this discourse produced a historical loss that my present work seeks to register. This was the loss of affect as multifarious and deterritorializing, affect attached to social asymmetries of dominance and exploitation parasitically, reiterating and theatricalizing those asymmetries. In chapter 3, I have more to say about such subterranean, convivial feelings. Here I want to mark the deployment of amalgamation as an act of ideological closure that opens out only onto the future of racially normative heterosexuality. Yet such positing of norms, as we have learned from Foucault, requires the simultaneous elaboration and policing of deviance.

If Peter Sewally and David Ruggles shared the streets of antebellum New York, they did so as antitypes: moral entrepreneur and transvestite streetwalker. The ludic and violent panic and pleasure of the amalgamation waltz drew upon both types. Insofar as American egalitarianism introjected the split between the bourgeois self and the grotesque body, both the bespectacled gentleman and the "man-monster" could throw the status of the public sphere into question.

If we try to retain an awareness of the dignity Sewally sought to draw around himself, standing in ridicule before the court of law, we might see how his transformation of shame might share the spirit of Ruggles's own victory "in night's eye." That both were engaged in performances of respectability only underlines the forever-contested content of that category.

3. Minstrel Trouble: Racial Travesty in the Circum-Atlantic Fold

The uneven ground of history ensures that social struggles are usually pitched not in terms of opposing discourses but in competitions over a single vernacular and improvisations upon a common repertoire. This is what "the amalgamation waltz" is meant to evoke: a momentum that spins the body into and out of the symbolic order, a performance that becomes a mirror in which seeing and being seen convene without ever quite converging. Historically speaking, as a metaphor of transformation, amalgamation appeared as a performed and potential transgression of the boundaries of blackness and whiteness. At the same time, it did so within a deployment of sexuality and a project of racialized governmentality. This places the affective labors of black anti-antiamalgamation on a somewhat different footing, though, insofar as they formed a bulwark against a national fantasy premised on the indefinite management of the black–white distinction. Against the pedagogic deferrals of a hybrid future, then, black anti-antiamalgamation proposed the performative inhabitation of the nation by a black dignity thriving outside the confines of its dialectical resolution.

The vertigo induced by the amalgamation waltz did not of itself undermine racializing practice insofar as love, shame, and desire served not as respites from governmentality but as a map of its coordinates. Against the deployment of amalgamation as a secret history of the nation, then, it is important to demonstrate how those affects migrate across divisions conventionally drawn between private and public, self and society. In shifting the corporeal site of this analysis from amalgamation panic to blackface minstrelsy, a fantasy of private corruption is pulled inside out to reveal the rough seams of an emergent public sphere, and bodies interlocked in conjugal union are dispersed across a profane and promiscuous stage. What repeats here are the affective outcomes of the grotesque body, that emblem of hybridity as figured especially in the social performances of the carnivalesque.

The carnivalesque, Bakhtin argued, was keyed in particular to an aristocratic order within which hierarchy was so naturalized that the most radical gesture was to imagine a reversal of fortune: the world turned upside down. But when these images of topsy-turvydom were refracted in the mirror of liberty, they took on a new valence insofar as democratic ideology professed an equality of condition rather than inherited, hierarchical status. Under such conditions, we cannot indeed resort to "old modernist insights into the nature of liminality, the place and time of betwixt-and-between, of carnival, rituals of rebellion and rites of cosmic renewal."[1] Instead we must account for how the carnivalesque might participate in the imagined liberties of a democratic national culture, operating itself as a mode of governmentality.

We might consider, in this respect, how such an operation was at play during the extraordinary rendition of a fugitive slave from his northern refuge in Boston. Anthony Burns's case was an abolitionist cause célèbre in 1854, not least because of the high drama of a slave's trial in the birthplace of American liberty. William Cooper Nell moaned that Burns had been "dragged back to slavery . . . marching over the very ground that ATTUCKS trod."[2] His case dramatized the national crisis produced by the Fugitive Slave Act of 1850, which reinforced and extended slaveholders' property rights nationally, exposing the futility of "free soil" ideology. This bore implications not only for abolitionists but for a broader swath of the white American populace who opposed slavery not out of sympathy for the slave but from a self-interested calculation that the spread of slavery would immiserate the white working class. The historical bloc that emerged to counter the slave power in the north and west could, as Eric Foner has shown, wed antislavery with antiblack racism.[3] While ultimately opening a path to the ascendancy of the Great Emancipator, the manner in which abolition was ultimately accomplished in the United States seems to fulfill William Cooper Nell's maxim that justice is done to black people only by mistake.[4]

We see these contradictions especially at one particular point in the tragedy of Burns: the conduct of the garrison charged with maintaining order. According to Charles Emery Stevens,

> A keen sense of . . . ignominy . . . filled the breasts of some. . . . Some were indifferent. . . . Others sympathized with the slavehunter and rejoiced in the opportunity to render him aid with ball and bayonet. . . . As they stood in line on the Common, they compromised the character of the whole corps by their free use of intoxicating liquor and the singing of ribald songs. . . . Filled with liquor, even to intoxication, they became lost to all sense of decorum, and, reeling upon their gunstocks, sang the chorus, "Oh, carry me back to Old Virginny."[5]

In a seemingly gratuitous cruelty, enlisted men obliged to follow orders threw their esprit de corps into the further dehumanization of their prisoner, mocking his fate to a minstrel tune. At the same time, however, Stevens depicts their singing and intoxication as reflecting both their dissensus as to the justice of those orders and their helplessness to do other than obey them. The ressentiment of their nostalgic, drunken singing performed their disidentification with the subject of the song pining for hearth and home. While the vexed story of blackface minstrelsy and the white working class does certainly not begin or end here, it does reach a certain pitch, driving home Stuart Hall's emphasis on the politics of accentuation.

"Carry Me Back to Old Virginia" was a song that had been popularized by E. P. Christy, born in Philadelphia and one of a number of northern men who drew fame for their musical and theatrical impersonations of blacks, a complex performance genealogy that gets the inadequate modern shorthand "blackface minstrelsy." That Christy's sentimental lines could be purloined for use in a state-sponsored kidnapping suggests something of the easy complicities of popular culture.[6] Burns's fate, and the leitmotif by which he was conducted to it, registers the space of performance as a charged palimpsest of history, tragedy, and power. It is never a dance upon "free soil." Danced and sung freedoms are always situated in relation to boundaries, limits, and thresholds.

In order to see this, we must shift from an abstract conception of liberty to the rendering of historically articulated zones of license, exchange, and dialogism that Joseph Roach has shown us how to think of as "the liberties."[7] The liberties name an actual and moral place on the map of the city, a boundary toward which certain abject but necessary activities, like the market and the theater, were dispersed. Through Roach's work, we see how this imagined zone of lawlessness and exchange could become a site for the resentful reinstatement of white over black. Might this easy complicity between carnival and the law help account for the compromised character of the militia? Did singing and drinking perform a triumph of market libertinage over human dignity? And in ordering the return of Burns to slavery, did the court not surrogate the work of the auction block? Thus asserting its own inner consilience with the soldiers' outward display of bad manners? The sober articulation of the agrarian south to the commercial north through a shared rule of law instated American liberty in the fleshly form of the human commodity. How could this process not find itself registered, reflected, and refracted in the participatory performance culture of its moment, particularly given the growing role within that culture of the principles of the market revolution?[8]

Performance, particularly the carnivalesque spirit associated with minstrelsy, can thus participate in a society structured in dominance. But what cultural work did it embody as an instatement of the national Thing? How did a shared history become a fraught scene or sound, shared by black and white, such as "Carry Me Back to Old Virginia" suggests? And what kind of historical writing can preserve this split rather than seek to "complete" or harmonize the difference between the melting pot and miscegenation? Above all, how might we refuse the temptation to read the exchange of differences in terms of the market itself, a system of equivalences that nonetheless reproduces inequality? In answering these questions, we must target minstrelsy as an important site where blackness and Americanness, identity and the marketplace, provocatively intersect and diverge on national and transnational stages.

Rich in Black Fun

In an 1823 letter of reminiscence of his travels to America, the British thespian Charles Mathews related news of the comic material that his interactions with black Americans would add to his repertoire. Mathews represented his travels as a sort of fieldwork into the mannerisms, colloquialisms, and peculiarities of American types, all of which might assist him in "the first popular antecedent of blackface acts" back home, as Lott describes it.[9] Finding much of what passes for American to be ultimately recognizable as Scottish, Irish, or some other already familiar type, Mathews selected black dialect as offering "one of the few instances of originality" upon which his "personation" might capitalize. In a phrase made famous by repeated commentary, he boasted that, having mastered these black roles, he will be "rich in black fun."

The specifically commercial context in which Mathews wrote gives the word *rich* multiple nuances, including the literal one. Blackness in the form of an "original" dialect becomes both a commercial and a performative medium. "I have several specimens of these black gentry," Mathews writes, tellingly mixing monetary and dramatic metaphors, "that I can bring into play."[10] Mathews capitalizes on character as caricature, bringing blackness into circum-Atlantic circulation in the hybridized form of a broken diction. To coin a phrase, Mathews's forays into black America serve him as a "primitivist accumulation," a foray into the accumulation of cultural and performative capital that lay in store a repertoire of phrase and gesture upon which to make a name. But, as Fred Moten might note, his fictions of black dialect rest on a further fiction that the experience of the human commodity is fully communicable, that black phonic materiality is just a broken down and ragtag version of ordinary speech. That such a capitalist stance toward linguistic dialogism nevertheless carves out a ready reservoir of wit and cross-racial identification in the face of the depersonalized disorientations of the market was Eric Lott's great insight. Insofar as capitalist relations cause all that is solid to melt into air, the specimens of black gentry that dialect humor brought into play could at once serve as a profanation of the sacred (in this case, the King's English) and projecting of the grotesquerie onto a black screen. It would not be the first time that capitalist culture would present itself as its own anodyne.

I emphasize here that the Atlantic "lore cycle" that Mathews helps inaugurate, to evoke W. T. Lhamon's useful phrasing, was also a commercial nexus. Fun, as a particularly American, particularly black, particularly marketable idiom, formed part of its idiom from the very start.[11] How might this observation lead us to reconsider Lott's influential thesis regarding minstrelsy's staging of the contradictions of freedom and slavery in the national popular? "In the broadest political sense," Lott notes,

we might say that blackface artists all at once found themselves staging a sort of unintended play about the slavery crisis, a play that
pointed up rather than papered over cracks in the historical bloc of
mid-century America.[12]

While Lott's treatment of minstrelsy's pointed accentuation of racial
contradictions remains definitive, I suspect that a better umbrella
category under which to place blackface is not, as he suggests here,
the theatrical. It is rather, as I discuss in this chapter, the carnivalesque. A critical aspect of this difference, as Bakhtin argues, is the
participatory, infectious spirit of carnival, which does not truly
come alive until it is taken into the mouth, shaken from the feet,
expelled from the body in odors and shouts. While blackface minstrels and comics indeed staged plays, no single genre could capture
what was specifically appealing about minstrelization: its facility
for inverting, burlesquing, and blackening anything. And no image
of theatricality—which must draw some workable distinction between performer and audience—can capture the specifically participatory character of the blackface craze, which disseminated along
lines that Barbara Browning has labeled "infectious." In early song
and dance crazes like T. D. Rice's "Jump Jim Crow," minstrelsy had
an enthusiastic audience mimicking its act from the start: turning
about, wheeling about, and doing just so. Minstrelsy's carnivalesque
spirit pervaded visual, print, and performance culture, disseminating
across the Atlantic as a kind of lingua franca that was recognizably
American.[13]

The carnivalesque, to be sure, is not carnival. It is carnival as refracted in the commodity mirror and transfigured by the commercial
nexus. If minstrelsy staged the crisis that was also, by the 1840s, dis-
tinctively American (Britain having ended slavery in its West Indies
possessions by 1834), it did so through a mode that insistently exposed the grotesque body in an environment for which we can call
on an unpredictable resonance of the term *hybrid*. Like the hybrid-
izing process of trees in botany, the carnivalesque was grafted onto
an American culture increasingly rich in black fun, instantiating at
the heart of a Protestant, individualistic, commercial, and democratically egalitarian culture a commodified effigy of carnival.[14] This aspect does return us to Lott's original insight, in modified form. In its
condensation of carnival spirit, space and time into the virtuosic gesture of exemplary performers, the carnivalesque can indeed be said

to "stage" a "play" for the viewing pleasure of an audience. Even as blackface coined a "specimen" of black gentry to set into "play," it quarantined a bit of the inadmissible in exchangeable form. Blackface and its heroes became the national thing. The riches of black fun accrued not only to the performer as culture hero but also to a popular audience organized around what would come to be called the possessive investment in whiteness.[15]

The carnivalesque, whether in literature or performance, establishes spectatorship as well as participation. This is why its role in the performance of imagined community has proved so compelling. Quite early on in the contemporary study of minstrelsy, Roediger borrowed George Rawicks's suggestive phrase, "a pornography of his former life," to describe the attractions the proletarianized white worker might have found in certain minstrel images of bucolic and contented country folk.[16] And while this borrowing misses the important presence of the urban dandies in early minstrelsy, it does at least disclose the cultural work of surrogation. Early minstrelsy did not simply surrogate blackness. It also surrogated whiteness in so far as it represented an image of life lived in heroic relation to the regimes of labor discipline, whether that life was figured as pre- or posturban, trickster or outlaw, buffoon or sentimental spectacle. But this process, beginning with men like Mathews, T. D. Rice, and George Christy, must be understood as commercial culture. It is not merely the content of minstrelsy to which we must attend, in other words, but its commodified and professionalized form.

How did minstrel as commodity and as national Thing point out cracks in the historical bloc of midcentury America? To answer this, we must consider a certain haphazard, postcolonial aesthetic attached to the United States in international settings. Consider one cosmopolitan response to American wares displayed at the Crystal Palace in London during the Great Exhibition of 1851:

> If the Americans do excite a smile, it is by their pretensions. Whenever they come out of their province of rugged utility, and enter into competition with European elegance, they certainly do make themselves ridiculous. Their furniture is grotesque; their carriages and harness are gingerbread; their carpets are tawdry; their patchwork quilts surpass even the invariable ugliness of this fabric; their cut glass is clumsy; their pianos sound of nothing but iron and wood. . . . Even their ingenuity, great as it is, becomes ridiculous when it attempts

competition with Europe. Double pianos, a combination of a piano and a violin, a chair with a cigar-case in its back, and other mongrel constructions belong to a people that would be centaurs and mermen if they could, and are always rebelling against the trammels of unity.[17]

A condescending attitude toward the pretentious, rugged, tawdry, clumsy, ridiculous, grotesque, hybrid, and rebellious are all gathered into and under the epithet "mongrel." All those words might also be used to describe the blackface minstrel, whose popularity abroad, by the 1850s, well accorded with such metropolitan disdain. But the "mongrel" nature of American attempts at elegance beyond the province of rugged utility, as can easily be seen here, could also be defiantly embraced as the source of a unique national culture, stripped of guile, skill, elegance, and refinement. If mongrel marked the threshold between man and monster, it is not surprising to discover its uses in promoting a certain mystique of the nation as powerful, unpredictable, rugged, hybrid, and for sale.[18]

An early illustration of Jim Crow, "The American Mountebank," depicts him in a pose whose circum-Atlantic genealogy has been traced by W. T. Lhamon.[19] As portly, self-satisfied men look on, Jim Crow sings about studying the legal commentaries of "Blackstone ebry morn & arter noon," while charming "de House where Chatham died and danc[ing] in de saloon" every night. Is this ramshackle stance not part and parcel of the minstrel appeal? Since Lott, we have been talking about "love and theft" in the blackface repertoire. Of what does their union consist if not of the attempted combination of two nonopposed terms into a single theoretical contraption, like a chair with a cigar case in its back?[20] Sloppy but not ragged, darkened but clearly not African featured, Jim Crow epitomizes at American rebellion against the "trammels of unity," equal parts arriviste and scoundrel.

So, what do we talk about when we talk about love (and theft)? Theft might helpfully index an overlooked moment in the history of anticapitalist critique, the polemic between Marx and Proudhon over the latter's ringing claim that "property is theft."[21] Can we think of blackness as a property similarly stolen, provided we admit, with Proudhon, that there is no original owner but that blackness, property, is constituted *through* theft? Cedric Robinson has helped here, resituating Marx in the context of contemporaries in anticapitalist critique and arguing their importance for a black radical project.[22] The theory of primitive accumulation is a particularly productive site

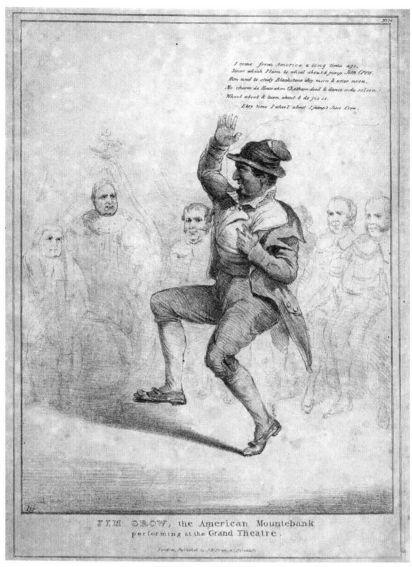

Figure 10. I. H., *Jim Crow, the American Mountebank Performing at the Grand Theatre,* circa 1828–33. S. W. Fores, 41, Piccadilly, London. Courtesy of American Antiquarian Society.

for a black radical revision. Despite Marx's insistence on the production of value through the labor process, his concept of "primitive accumulation" retains a sharp Proudhonesque tone to it insofar as what was being "accumulated" was land and resources formerly held in common or bound within precapitalist moral economies, and what was "primitive" was its violence. Violence is papered over in most of the pious histories of capitalist development. But slavery exposes this contradiction, most obviously by presenting the spectacle of property rights *in* the individual, thus taking a theft that had supposedly been ushered into the gloomy past and restaging it at the center of modernity. But it also shows it in the entr'acte between slavery and freedom that I call the circum-Atlantic fold, in the kind of "primitivist accumulation" witnessed in minstrelsy, which heisted an image of blackness that did not exist prior to its theft but that was constituted through this theft.

Negro Eccentricities and the Antislavery Wall

At the Crystal Palace in 1851, at least one American entry tried in a clumsy fashion to present itself as antislavery. Among the mongrel objects entered into competition with European elegance was Hiram Powers's statue *The Greek Slave,* purportedly an image of oriental despotism in the Old World, a white bondage from which the New World had heroically freed itself. Exhibited throughout both north and south in the late 1840s, when sectional conflicts over slavery were reaching a fever pitch, Hiram Powers's depiction of white slavery in the Orient had been embraced by the American public as art in its image, its relevance to black slavery in America hysterically denied. The sturdiness of this stance was tested in a caricature printed in a British humor magazine. In the *Virginian Slave,* the ideal female beauty over which audiences cried was rudely replaced with a pointedly black female body. Displacing the ethereal with the earthy, the cartoon created a sense that something pure had been defiled. The *Virginian Slave* seems to necessitate more draping than the original. The parody, unlike the allegorical original, could not sublimate her sexuality.

Such British criticism of American hypocrisy lacked a clear abolitionist stance. But the ambiguity of the cartoon's message did not prevent the black American abolitionists William Wells Brown and Ellen Craft from brandishing it as part of their agitprop disruption of the London exhibition. Like Nell's revised images and enactments of the Boston Massacre, Brown and Craft choreographed a response that signified on both the *Punch* cartoon and American neoclassicism.[23] After dramatically placing the cartoon next to the offending statue, Craft's prominent promenade through the Crystal Palace performed black femininity as ladyhood, disputing the degraded image of the Virginian slave at which Londoners were invited to either laugh or sneer. Craft thus reaccented the *Punch* cartoon that, while nominally anti-American and antislavery, was also rich in black fun. The fun of blackening Powers's virginal image was the aggressive, bawdy fun of minstrel debasements, to which Craft responded with a black abolitionist performance of respectability.

Mary Webb, the African American dramatic reader who declaimed from *Uncle Tom's Cabin* and *Song of Hiawatha* in the salons of Philadelphia, Boston, and then London, similarly transfigured the image of black femininity disseminated on the minstrel stage into a dignified alternative. But, like Craft's use of the cartoon, her respectable performances drew upon their minstrel antitype. Her performances could not risk a lack in the richness of black fun. Indeed, one Philadelphia reviewer found Webb's "Negro Eccentricities" so "near perfection that our mind was carried back to our native State, where we had heard and seen the genuine 'darkies' of the South act naturally, that which Mrs. Webb had acquired by practice and study."[24] How was Webb able, in performing dialect humor, to send the metamessage that she was a skilled performer adopting rather than exemplifying black traits?

As Paul Gilmore has provocatively argued, so pervasive were the cultural associations between blackness and blackfaced artifice that black activists and abolitionists like Brown and Webb were obliged to engage the minstrel repertoire in order to attract attention to their critique of American slavery and racism.[25] In the funhouse mirror of liberty, a black actor could demonstrate comic skill by mimicking through "practice and study" the malapropisms of the genuine darky. The roots of both Bert Williams and Paul Laurence Dunbar lie here, in a virtuoso performance of the supposedly congenital. Gilmore argues that for Brown (and we may add, for Webb and Craft as well) "the minstrel show offered particularly expansive representational possibilities because its commercialized images foreground the slippage between performative and essential notions of blackness and manliness" (and femininity).[26] Much of the revisionist literature on minstrelsy has made a similar effort to recover its subversive edge, whether in the name, as here, of antiessentialism or, in a not wholly implausible supplement, in the name of anticapitalism. At stake here is the place of enjoyment in history, particularly popular and convivial

Figure 11. *Mrs. Mary E. Webb, 1856. Illustrated London News.*

forms of enjoyment that resist the censoriousness of bourgeois culture, which are deliberately offensive and crude.[27]

At stake also is the image of black culture in historical perspective.
The politics of respectability, which censure minstrel buffoonery on
the one hand, on the other now reprimand hip hop and baggy jeans,

black English and ghetto fabulousness, and in general, place black working-class culture beneath its contempt. Herein lies the plausibility of Lhamon's paean to the lumpenproletarian solidarities that minstrelsy supposedly instilled. But if minstrelsy is to take its place in the "old, weird America" as rebellious counterimage to the nation's official culture, then its carnivalizing spirit must be much more seriously interrogated than some latter-day romantics are prepared to do.

In our contemporary moment, to speak of a performance as minstrelized is to refer to a felt residue of the subservient, ingratiating, and degrading still clinging to present-day performance, a lingering half-life emanating from minstrelsy's radioactive core. But this present-day use treats the minstrel complex as it might be condensed in a Kara Walker silhouette: the racial phantasmagoria of the peculiar institution. But once the genealogy of minstrelsy is situated in an emergent U.S. national popular with global reach, the stability of this minstrel icon dissolves. Jean-Christophe Agnew has demonstrated the historical and spatial linkages between the theater and the market in Anglo-American thought.[28] We might use his perspective to reconsider the enduring affinities of the carnivalesque and the commodity form. This in turn may produce a more complex picture of the critique developed by black activists and abolitionism of minstrelsy, one based not simply on bourgeois disgust for profane and popular culture but also on experience on both sides of the commodity, an experience that supplies a powerful critique of bourgeois, market, and capitalist values.

Rather than hastening to add minstrelsy to the old weird America, we should investigate how the performance of "negro eccentricities" figured into the building of a black antislavery wall, to use R. J. M. Blackett's useful phrase.[29] Part of answering this question entails foregrounding a perspective usually shunted to one side or overly simplified: black commentary. Kevin Gaines's history of black leadership in the twentieth century has begun part of this work, but he picks the story up at a point, the early twentieth century, by which a half century of blackface and the incorporation of American culture had produced what I think of as a "late minstrelsy," with its own particular set of historical coordinates.[30] What of "early minstrelsy," that supposedly more mongrel, subterranean, and rebellious form, before it was co-opted by parlor sing-alongs, Rotary Club fundraisers, and *The Jazz Singer*? Cockrell, in his defense of minstrelsy, draws a dividing line as early as 1843. Early blackface, he argues, challenged "knowledge acquired through reason and print" with the "moral capital" of "the community's stories, songs, and homilies." He even claims in response to the historical emphasis on the act of blacking up that "Blackface subverted 'knowing' gained through image" because blackface "was really the secondary signifier, at least from the perspective of the common people. The *noise*—the *ear*— that which always accompanies ritual representations of blackness, is a much richer indicator of the presence of inversion rituals than mere blackface." After 1843, he continues, minstrelsy took a turn for the conservative, from noise to representation, and from social real to the commercial deception.[31] Cockrell suggests that bourgeois culture was threatened by this ear culture of the masses. And indeed one witnesses in early black accounts of minstrelsy similar descriptions of the genre's disrespectability. But since white supremacy affected African Americans as a group, the politics of respectability and uplift cannot be read simply as a "middle-class" imposition upon the black working class. Respectability came to the fore as response to potentially degrading behavior and spectacle. On the one hand, respectability relates to class in that bourgeois society defined itself, against both the unwashed masses and the decadent aristocracy, as decent and respectable. On the other hand, respectability and religious piety were potent resources among African Americans, who employed them to protest their oppressed status. Insofar as, in principal, any individual could choose to act respectably, respectability could be detached from its class connotations and itself become a performative tactic of class struggle.

Respectability, to specify a vague term, historically referenced the volitional aspects of class and race, that is, the part the individual or family might voluntarily choose to alter or change. As a vehicle for social change, it undoubtedly colluded with the bourgeois values: abstaining from immorality, dancing, alcohol, and gambling. Insofar as it did so, there is the temptation to see, as Foucault warned against, the mirage of symmetrical hypocrisies, bourgeois and subaltern. But against such an explanation one might mobilize an argument that in claiming practices from the bourgeois, respectability also resisted the automatic equation of poverty or race with degradation. The long history of the working-class and African American pursuit of dignity, at work and in society, speaks to this complexity. Today, critical intellectuals sometimes identify romantically with working-class rebelliousness, vulgarity, and disdain of bourgeois restriction. But such a romantic identification with the mongrel past forgets the resources of dignity the poor and racialized have wielded against their oppression, such as I argued for in relation to Peter Sewally. Vernacular culture is not intrinsically vulgar or carnivalizing, any more than it is intrinsically respectable. Carnival masks and one's Sunday best are both moments in the cycle of plebeian life. And furthermore, the work of gender in these matters must be emphasized: working class masculine culture cannot be made to stand in for working class culture as such.

What is more, the very "demons of disorder" lionized by some historians as champions of a subterranean American culture themselves well knew how to negotiate this language of deference as much as "bourgeois" black reformers did. I discussed earlier T. D. Rice's response when one of his plays was attacked in the *New York Mirror*. The heteroglossia of his published response—which veered between miming black dialect and lampooning the regular diction expected in print—destabilized his own racial identity and blurred the line between performer and role.[32] Referring to himself as "Jim Crow" and calling for support from his "brudder" actors, Rice opined at gratuitous length on topics ranging from the redeeming social merits of his production to attacks on the credibility of his critic. If Rice's claiming a reformist mission for his bluster and stomp was surely spurious, it was so in a characteristically antebellum way. To grasp this dynamic, we must be reminded of Rosemarie Bank's observation that it was "perhaps a uniquely theatrical approach to meet the titillating and moralizing text" of "the gentrification campaign in nineteenth-century America . . . with an invitation to perform the appearance of respectability."[33] Popular pleasures and vices made recurrent use of reform as an alibi in this time period.[34]

Rice's bogus tribute to white respectability was mirrored in black uplift politics, which also looked to blackface minstrelsy as an object lesson in what not to do. If the dominant image of blacks in both free and slave states was as servants and drudge laborers, attached to and servicing white households and economies, then the counterimage produced in the black public sphere required the imaginative construction of modern black selves no longer attached to or dependent upon white households.

Gender was critical in this black rearticulation of domestic and sentimental values, not only because women were presumed to be the makers of home but because black men as proud householders offered a powerful counterimage to the rootless, vagabond image of the black man advertised on the minstrel stage. If the home was at the core of ideologies of respectability and uplift, as Robert Reid-Pharr argues, then the streets, theaters, and public spaces were zones where they would be tested. Key in black reformers' encounters with everyday life were the public and homosocial entertainments of early blackface performance. If the presence of cross-dressing highlighted the absence of women from antebellum minstrelsy, this merely underlines the gendered stakes in the confrontation between a respectability grounded in domesticity and proper roles for men and women and the promiscuous street life the genre perilously engaged. Insofar as antebellum minstrelsy not only represented nostalgic images of bucolic country life, as was formerly thought, but rather celebrated strong and dangerous urban rebels and heroes, that would only have produced further worry in the reformer's mind. Attacking the excesses of a popular vulgarity that was explicitly and excessively masculine formed a frequent strategy in an abolitionist movement in which black and white women took prominent and increasingly independent roles.[35]

The respectability pursued by black male and female activists was virtual, a respectability to come. It was not based in a defense of extant social relations but enacted through a mimetic performative intervention into those relations, upon terms they well knew white supremacy might find unacceptable. Builders of the antislavery wall claimed respect in the face of its quotidian denial on both sides of the Atlantic. In politicizing respectability, they moved the domestic into the political sphere. We see this move especially in the antebellum black press, a resource largely overlooked by most contemporary historians of minstrelsy.

The Blackface Image in the Black Counterpublic Sphere

Debates in the black press, which were public conversations about the condition and destiny of black people as a community, reflect this paradoxically public privacy and peculiarly political domesticity. In the Civil War era, a letter writer to the San Francisco black newspaper the *Pacific Appeal* described minstrelsy as "a moral ulcer" and called for its "abolition."[36] The *Pacific Appeal* argued that black civil rights and the popularity of blackface performance were inversely proportionate to each other. "In those cities and communities where the rights of the Colored man are mostly respected," the paper wrote, "those burlesquing exhibitions are never tolerated. While in those cities and communities where their rights mostly are disregarded, these exhibitions in ridicule are of common occurrence."[37] The writer underscored his reading of minstrelsy as an attack on manhood. "Is there a man among us," he asked, "who has not witnessed these exhibitions and has not felt his manhood outraged while gazing upon them?" I find it suggestive that he places the comment in the form of a rhetorical question to his readers, challenging them to participate in his disgust:

> Or are we, in the midst of a community of Colored men, so morally depraved as not to feel an intuitive uprising of their manly nature, in revolt against such ridiculous performances?

Repeating key emotive terms like *uprising* and *revolt,* he sought to associate with them a manliness modeled on bourgeois restraint and dignity.

But the author also exhibited doubts as to whether such an "intuitive" response to minstrelsy was in fact intuitive to his audience. He sought to interpolate his readers into a potential "community of Colored men" who would both feel disgust at the sight of minstrelsy and recognize that disgust as natural. The virtuality (or ideality, as Maurice Wallace might put it) of this black manhood displayed itself in differing modes according to race and respectability.[38] While the white men traducing the black image might merit only "a nettled brow of scorn," he claimed, "the eye moistens with a tear" when discovering "that men, naturally black . . . have been induced through ignorance, lack of principle, or sheer cupidity, to be a party in representing by public entertainment their own degradation and that of their unfortunate race." Modeling the proper affective response for his reader—a lip curled in scorn, a tear-laden eye—he proposed that respectable black masculinity would be cultivated through a series of identifications and counteridentifications with the "public entertainment" from which other African Americans, through "ignorance" or greed, would seek to profit.

This response bore continuities to that published two decades earlier in the *Colored American*. In 1841, two years before Cockrell's fateful turning point, editor Samuel Cornish noticed and sought to augment an emerging class schism between theatrical venues catering to the working class and those to which respectable black men and women might seek access. He wished his black readers to avail themselves of this divergence and get on the right side of that division. Representing theatergoing in the same language with which reformers indicted drinking and sexual promiscuity, Cornish called one inexpensive theater house "a temptation to the poorer and the lower classes." Such reformist rhetoric was pitched to a black community that painfully understood itself to be lumped together into a single category in the eyes of whites and therefore to enjoy class status primarily in the eyes of each other. Respectability among free black people was a fluid concept related to but not *reducible* to class or income, a relational category that negotiated two publics simultaneously: the general public and the imagined "community of Colored men."

The *Colored American* dealt with the problem of a black presence in the audience for minstrelsy. Cornish based his report on a "friend's" attendance of a "vile haunt" from which he "came away disgusted" and indicted the performance in morally charged language:

> The actor came from behind the curtain, lost to all self respect, and sunken in the lowest depths of degradation and vice, with his face painted to represent a colored man, and there acted out scenes, the like of which, no human being, but some one as lost to all sense of honor as himself, ever acted.

In such language, the role of actor and the device of blackface are conflated in a vision of degradation and vice redolent of the stock figures of reformist invective. Cornish evoked a racially bifurcated class structure of respectable black and white men, equally and independently honorable, and a popular class sunk to the lowest depths of degradation, even to the point of losing their sense of racial distinction:

> But what crowned the whole, our informant said, he never saw so many colored persons at the theatre in his life, hundreds were there, and among whom were many very respectable looking persons. O shame! paying money, hard earned, to support such places and such men, to heap ridicule and a burlesque upon them in their very presence, and upon their whole class.[39]

Respectable-looking people brought home the dangerous polyvalence of class appearances. Here the fruits of "moneymaking" are revealed in the base coinage's hasty return to its natural level. The respectable-looking black persons in the audience were at least aspirationally of a different class than the others, but in a metropolitan environment of strangers, in which class mobility in both directions was an unavoidable element of life, neither race nor class could easily serve as a stable point around which the other might pivot. Instead, race and class merged into each in and through the performance vortex of minstrelsy, spaces in which would-be race reformers could picture themselves "in the midst of a community of Colored men," correcting and chastising that community by modeling proper affective deportment in relation to popular culture and the other temptations of vice.

In order for this pedagogic scenario to work, however, the degrading implications of minstrelsy would have to be rendered explicit. It is significant that this effort was already underway in the 1830s. In 1837, Cornish reprinted a speech T. D. Rice himself gave after a performance at the Holliday Street theater in Baltimore, Maryland, a slave state, upon his return to the United States after a successful tour in England. In the speech, originally published in the *Baltimore Sun* (thus serving as another instance of black Atlantic eavesdropping), "that most contemtible [sic] of all Buffoons," as Cornish called him, claimed that the popularity of his performances had increased support for the southern slaveholding class abroad. Cornish remarked, "I sincerely hope after reading the following no colored American will ever again so disgrace himself, or his people by patronizing such performances, nor even the theatres where they are exhibited."[40]

In the original article in which the *Sun* had printed this speech a month earlier, it had called Rice "supereminently a favorite of the sovereign people," thus affirming the status of early blackface within a (white) national popular. Claiming its own right to nevertheless reprove the unwashed masses among whom Rice numbered, the *Sun* sardonically noted that

> Crow has decidedly improved by his travels. The coarse "yaw! yaw!" and the shrill "whew!" we perceive as much softened, and his wonted vulgar and unmeasured jumps, uncouth hops, and "plank downs," are exchanged, we are pleased to observe, for more graceful leaps, more refined "turnabouts" and "wheelabouts," and infinitely more defecated [sic] attitudes.[41]

Almost certainly tongue-in-cheek, the article facetiously equated Rice's foreign travels with the traditional European tours taken by elite American men. If E. W. Clay's European trip represented that residual culture, Rice's contemporaneous tour bespoke the emergent role of a globalizing American entertainment that the *Sun* did not know exactly how to handle and so chose to read in familiar terms. Seeming to recognize that indeed the reverse of a finishing tour had happened, and that instead of being refined by Britain, Jim Crow had only spread his coarse *yaw yaw* and shrill *whew,* the *Sun* took refuge in the patriotism of his after-performance speech, one that rendered his performance legibly proslavery and antiblack.

The speech does indeed read like the smoking gun Cornish took it to be:

> Ladies and Gentlemen: Before I went to England, the British people were excessively ignorant regarding "our free institutions." (hear) They were under the impression that negroes were naturally equal to the whites, and their degraded condition was consequent entirely upon our "institutions;" but I effectually proved that negroes are essentially an inferior species of the human family, and that they ought to remain slaves.—(Some murmurs of disapprobation from the boxes, which was quickly put down by the plaudits of the pit.) You will never again hear of an abolitionist crossing the Atlantic to interfere in our affairs. . . . Ladies and Gentlemen: It will ever be a source of pride to me that, in my humble line, I have been such signal service to my country![42]

Rice's speech couched antiblack racism within a string of patriotic verities, delivered in the educated register he subverted in his earlier letter to the *Mirror*. Its tenor seeks to persuade the ambivalent, to assign performance a clear and unambiguous political meaning.

But Rice's argument that minstrelsy proved black inferiority is almost as surely preposterous as his prior claim that it could cure white women of their attractions to dandies. Rice's speech, and Cornish's admonitory publicizing of it to a black readership, may be certainly read as evidence of the desire to assign the liminal space of performance a determinate political meaning, much as the notations of "dialect speech" fix popular ear culture in mocking print. This does not provide an exhaustive account of the particular problem minstrelsy presented to early black activists. For this, we must turn to their more ambivalent responses to minstrel performance.

Paul Gilmore argues that certain black abolitionists drew upon minstrel convention to embrace a performative blackness. But the overly neat distinction between performative blackness and essentialist blackness he posits may not be sufficient. Here Daphne Brooks's alternative concept of "afro-alienation acts" proves a more capacious category under which to gather both "performative" and "essentialist" modes of doing blackness insofar as the essential and/or real destabilizes the social instatements of race.[43] In particular, Gilmore's adoption of Frederick Douglass's manly self-fashioning as his example of black masculine essentialism undercredits one of the most complex and protean of figures. Douglass's self-fashioning as a representative race man has often been oversimplified, in part due to the literary critical habit of restricting exegesis to his canonical autobiographies. To fully engage Douglass's relationship to minstrelsy, we must take up a fuller consideration of his archive and place specific and familiar statements within the arc and context of his life.

In 1848, Douglass rendered a characteristically pointed judgment on the nascent popular phenomena of blackface minstrelsy, already connecting it to the spread of market culture. He described its performers as

> the filthy scum of white society, who have stolen from us a complexion denied to them by nature, in which to make money, and pander to the corrupt taste of their white fellow-citizens.[44]

In this most familiar of Douglass's views on blackface, he emphasizes the commercial calculations he sees at work in the genre, literally characterizing blackness as a property that has been stolen for purposes of moneymaking. While this undoubtedly expresses an essentialist view of race, it also expresses an equally essentialist view of money, and understanding how these two essentialisms interact in his statement opens out an otherwise neglected commentary on its cultural moment. I will return to and complicate this particular view of Douglass's by offering other comments he made, but before I do, I would like to expand upon this particular claim.

As we saw in the hostile press attention to Peter Sewally in chapter 2, "moneymaking" was a particularly unstable site within capitalist relations. While theft is obviously proscribed in order for market relations to flourish, the cash nexus has few bars against the circulation of ill-gotten gains. This makes the presence of urbane confidence men like David Ruggles, seeking to procure "property" from visiting slaveholders, and painted ladies like Sewally, seeking to pick the pockets of lusty lads, so worrisomely equivalent. And the ability to procure money illegitimately indexes a further illegitimacy internal to the money form itself. As Gilmore and especially Michael O'Malley explore, the particular conditions of specie circulation in antebellum America produced high anxiety over the authenticity of paper money. Given the absence of a single national currency, there was an omnipresent temptation to counterfeit and the understandable temptation to prefer a good counterfeit note from a prominent bank over a real promissory tendered by a less well-known institution. William Wells Brown himself issued bank notes for a time, Gilmore shows, learning in the process how truth so often lies in appearances.[45]

Anxiety over the dependence of a market economy upon the trust-worthiness of strangers and the legal fiction of paper notes led to a search for "natural facts" as a counterweight to social flux, O'Malley argues. Both the gold standard and the doctrine of black inferiority were presented as two such natural facts buttressing an otherwise turbulent period. Gold and blackness were instated as contrasting natural certainties. Just as inferior metals could debase gold coin, "amalgamation" with the black race could debase the nation. Social conservatives explicitly linked the granting of citizenship to blacks in the postwar reconstruction to the elevation of a national paper currency, O'Malley recounts. Both black citizenship and paper money were represented as governmental frauds perpetrated upon society.[46]

Seen in this light, we can understand Frederick Douglass to be signifying on the supposedly essential qualities of blackness, which he shows ironically to be as much a source of performative value as gold. And his juxtaposition of the value of blackness and the value of gold/money is quite deliberate insofar as it is also the juxtaposition between labor and capital. Douglass relished the affinity his chosen surname gave him with Scotland, and he frequently read and quoted the romantic poetry of Robert Burns. A particular favorite of Douglass's, which he frequently quoted, was "For a' That and a' That."[47] In its perhaps most memorable couplet, Burns assured that "The rank is but the guinea's stamp; / The man's the gowd for a' that" (gowd = gold). Gold coins called guineas derived from the early modern traffic in slaves and gold from West Africa. Asserting with Burns that the source of value was not the sign or stamp on the coin, but the labor (here gendered as male), Douglass joined Burns's satire of economic and racial essentialism.[48]

Douglass's strategic essentialism was further complicated by much more ambiguous comments he made about minstrelsy on other occasions. He could also jocularly evoke minstrelsy as proof of white American affection for blacks, as he did in an 1852 speech (reported partly in the third person):

> In Ireland and Scotland he had heard the highlands and lowlands vocal with the *native* music of Liberty—music *original* with the People, but, said he, in America the masses can only sing *Nigger songs*. (Applause). I don't believe you want to get rid of us after all.[49]

Here Douglass registered an awareness of precisely the dilemma later historians have struggled to articulate: the antithetical manner in which mass or popular culture evoked an awareness suppressed in official culture. Sarah Meer, in her fine study of minstrelsy and abolition in transatlantic perspective, directs our attention to another speech from 1855 in which Douglass suggested to the gathered Rochester Ladies Anti-Slavery Society that "we have allies in the Ethiopian songs."[50]

> It would seem almost absurd to say it, considering the use that has been made of them, that we have allies in the Ethiopian song; those songs that constitute our national music, and without which we have no national music. They are heart songs, and the finest feelings of human nature are expressed in them. . . . They awaken the sympathies for the slave, in which Anti-Slavery principles take root, grow up and flourish.[51]

Meer notes Douglass's preference for the sentimental end of the continuum of minstrel songs, Stephen Foster's "Old Kentucky Home" rather than Old Cornmeal's "Long Tail Blue." But unlike bourgeois white critics of minstrelsy, black critics like Douglass did not fail to notice at least implicit possibilities of interracial affective transactions on the minstrel stage. His sentimentalization of minstrel efforts to sing a national music dovetails with Walt Whitman, who also saw in minstrelsy the possible beginnings of a national music.[52] What seems to mark out Douglass from Whitman is the presence, alongside this romantic attitude toward a prospective fusion, of a powerful political critique of proslavery and racist ideology, which Whitman was never able to develop.[53] Douglass's self-making was based on a critical and partly sympathetic spectatorship of minstrelsy, but to observe how he drew his own self-presentation in contradistinction to blackface grotesqueries is a very different thing than to assert that his was therefore an essentialist rather than a performative blackness.

Certainly, the performativity of Douglass's race man persona was recognized at the time. On the release of his first narrative in 1845, the Hutchinson Family of white antislavery singers composed and performed "The Fugitive's Song," which circulated as sheet music with a lithograph of Douglass, in the pose of a runaway slave, on its cover. John Stauffer convincingly relates how troubled Douglass was by such caricatured representations of himself and shows compellingly how in response Douglass embraced the then nascent medium of photography in which he could project an alternative but equally performative self.[54]

Douglass's pursuit of "essentialist" respectable manhood brought him into continued conflict with a racist public. Failing to meet their perceptions of appropriately servile black behavior, Douglass was seen as insubordinate. In the spring of 1850, Douglass and his English friends, the sisters Julia and Eliza Griffiths, were assaulted in Manhattan while attempting to board a steamer to Philadelphia. Given Douglass's recent trip abroad, the attack drew international attention, and the *London Times* reprinted in astonishment an article from the *New York Globe* that had rendered the story as a miniparable about the triumph of white male honor over Negro insolence. The *Globe* recounted how Douglass, "the impudent negro who has of late taken upon himself the privilege of abusing our country," had "the audacity yesterday morning to walk down Broadway, the principal promenade in our city, with two white women resting on his arms." "Several citizens" began to follow "the impudent scamp" and his companions "to the Battery," where one was further "provoked" when Douglass began "laughing and sneering at the gentlemen" who were following him. Asking the women to step aside, this "indignant and insulted gentleman administered to the back of the negro a 'dressing' that he will have occasion to remember some time hence."[55]

The *London Times,* in response, professed "unbounded indignation, disgust, and astonishment" at this treatment of a "negro gentleman" by "our Transatlantic brethren" and asserted the incident had effected shock "upon the whole English people—not merely upon Abolitionist writers and speakers—not merely upon subscribers to the Anti-Slavery Society—but upon every human being not American in this country, man, woman, and child." It saw the incident as revelatory of a worrying divergence of Americans from "the whole great

Anglo-Saxon family." The attack, it went on to say, was even worse than a recently reported case of man-stealing in Ohio, for in that case the assailant was at least motivated by "the desire to obtain his property," which was understandable, whereas the attack on Douglass was caused by "a general ungovernable sense of insult pervading a whole population." "We in England," the *Times* puffed, "happily have never been subjected to influences which could lead to a state of mind so unjust."

This editorial line was quintessentially liberal in its sacrosanct commitment to civility and property rights, both of which easily trumped concerns of social justice, as illustrated by the *Times*' hostile reaction two years later to Harriet Beecher Stowe's incendiary novel *Uncle Tom's Cabin* and especially to its stage popularizations.[56] By posing the problem as one of a "general ungovernable sense of insult" among Americans, the *Times* distanced England and its Anglo-Saxon heritage from any complicity in either slavery or racism, seizing the occasion to tout liberalism's ethic of tolerance.[57] It thus propelled what David Kazanjian has termed an "imperial citizenship" of a whiteness extended across national borders, uniting the metropole with its former settler colony in one great Anglo-Saxon family.

Douglass, for his part, used the incident to radicalize his theory of American racism, to demonstrate the absurdity of the idea that black people were objectionable *because* of their color:

> Properly speaking, *prejudice against color* does not exist in this country. . . . While we are servants, we are never offensive to the whites or marks of popular displeasure. . . . On the very day we were brutally assaulted in New York for riding down Broadway in company with ladies, we saw several white ladies riding with *black servants.* . . . They were there as appendages; they constituted a part of the magnificent equipages.—They were there as the fine black horses which they drove were there—to minister to the pride and splendor of their employers.[58]

Douglass's comparison of black servants to black horses was pointed. What he described here was the shared reification of black people and domestic animals. They were both treated as objects of labor and conspicuous consumption. Rank and race were the guinea's stamp, which was why blacks could circulate unproblematically among whites so long as their status was clearly assigned. It was the manner in which he and the Griffiths symbolically disrupted this process of reification, exposing its social rather than natural foundations, which gave offense, not the disharmony of their color. Their crime was the interaction of black and white on terms other than those that reproduced the subservience of the former to the latter.

In a polite letter to the *Times,* Douglass carefully parried the suggestion that the attack against him could somehow be blamed upon coarse lower classes or ungovernable ex-colonists. "Gentlemen" who "might shrink from the performance of the deed itself," Douglass pointed out, could nevertheless "applaud" it, because it reinforced the "aristocracy of skin" that kept poorer men content, as long as they could be white. His offense was social equality, Douglass insisted. Where the *Times* used the incident to promote a sense of innate Anglo-Saxon civility and tolerance from which Americans were inexplicably (and hypocritically) diverging, Douglass insisted that no such innate civility could be counted upon.[59]

Douglass's success at performing respectability made him a convenient target for political invective. In the 1858 senatorial campaign, Stephen A. Douglas used Douglass to frame black ambition as an illicit desire that would ultimately degrade whites to their level. In his famous debates with Abraham Lincoln, Douglas baited his audience with what he hoped would be a particularly incendiary image of what he had previously termed "political amalgamation":[60]

> The last time I came here to make a speech . . . I saw a carriage, and a magnificent one too, drive up and take its position on the outside of the crowd, with a beautiful young lady on the front seat, with a man and Fred. Douglass, the negro, on the back seat, and the owner of the carriage in front driving the negro.[61]

This topsy-turvy image of blacks on top was pitched to a democratically minded audience who would rebel at this return of European-style hierarchy. Placing Douglass outside and slightly above the standing crowd, seated in a privileged, privatized space even while attending an open-air, public meeting, the senator's imagery evoked a class privilege that violated the populism of post-Jackson electoral politics. It mobilized a resentment that targeted the wealthy and the enslaved alike, who were seen as joined in a conspiracy against the common man.

Stephen Douglas employed rhetorical inversions to underscore the absurdity of racial equality. He positioned the United States in a sea of already existing amalgamation, an island of herrenvolk democracy that was in danger of submerging back into the mongrelism from which it had long struggled to arise:

> In Mexico, in Central America, in South America and in the West India Islands, where the Indian, the negro, and men of all colors and all races are put on an equality by law, the effect of political amalgamation can be seen. Ask any of those gallant young men in your own country, who went to Mexico to fight the battles of their country, in what friend Lincoln considers an unjust and unholy war, and hear what they will tell you in regard to the amalgamation of races in that country. Amalgamation there, first political, then social, has led to demoralization and degradation, until it has reduced that people below the point of capacity for self-government.[62]

Far from assuming amalgamation to be a horrifying hypothetical, Douglas conjured up an image of the United States as a lone white republic in a hemisphere of amalgamation and thralldom. Through his reference to the Mexican–American War, Douglas justified his opposition to amalgamation through an appeal to Manifest Destiny. Amalgamation provided a motif for the insurgent chaos that American empire must quell. The people would be degraded "below the point of capacity for self-government." The consequence of the false coin of racial equality would be the real destruction of political liberties.

The threat posed by amalgamation was externalized, so its domestic advocates became internal aliens. Particularly in the western states—where, as Frederick Douglass acidly put it once, "Opposing slavery and hating its victims has come to be a very common form of Abolitionism"[63]—blacks could be viewed as a "a foreign and discontented people" intruding upon a white man's country.[64] "Black" nations such as Haiti and "mongrel" nations such as Mexico posed an identical threat to white racial purity, and southern politicians blocked diplomatic recognition of nation-states they feared might send colored ambassadors to Washington. White supporters could find themselves blackened by association and made agents of amalgamation as well. Placing the black orator beneath contempt, Senator Douglas also managed the embarrassing implications of the very resentments he sought to mobilize. The black man's efforts to attain social equality with white men had to be insisted upon, even exaggerated, by the Senator, but they also had finally to fail. Only a fellow white man such as Abraham Lincoln merited the mutual recognition of debate. Douglas "blackened" Lincoln, making him a surrogate for Douglass. The "Black Republicans," Douglas charged, were violating the sanctity of democratic politics by bringing out "men to canvass the State of the same complexion with their political creed." This metonymic slippage between Abraham Lincoln and a body of black Republicanism constituted in Douglas's rhetoric another form of political amalgamation: Lincoln's campaigners and backers were nothing but "a drove, white, black, and mixed."[65]

Like other "foes" of amalgamation, Stephen Douglas repeatedly recited its parade of horribles as fount of both lure and loathing. Such disciplinary deployments of a world turned upside down, precisely in order to draw popular support, made use of the minstrelized idiom of the carnivalesque. If T. D. Rice's paean to white supremacy was probably balderdash, Stephen Douglas's was no joke. The work minstrelsy undoubtedly did in exposing the social construction of race could never have simply congealed for abolitionists like Douglass and Wells Brown into a "performative" alternative to essentialist accounts of race, status, or gender. Rather, it disclosed the national popular as a tricky and unstable terrain.

The Native Music of Liberty

If the richness of black fun and the abjection of black ungovernability were both indexed in broken dialect and hilarious malapropism, then the cultivated cadence of the black orator, of which Douglass remains exemplary, was an exercise in sly civility. Douglass recounted in his 1845 autobiography how he first grasped the injustice of slavery while reading a popular elocution manual, the *Columbian Orator,* one of the most universally read textbooks of the early republic.[66] Douglass recalls discovering in it "a dialogue between a master and his slave" in which "the whole argument in behalf of slavery was brought forward by the master, all of which was disposed of by the slave." Douglass read the entire text of the *Columbian Orator* "over and over again with unabated interest."[67] He leaves unmentioned, however, another text relating to slavery in the same compendium, a text that he surely also read and reacted to. This short play, *Slaves in Barbary,* tells the adventures of a crew of circum-Atlantic sailors held captive by a Tunisian tyrant. The play was part of a genre, then popular, in which American sailors were held captive in North

Africa.[68] One of the white captives is held in bondage alongside his own slave, Sharp. Sharp possesses none of the eloquent dialogical style that so amazed and encouraged Douglass and instead speaks in servile dialect. His inability to articulate the injustice of his enslavement allows the play, like Powers's statue, to attack slavery for whites while excusing slavery for Africans. When some white captives are redeemed, Sharp is portrayed as being satisfied merely with getting a kinder master.[69] Black inferiority operates as a sort of political unconscious for republican antislavery rhetoric, laying the groundwork for racial governmentality.

Situating this play within Douglass's reading of the text in which it appeared helps account for Douglass's famous ambivalence toward slave culture. At the same time, it inflects his paradoxical interest in minstrel songs. While he avoided slave dialect, Douglass did not fully embrace Standard English either. Alongside this he cultivated a taste for Scottish English, and particularly for the dialect poetry of Burns.[70] As another unlettered autodidact, and a minstrel in the sense of a singer, Burns illustrated the relativity of condition rather than the essential difference of the races. Whence came this interest in Scotland and Burns? Alisdair Pettinger has argued that it was part of Douglass's effort to refigure the longstanding identification between the American south and Scotland. "Scotland lies at the heart of the South's most emotive symbols:" he notes, "the Confederate battle flag, which incorporates the St. Andrew's Cross, and the 'fiery cross,' a Highland tradition appropriated by the Ku Klux Klan." Douglass's interest in Burns was, he argues, therefore linked to a desire for "an anti-slavery Scotland." By making Burns a champion of the lowly, a rebel against aristocratic privilege, Douglass constructed a Scotland "no longer set against the abolitionist North but now firmly in opposition to the slave South."[71]

In looking to Burns and Scotland, Douglass performed what José Muñoz calls a disidentification. Disidentification, Muñoz writes, can operate as a "tactical misrecognition" that "permits a subject to demystify the dominant publicity."[72] Rather than accept the identity one is granted within the symbolic order, or fleeing it into a space of nonidentity, disidentity works on and through identity, enacting perverse and unexpected affiliations. Renaming oneself, as Douglass did, is often a signature act of disidentification. His performed affinity for Scottish language and culture as an alternative source of antislavery feeling was another. Turning away from the copious literature of American and British abolitionism, from poets like John Greenleaf Whittier, and from the recurrent imagery of the heroic and/or grateful and/or Christian slave, he even ignored Burns's own modest effort to contribute to this genre, "The Slave's Lament."[73] He instead made a subterranean connection with Burns's robust images of Scotland. Noticing in particular how Burns revolted in spirit and language against the confines of his society. Douglass found in Burns's relationship to the English language and culture an analog for his own.

Seen only in the black–white framework of the American context, Douglass's disidentification becomes almost totally invisible. One critic has even suggested that his citation of Burns amounted to a mimetic effort to demonstrate his "familiarity with classic white writers."[74] Douglass's use of Burns was in fact a kind of antierudition, a hostile weapon against both abstract liberalism and racial particularism. In romantic poetry, Douglass was able to find the full range of rhetorical expression, from abstraction to intimacy, from reason to emotion, without reinforcing race by using the folk idiom of African American slavery, which would have been seen as the natural source for him to have used. Douglass found in Burns's Scots English a substitute, within and against the dominant tongue, in but not of Anglo-American culture. He did this to flee not blackness but blackness as seen in the commodifying, racializing gaze, blackness as appropriated as the "native music of liberty."

To an antebellum black activist like Douglass, blackface minstrelsy reinforced the popularity of the color line by insisting that black men and women were coarse and ragged of speech and conduct. It reduced them to a collective body of malapropisms, however boastful, thrilling, or dashing. And yet, they also recognized how blackface signposted the inclusion of black culture into the national popular. The democratic sovereignty of popular taste was an obstacle to racial justice insofar as that popular taste embraced blackface and oppressed blacks. But the scorn heaped upon it by black activists and abolitionists was not unmixed with a sense of its possibility. The white attraction to black song and dance, which fed into white supremacy as black abolitionists well knew, was paradoxically also the grounds upon which a challenge to that supremacy could be mounted, precisely insofar as minstrelsy refused to imagine an America without blacks.

Douglass's antagonistic cooperation with minstrelsy is best witnessed in his reaction to black performers trying their hand at the native music of liberty. In an 1849 review of the Gavitt's Original Ethiopian Serenaders, a troupe of black minstrels, Douglass wrote,

> We are not sure that our readers will approve of our mention of these persons, so strong must be their dislike to everything that seems to feed the flame of American prejudice against colored people; and in this they may be right; but we think otherwise. It is something gained, when the colored man in any form can appear before a white audience, and we think that even this company, with industry, application, and a proper cultivation of taste, may yet be instrumental in removing the prejudice against our race. But they must cease to exaggerate the exaggerations of our enemies; and represent the man rather as he is, than as Ethiopian Minstrels usually represent him.[75]

Douglass senses blackface performance here to be caught within a commodity circuit of exchanges in which the simulacra is preferred to the real. But we should not oversimplify his wish to see the black man represented "as he really is." Nor ought we minimize the sense of moment he associated with what occurs "when the colored man in any form can appear before a white audience." Douglass directly contrasts his position with those of his readers for whom minstrelsy was simply beneath contempt. Unlike them, he understood there to be a potential present even within its degraded popular sphere, and consequently, a need to examine and discuss it in order, conceivably, to make it "instrumental" in the struggle against racism.

Douglass's engagement with the Gavitt's Original Ethiopian Serenaders differs from the approach of later defenders of the respectability of the race, in part because the moment in which he lived articulated minstrelsy differently than subsequent moments did. If the critique of "late minstrelsy" presented the genre in terms of the commodity fetish, focusing on the object hardened into a stereotypical silhouette and the face reduced to a blackened icon, then the critique of early minstrelsy might alternatively focus on the performing body as a site of primitive, even primitivist, accumulation. Burns's image of commodified humanity and the "gowd" shining through essentialist fictions seem to guide Douglass's approach. Our critique could take Douglass's lead and historicize the romantic nineteenth-century drive to transfigure folk forms into national forms, without neglecting the crucial opening that this process provided to the emergence of the exemplary performer as an entrepreneurial, calculating individual. It would also track the promiscuous disidentifications across nationality, within which minstrels—"Ethiopian" and Scottish alike—disclose race and rank as the guinea's stamp, marking the body out for its commodified itinerary.

4. Carnivalizing Time: Decoding the Racial Past in Art and Installation

If my argument up to this point has observed a roughly historicist shape—moving across three moments that all lie within what I have called the circum-Atlantic fold—I want to now take up what Slavoj Žižek calls the "parallax view" and reconsider that antebellum moment from the perspective of historical memory.[1] This shift is not an attempt to bring my narrative up to date. Indeed, I make no attempt to do justice to events after 1877, the events of the "American cycle" of the long twentieth century, as Arrighi and Baucom have called it.[2] My concern in this chapter is not with historical sequence or causation but rather with the presence of history-making as a cultural practice in the present. It is to the image of the antebellum as figured in contemporary practices of commemoration, a theme I have already considered in its historical aspect (as in the antebellum commemorations of Crispus Attucks), that I now turn.

Hybridity remains my focus here, as it has been articulated through Bhabha's disjunctive temporality as well as Foucault's carnivalizing of time. I use both to consider the split subject of historical memory. Thinking through this split subject in terms of race, racial heritage, and cultural hybridity requires extending an argument most recently developed by Darby English, who has drawn on both W. E. B. Du Bois and Frantz Fanon to theorize what he calls "black representational space." English's arguments are instructive, I argue, for thinking through the historicist turn taken by some prominent contemporary African American artists, artists who are discussed in his monograph, some of whom I also consider here. I draw from English's insights to begin to think about a black representational space *in memory* and to ask how it might figure—and be figured by—the structures of feeling and genealogies of performance I have discussed so far.[3]

The parallax view permits a break with the organic and continuist motifs of embodied memory that populate African American studies. My interest here is not with the endurance of oral tradition or collective memory beyond or outside the official transcript. Neither is it with the aporetic trauma of an ostensibly unrepresentable past, such as critical discourse increasingly characterizes the historical experience of slavery. Rather, my interest in historical memory as a cultural practice of the present is meant to take up Foucault's challenge to the genealogist not to be too serious to enjoy the "carnivalizing of time" that acts of popular historical transfer can so often occasion. This carnivalizing of time, with its hybrid aesthetic, is my primary concern here. And my question remains Foucault's: Can such masquerade be pushed to its limit? Can historical contact conjure not "the identification of our faint individuality with the solid identities of the past, but our 'unrealization' through the excessive choice of identities"? In taking up the mask, as Foucault suggests, can we revitalize "the buffoonery of history"?[4] It is the carnivalizing of the past, and the possibility of becoming history's buffoon, that I gather under the rubric of "mistaking memory."

Most accounts of historical memory are preoccupied with truth: the possible deviation from the recorded truth that memory affords, the performative acts of reconciliation that truth-telling ostensibly effects, or else the higher truth that embodied, experiential memory somehow obtains over dry, written documents. By contrast, I am preoccupied not with the virtues of getting it right but with the ethical chance that may lie within getting it wrong. What does it mean to mistake a memory, to remember by mistake, or even to remember a mistake? And how do such acts figure in a theory of hybrid agency? While inspired by Foucault and Bhabha, these questions also take me beyond them.

Beyond Foucault and Bhabha, the theorists who assist this investigation are Walter Benjamin and Jacques Lacan. I intend no exegesis of the work of either; but I seek to exploit what I perceive to be an affinity between their work. That affinity is between Benjamin's radicalization of historical materialism and Lacan's radicalization of the Freudian subject. An affinity lies in their shared perception that the interval between past and present is a kind of rupture or, in what amounts to much the same thing, a point of stasis. That is to say, both radically oppose traditional organicist, continuist, and subjective approaches to memory. They instead position themselves as ethicists of estrangement and even discord—Benjamin through his commendation of "hatred" as an appropriate orientation toward the past and Lacan through his reinterpretation of the Freudian "Id" as the letter's agency in the unconscious past. While no ultimate harmonization of their mutual approaches to history and memory seems likely, their shared interest in a subject constructed out of an antagonistic cooperation with a past that does not belong to it has bequeathed to us useful tools for thinking through the aesthetic and performative construction of black representative space in American memory.

The Buffoonery of History

How does history make us its buffoons? Civil War reenactors pursuing a "period rush" to the point of infecting themselves with lice provide one answer to this question. But even those of us who do not relish history beyond the printed page are caught up within a continuous present out of which fragments of the past occasionally and unpredictably explode. This explosive, affective quality of past time was the great theme of the late writings of Walter Benjamin, whose famous theses on the philosophy of history continue to instruct and illuminate.[5] And the buffoonery into which historical affect can drive the subject was also visible in an unexpected and unsettling sojourn taken by a former NAACP local official, H. K. Edgerton, who reacted to what he saw as the desecration of the Confederate Battle Flag by a contemporary black artist, John Sims, by conducting a "Historical March across Dixie."[6] From Asheville, North Carolina, to Austin, Texas (ironically enough, two southern cities known for their progressive values), Edgerton walked on foot, dressed in his Confederate grays, seeking to call attention to the threat contemporary art presents to southern values and history.[7] Admittedly an outlier in terms of sentiment among southerners of African descent, Edgerton's wholly committed embodied response to a work of contemporary art arrests the attention and impels further investigation. How exactly does the past so threaten a body in the present if the two are, as we typically think, wholly distinct? What is the inner principle animating Edgerton's endurance feat, even if the particulars of his motivation entitles us, with some caution, to pronounce his values deeply skewed?

Figure 12. H. K. Edgerton, film still from *Recoloration Proclamation*. Courtesy of John Sims.

The perils and possibility of embodied memory lie precisely in this hazy zone where the ideologically correct and wholly suspect intermingle and blur. Edgerton's passion would have been less unremarkable had he, as one academic showboat did, merely reenacted a fugitive's escape from slavery nailed into a box.[8] While the latter act merely sounds difficult and uncomfortable, Edgerton's march strikes us as deliciously deranged. I am interested in the parallax view that the juxtaposition of these two acts of historical "buffoonery" provide. And I suggest both provide a view into the character of memory as ridden with glitches and mistakes, a character driving us ultimately to break, as Benjamin did, with a conception of history as presenting the past "as it really was."

We understand Edgerton's intensity, even as we accept that it is misplaced, because he is a black man from the south with intense feelings about race and American heritage. African American historical memory is indelibly structured by slavery and its legacies. The overwhelming character of this experience, the unimaginable horror of becoming enslaved, and the impossibility of bearing witness to the fullness of its traumas, seems to render the history of slavery at once unavoidable and incommunicable. In order to articulate this tension, many scholars have adopted Toni Morrison's word "rememory" to express this involuntary and traumatic character. Of the many commentaries on this idea, perhaps the most apropos to my current concern is Kathryn Bond Stockton's adaptation of Morrison to affective and cybernetic theory in her account of rememory as "viral memory." After all,

> we know the dead live, for they reside, with strange intermittence, behind our eyes, in the room of our brain. We wonder how they breathe inside us, at the length of such an intimate remove. Really, the dead are a cybernetic problem. Alive in the virtual world of ideas—we think of them often—they pose a problem of storage and transfer. And they do spread.[9]

Stockton's "strange intermittence," something like the decaying blink of a radioactive half-life, resonates with Lacan's account of the agency of the letter in the unconscious, in which is also posed both the problem and possibility of storage (archiving) and transfer (performance). Stockton sounds this Lacanian note when she reads *Beloved* as a material linguistic object:

> The point is this: a sign, in order to be a sign to you, must get inside your body. Actually, it must enter your body through an orifice, usually ear or eye. In *Beloved,* it even enters the body through the gullet. Ingestion, that is, is the site of a struggle where a daughter restructures her mother's brain.[10]

Stockton's account helps us see how Morrison's "rememory" bears comparison with, and further illuminates, Lacan's concept of the "signifying chain," which he uses to describe a form of inorganic, impersonal, extrinsic "memory" that exists outside of the subjective individual and collective experience we ordinarily call remembering. Rather than the object of personal identity, as held in the classical romantic theory of the individual and the emotions (recall Wordsworth's definition of poetry as "emotion recollected in tranquillity"), historical affect invades and restructures the present with a strange intermittence that is both uncanny and, as Stockton insists, queer.[11]

I proceed no further in the exegesis of Morrison's remarkable novel. Instead, I use her theoretical model of the daughter restructuring the mother's brain in an affective, cybernetic loop to think through the aesthetic and political strategies of artists working at the intersection of performance, visual art, and collective memory. I am especially interested in the dead as a cybernetic problem, that is, by the unpredictability of their agency in our political unconscious, an unpredictability that spills over the boundaries of our attempts to pedagogize the past through museum and gallery displays. Against the pedagogic imperative to teach us to remember and to inculcate a proper reverence for a rapidly vanishing past, these artists champion a performative disruption of the official modes of memory that evince the invasive and disruptive agency of the past in the present, an agency that bears witness to Benjamin's powerful image of history as an accumulating catastrophe.

The incident that prompted Edgerton's march may now come into focus as a conflict between pedagogical and performative views on history. John Sims, the artist whose work incensed him, and to whom I now turn, has specialized in exploring the formal properties of visual signs as mnemonics of culture, history, and identity. With a training in mathematics, he is especially attuned to the arbitrariness of the sign. At the same time, his work evokes anything but a dry or unemotional reaction to the past. His pieces are almost overfull with triggers of intense affectivity. Sims is an artist whose medium is the sign that enters your body via the eye and exits from the skin, trembling with rage, or shouting from the mouth, or through fingers excitedly typing or scrawling their incensed reaction. It is work at the seam of the historical past and present, engaged in an aesthetics of unexploded ordnance.

The *Recoloration Proclamation,* Sims's film in progress, documents some of his provocative responses to historical memory in the circum-Atlantic fold. His full title—*Recoloration Proclamation: The Gettysburg Redress*—slyly conflates two of the most familiar acts of the U.S. Civil War presidency of Abraham Lincoln: the Gettysburg Address, delivered at Gettysburg, Pennsylvania on November 19, 1863, and the Emancipation Proclamation freeing slaves in the rebelling states, the final version of which was issued in January of that same year. Sims evokes Lincoln less to comment upon his legacy directly and more as a medium for the artist's ongoing response to the controversial use of the Battle Flag of the Confederate State of America as a widely circulated and commodified symbol of southern heritage.[12] I return to this peculiarly fruitful "mistake" in which Lincoln and the Confederacy are fatefully condensed and conflated. First, however, I want to examine how Sims's project works as a performative intervention into historical memory, one focused not on getting facts right or doing justice to the past as it really was, but on seizing upon an intensely affective trigger as it flashes up in a moment of danger.

Naming this ongoing multiform project the *Recoloration Proclamation,* Sims signifies upon political performativity in more ways than one. The Emancipation Proclamation, after all, is remembered primarily for clarifying publicly for the first time that the U.S. Civil War was being fought over slavery and that the consequence of a Union victory would be its overthrow. The Gettysburg Address, by contrast, accomplished no such specific world historical task but is instead widely admired as a masterpiece of political rhetoric, indeed as "the words that remade America," in the judgment of one influential historian.[13] The two acts thus present an interesting contrast: the Emancipation Proclamation was a relatively dry executive order; the Gettysburg Address was a short but intensely memorable dedicatory speech. By conflating and contrasting their performative efficacy, Sims intervenes in the complex task of remembering the ending of U.S. slavery, an event now beyond living memory but one that nevertheless continues to structure our contemporary reality. Specifically, he draws attention to the contrast between historical memorability and historical efficacy, in the very process of fruitfully entangling them. The ambivalence in his title's double referent suggests that our patterns of remembrance may have little to do with how history was actually made, that behind the "pageant of time" reproduced in most historical pedagogies, there subsists a more elusive pattern linking events and causes, words and actions, past and present. This elusive and hidden agency, obtainable only retrospectively and through indirection, is the important subject of this work.

Sims's *Recoloration Proclamation*—as an aesthetic practice of negative heritage—specifically responds to the use of the Battle Flag as a symbol of southern heritage and rebellious white masculinity. It revisits the question of how an unremembered past choreographs our present.[14] For the Detroit-born Sims, seeing the flag during trips south was a shock, one that was intensified by what he perceived to be black southern indifference or even acceptance of its frequency. As a commentary on such a state of affairs, and in an ostensible effort to accelerate a new, nonracist southern and national heritage, Sims created several new recolored versions of the Battle Flag, most memorably one that exchanges the colors red, white, and blue for the red, green, and black of pan-Africanism. Black artist David Hammons pioneered this technique with his "African American Flag" (2000), which recolored the Stars and Stripes. In displacing the Eurocentric red, white, and blue with the Afrocentric red, green, and black, but retaining the design of the rebel Battle Flag, Sims created a similarly ambiguous symbol of race, nation, and cosmopolitanism. It overlays two forms of symbolism in a way that deprives the viewer of accepting either, presenting a flag to which no one can possibly swear allegiance. Interrupting the stale debate over whether the flag represents "heritage" or "hate," Sims's recolored and rewoven flags reveals its power to rest precisely in the indeterminate space within and between the two options, locating its meaning less in what it *is* than in what it *does*.[15]

Sims's choice to blur the historical symbol of the Slave Power with the effigy of the president who defeated it is telling, given the rich ambiguity that the figure of Lincoln obtains in black collective memory.[16] As the Great Emancipator who wished until fairly late into the Civil War that the national "race question" could be solved by convincing the freed slaves to emigrate, a man Frederick Douglass himself affirmed treated black people as his equals, but who feared that social equality between the races was neither desirable nor possible, Lincoln is a commanding cipher who occasions both sincere affection and subtle antagonism. This ambiguity is evident in the playwright Suzan-Lori Parks's recurrent incorporation of his assassination into her widely noted and award-winning plays, most notably in *Topdog/Underdog* (2002) (whose principal characters are named Lincoln and Booth) and *The America Play* (1994), in which fairgoers pay for the privilege of pretending to shoot a Lincoln impersonator. The impulse to take a pot shot at the embodiment of authority, even an authority so closely associated with emancipation, is also present in Sims's *Recoloration Proclamation*. The uses of Lincoln by both Sims and Parks suggest the capacity of parody to bring the parodied closer to our affections.[17]

Much as Parks's plays call attention to how much of the past we have forgotten and articulate the insufficiency of the standard modes through which we seek to remember, Sims's work is also a commentary on the pedagogic mode of communicating the past. If the Lincoln effigy in Parks's plays serves as the instatement of a social forgetting, via the very recognizability of that face, then Sims's investigation into the construction of the political signs shows us how such a teaching to forget proceeds through a process of detachment. In testing how far we can detach the pan-African colors from the pan-African flag and hybridize them onto the Confederate Battle Flag, Sims deliberately played with fire. In his film, one incensed man insisted that despite its recoloration, it was still clearly a Confederate flag and therefore still clearly a symbol of white supremacy. To claim anything else, the man declared in a phrase that was surely music to the ears of a mathematician-turned-artist, would be like asserting that "2 + 2 = 5." Once taught, as Sims's interlocutor well understood, arbitrary symbols become anchored in reality. Indeed, they *are* our anchors in reality. As Deleuze and Guattari write in *Anti-Oedipus,* "the first signs are the territorial signs that plant their flags in bodies."[18]

Sims's historical performativity contrasts with the established mode of experiential historical pedagogy that teaches proper subjects to remember. Ordinarily, a pedagogy of memory would seem counterintuitive or possibly even deceptive. Teaching, after all, is supposed to transmit knowledge, whereas memory is commonly supposed to be an intrinsic faculty one might at best work at improving but which cannot or should not be "filled in" by an external curriculum. And yet, when we consider the "social frameworks of memory," we see the range and depth of pedagogies that seek precisely to buttress and perpetuate memory, pedagogies that seek to memorize memory, as it were.[19] Contemporary artists who signify upon this pedagogy necessarily raise questions regarding the archive and its interpreters. They also broach questions regarding the contemporary and its relation to the past.

Aesthetic efforts to engage the social frameworks of historical memory assume a political significance when, as with Sims, they confront a highly pervasive amnesia. But the effort to shore up this missing information, to teach us to remember slavery, entails its own set of internal contradictions that can be traced along the fissure between the archive and collective memory. These fissures are most visible in mistakes or glitches in the mnemonic process. The ordinary distinction between memorization and memory reflects the relation between a rote, machinic, objectivizing process and an intensely subjective experience. Turning this relation inside out, contemporary artists of memory have proposed taking collective memory as a set of instructions to be mechanically repeated, introducing deliberate "mistakes" in the process to expose its arbitrary nature.

What drew national attention to Sims's efforts in this was not his recolored flag but a 2004 installation in which he proposed to hang the Confederate flag from a thirteen-foot outdoor gallows on the lawn of Gettysburg College. The piece, titled *The Proper Way to Hang a Confederate Flag,* was widely described as a "lynching" of the Battle Flag, but it might more accurately be seen as a pointed fulfillment of the ambiguous instruction "to hang." Much as his flag could be thought of as the product of garbled instructions, *The Proper Way to Hang a Confederate Flag* posed the pedagogy of heritage a difficult question to answer: if not this way, then how? Sims's planned installation drew enough heat from groups as various as the Sons of Confederate Veterans and the Ku Klux Klan that the college bowed to pressure and moved the exhibit, reduced in scale, into an indoor gallery.[20] In response, Sims boycotted his own opening but sent a film crew to tape the proceedings. That crew recorded, among other protestors, an incensed H. K. Edgerton.

Sims's deliberate error in the performance of the hanging ritual suggests an unspoken qualifier to the question it poses. What is the proper way to hang a Confederate flag *now?* What is the correct way, if at all, to remember or reenact identities forged in the shadow of slavery? This address to the present as that which is both produced by and potentially transcends the past is part of the contemporary artist's complex aesthetic itinerary. It is only relatively recently that black and women artists have enjoyed access to the institutions that credential artists to make such commentary upon the contemporary, and as Darby English's work argues, the way in which the institutions of criticism reproduce a horizon of aesthetic concern within which to circumscribe black artists remains an ongoing predicament.[21] The genealogy of the contemporary is thus intertwined with the exclusion of minoritarian and gendered voices from its unfolding question. Because this is so, an aesthetic "redress" of history can never simply restore missing voices but must continuously strive to think the genealogy of a contemporaneity characterized by its relations of exclusion. It must work to shape a black representative space in memory.

Confronting Legacies, Decoding the Past

I turn here to two major museum history exhibits that engage contemporary art practice by minoritarian artists: the *Mining the Museum* exhibit (1992–93) at the Maryland Historical Society, and *Legacies: Contemporary Artists Reflect on Slavery* (2006–7) at the New-York

Historical Society. Each exhibit serves as a useful questioning of the necessity and impossibility of pedagogies of remembrance, of memorizing memory, and reflects a variety of artistic and curatorial responses to this dilemma.[22] I select them because they stand at different stages in the development of a new rapprochement between black artists and the historical museum, the latter very much a benefactor of the great success of the former. I also select them because they reveal some of the fault lines that remain embedded even in this newfound and well-meaning attempt to incorporate the outside and produce a new, amalgamated history of American race relations. My intention is not to criticize either as unnecessary or as insufficient but to point to the dilemmas intrinsic to the project of teaching to remember.

Fred Wilson is a Bronx-born conceptual artist whose work blurs the boundaries between art-making and art-exhibiting.[23] Working with a series of historical collections, most famously that of the Maryland Historical Society in Baltimore in 1992, Wilson foregrounds the act of presenting, titling, and juxtaposing objects of historical and/or aesthetic value, a process that frequently involves the employment of sarcasm, inversion, and humor in spaces where solemnity, pedagogy, and being politely bored are more customary phenomena. His ludic, antagonistic sensibility seeks to highlight this omission rather than rush to fill it.

In *Mining the Museum,* Wilson was invited into an institution that was actively seeking to recast its relation and its relevance to the City of Baltimore and State of Maryland. The site of the exhibition was key to the shape of Wilson's intervention. The Maryland Historical Society, Lisa G. Corrin writes,

> is similar to many of the nation's first historical societies, which appeared just after the American Revolution. These institutions, founded by amateur historians and naturalists from "distinguished" families, were created as a response to the circuslike environment of dime museums. Thus, the Maryland Historical Society's early collecting efforts reflect a "gentleman's" interests of the antebellum era.[24]

A reprieve from the carnivalesque national popular for which blackface minstrelsy would come to serve as a signature, the historical society as representative space modeled its ideal patron as an aesthete standing before a cabinet of wonder. The collusions and confusions between natural history, exotica, and tasteful objects are reflected in the collections and archive of the Maryland Historical Society, which contain everything from arrowheads and precious silver to children's dolls and oil paintings. In one sense, one might read Wilson's re-contextualization of these holdings as precisely the infiltration and democratic victory of the "circuslike environment of dime museums" against which it was built as a bulwark. But in the mixed lineage of such elite activities as the cabinet of wonder suggest, Wilson's curatorial regimen might also represent a certain reversion to type, restoring to the collection its own repressed, variegated colors.

Mining the Museum was restricted to those objects already in the holdings of the Society, which was to be subjected to an archaeological critique. If Wilson was to indict the residual culture of this institution, it would have to be hoisted on its own petard with rope in its own possession. Wilson's method, in part, was to locate discomfiting material that had never before been exhibited, ranging from a Ku Klux Klan hood, to slave shackles, to a whipping post. He then found startling methods of exhibiting them, placing shackles, for example, in a vitrine alongside fine silver, and the hood in a baby carriage. Not simply excavating the shocking and uncanny, Wilson also reconsidered the many objects already prominently and pridefully displayed by the museum, calling attention to their many silences and omissions around race. Among his most remarkable of curatorial discoveries were the many images of black children, going back to the eighteenth century, who were represented alongside the white families that held them in slavery and thus were literally related to the iconographic tradition of the portrait through their exclusion.[25] In one portrait from 1710, a black child stands just adjacent to the white male sitter, wearing a metal collar. Wilson placed motion detectors that cause a spotlight on the black boy to be triggered upon approach, and a (possibly quite ominous) recorded voice asked the questions "Am I your brother? Am I your friend? Am I your pet?" Black likenesses that were intended to endow portraits with verisimilitude or local color were thus highlighted in a way that did not so much foreground the history of the new subjects as much as insist that their visual presence was also a historical absence. The audio and light triggers—obvious devices of theatricality—thus rechoreographed quotidian interaction with the piece, enlivening and presenting the past to the present with a series of unanswerable, haunting questions.

Alongside such plaintive strategies as the ghostly voice, which

Figure 13. Fred Wilson, *Metalwork, 1793–1880*. From *Mining the Museum*, 1992–93, Maryland Historical Society.

Wilson accounted for in terms of his effort to imagine himself in the position of the black sitters for these paintings, more directly sarcastic tactics were employed, such as providing, as an alternative title for *Country Life of a Baltimore Family* (c. 1850) by Ernst Fisher, *Frederick Serving Fruit*. This biting retitling, which similarly directs attention from the foregrounded family to the enslaved child bearing their refreshment, playfully reimagines history from below, but without necessarily filling in the details or even suggesting that such a task is doable. An exhibit titled *Cabinetmaking, 1820–1960* included armchairs, side chairs, and a whipping post, and here the sarcasm is much more despairing, as is the case with the simple presentation of a bootjack made in the shape of a naked black female. The shock here depends on recognizing the use to which the object was intended. Once this happens, the intended humor of the figure hits the contemporary viewer like a slap, inciting, as I have argued elsewhere, a powerful urge to destroy the offending object.[26]

Wilson's ludic inhabitation of the space of official archiving and memory, like Sims's transgressive fidelity to the instructions for patriotic display, pose blackness as exception, included in the repository from which it is nonetheless excluded. Staging rather than resolving this tension, his work for the most part avoids answering the pained questions it raises and thus shows the process of historical exclusion rather than outlining its remedy. His affective strategy partakes of the sentimental tradition of liberal protest. And, as Darby English has argued, the ways in which the museum positioned Wilson's work, as a representative black voice, simultaneously obviated his more radical project of negative heritage and cordoned it off from the main proceedings of the museum as the work of a single, identifiable troublemaker. But the power of the project suggests that Wilson's artistic medium is not simply "the museum" but "the archive" in the expanded sense in which Foucault invites us to think it: the entire ensemble of practices and institutions through which the past is projected into the present. *Mining the Museum* was not simply an exhibition. It was also an instruction piece, communicable through a suite of sharply refined ideas that themselves depend upon and demonstrate the subversive potential immanent within the pedagogic.

Legacies: Contemporary Artists Reflect on Slavery was held at the New-York Historical Society in 2006, another august historical institution that appears to have learned the lesson that Wilson's success and influence in Baltimore would teach. *Legacies* invited a range of artists into an imposing edifice fronting Central Park, a space usually devoted to historical exhibitions of a more triumphal character. The show came after, and was indeed prompted by, a very successful *Slavery in New York* exhibit, a more traditionally conceived and executed historical exhibit billed as the first of its kind. If *Slavery in New York* borrowed some of the curatorial strategies of defamiliarization popularized by exhibits like *Mining the Museum* (such as an exhibit showing an entire room of antiques, none of which obviously referenced slavery, accompanied by wall text explaining that everything in the exhibit might have been touched by a slave and that therefore the absence of signs of slavery is also their presence), *Legacies* went further in turning the main exhibition space entirely over to contemporary artists with no pedagogical obligation.[27] This release from the ordinary protocols of the historical museum was embarked upon in hopes of getting closer to the truth of that experience.

Rather than exhaustively detail the show, I concentrate on some pieces that gained new significance when presented in a context such as that of *Legacies,* explicitly concerned with the construction of black representative space in memory. That is, although none of this work was created for this specific show, or for explicit historical pedagogy, each gained a new "aura" when entrusted with the task of doing justice to historical memory. They were positioned between aesthetic and historical representation in a sedate setting that nonetheless could not fully forestall the controversies to which such a hybrid act or mixed message can give rise.

Leonardo Drew's installation of a huge square of stacked cotton bales in one gallery, to anyone familiar with the minimalist sculptures of artist Tony Smith, set an initial tone of pugnacious and sarcastic autoreferentialism. The meditative, allusive theatricality of a piece such as Smith's *Die* (1962), a steel cube seventy-two inches tall, wide, and deep, represented aesthetic minimalism's interest in the luminous property of radically simplified artistic gestures. Drew's cotton bales, simultaneously funny and shocking, permitted no such luminous meditation on form, instead sending a very mixed message about the possibility of abstract art when the conditions of artistic production are so inescapably yoked to profane histories of coerced labor. The object, to borrow from Fred Moten, here resists its status as an abstraction, succumbing precisely to the "theatricality" art critic Michael Fried disliked about minimalism in general. To this theatricality was added the further politics surrounding a form of racialized labor that did not simply construct objects but was itself objectified and commodified. Drew's installation refused the decontextualizing gesture so characteristic of contemporary art, which dislodges the signs planted on our bodies, only to hook them to the stars of the art world stratosphere, dissolving the semantic content of the social into the syntax of aesthetic reference. The recontextualizing of the commodity form—from which so much of contemporary art has become indistinguishable—has long been a preoccupation of black artists (consider Bettye Saar's recontextualizations of Aunt Jemima).

What a specifically historical setting adds to this aesthetic politics is a reminder that the complacencies of realistic historical representation are only seemingly to be distinguished from such art world flights of fancy. As Benjamin argues, in a rich exchange with Adorno over the terms of "phantasmagoria" as a historical index, "The commodity economy reinforces the phantasmagoria of sameness." "The commodity empathizes," he continues, "not only and not so much with buyers as with its price."[28] It is only through affective intensification and rough juxtaposition that this hidden empathy is exposed and the steadfast narration of time as empty and homogenous is exploded. Through such a dialectical image, of which I argue Drew's cotton bales stand as exemplary, contemporary art touches upon a technique Benjamin located in nineteenth-century phantasmagoria.[29] As Daphne Brooks puts it,

> For many, the fundamental attraction of the phantasmagoria show resided in its ability to stage the illusion of ephemeral bodies. . . . Appearing to be both riddled with ontological breaks and ruptures and yet fluid and concatenate, these metamorphic and "discontinuous" bodies floated through an evolving English [and American] popular cultural imaginary.[30]

The piece in *Legacies* that most closely approaches the nineteenth-century world of wonder that Brooks here describes was Ellen Driscoll's *Loophole of Retreat* (1991–92). Inspired by Harriet Jacobs's *Incidents in the Life of a Slave Girl* (1861) in which Jacobs described living for seven years in a small crawl space in the attic of her grandmother's house, Driscoll's *Loophole* was a wooden cone into which the museum visitor was invited to walk, therein to view images projected into the darkened interior. Simultaneously claustrophobic and magical, the phantasmagoria of *Loophole* cleverly cited the growing demand to be permitted to directly experience history while savagely lampooning the idea that such a skin could be so quickly tossed on and back off again. The museum tempo of seconds or at best minutes ironically contrasted with the impossible duration of Jacobs's fugitivity. Rather than an experiential narrative or explanation, past and present time came into a dialectical collision inside Driscoll's cone, which confronted the visitor with the necessity and impossibility of communicating Jacobs's experience. *Loophole* underscores a realization that knowing that Jacobs survived for seven years in such a cramped space is not the same thing as understanding it.[31]

These sparse examples stitch together past and present in a fashion that defies ordinary narration, recollection, or affective engagement. They are aesthetic and historical hybrids that refuse or at least defer the proper objectives of pedagogic mnemonics and insert "mistakes" into the routinized procedure through which history museums pretend to present their visitors with an experience of the past. Rather than confirm a heroic tale or weep before a tragic spectacle, these art works produce a message that mixes historical time with the time of the now. Rather than transport their witness into a mythified historical time, they gather up the past in the accumulation of the artist's assemblage.

Figure 14. Ellen Driscoll, *Loophole of Retreat,* 1991–92. From *Legacies,* exhibit installation of the New-York Historical Society. Photograph by Glenn Castellano. Collection of The New-York Historical Society, negative 79387d.

That the stakes behind such a production of black representative space in memory remains controversial was inadvertently exposed during the course of the *Legacies* exhibit when some viewers took issue with a particular piece. Like H. K. Edgerton, these viewers found the exhibit in question to be historically inaccurate, but unlike the latter-day black confederate, they were credentialed experts in the field of American history. Their complaint lay with the exhibition of a design for a proposed memorial to Frederick Douglass, to be built in Harlem, in which the artist had incorporated three African American quilting patterns. "Drunkard's Path," "Migrating Geese," and the "North Star" were all to be rendered in multihued granite in a plaza commemorating the famous black abolitionist. Algernon Miller's memorial design—which won a design competition in 2003 organized by the Studio Museum in Harlem—drew no negative attention when it was initially exhibited. But controversy ensued when news emerged during the actual construction of the memorial in early 2007 that a plaque on the sight would claim that the quilting patterns rendered in granite represented a secret visual code fugitive slaves used to escape from the south. This particular theory had come to popular awareness with the publication, in 1999, of a jointly authored book entitled *Hidden in Plain Sight,* which drew media attention and, according to Miller, provided creative inspiration for his winning design. Historians quickly objected to this public legitimation of what acclaimed historian David Blight described to the *New York Times* as "a myth, bordering on a hoax."[32]

On the surface, the controversy appears to be what the *Times* presented it as, a conflict between folklore and fact. And indeed, participants in the debate did sometimes see themselves as engaged in such a stark confrontation between the archive and memory. In response to the skepticism of the historical profession, partisans of the "hidden in plain sight" theory argued that there is no written evidence for their claims because slaves were denied literacy. They pointed to the longstanding dismissal of oral traditions identifying Thomas Jefferson as the father of numerous slave children, a claim historians also denounced as a myth and a hoax until quite recently, when DNA evidence pointed very strongly toward the accuracy of black historical memory.

By contrast, the rapidity with which historians leaped to criticize what was, after all, an artistic and commemorative effigy of Frederick Douglass bespoke their privileging of the archive as a source of historical meaning. The public discussion they conducted, on online discussion boards, centered around a process of debunking: pointing out errors, lapses, invented or imaginary sources, and hand-wringing over the dissemination of these myths about the slave past in educational and pedagogic settings, despite their refutation by credentialed interpreters of the archive. Although relatively harmless in itself, the offending plaque stood in for a larger array of African American folk beliefs and urban legends about the slave past that historians recognized as being in direct competition with their professional practice.

Upon further reflection, however, the "hidden in plain sight" theory fits only imperfectly into the "folklore and fact collide" framework. First, the theory was not folklore at all but a fairly recent urban legend. Its postmodern origins in the 1990s in a popular book, its dissemination on national television, and its incorporation into official designs sponsored by major cultural institutions are all signs less of a competition between "elite" and "folk" knowledge and more of a competition between academic and mass culture over the pedagogic stakes of remembrance. What was at issue was less a choice between the archive and memory and more a contest over black representative space in memory, a contest that was itself being transformed by new mnemonic technologies like the Internet.[33] Rather than cast the dilemma in the pedagogic terms preferred by historians—How can we stop people from perpetuating myths about the past?—it would be preferable to address the performativity of the quilt legend and to identify its basis in the dynamics of social desire. If history made buffoons on both sides of this quarrel, there was a larger lesson that lay "hidden in plain sight," above and beyond the quite doubtful claim that quilting patterns guided fugitives to freedom.

The very idea of a quilting "code," I would suggest, bespeaks a popular apprehension, spoken in a vernacular cadence, of the discontinuous and interruptive image of the past I have identified with Benjamin and Lacan. This apprehension of an encoded past, we might note, emerged at the same moment as the best-selling novel *The Da Vinci Code,* which similarly detected a secret history and captured national and indeed worldwide attention with its sensational claims about hidden messages in famous paintings and works of architecture.[34] The popularity of such narratives of historical decoding resemble but ultimately break with the kind of verisimilitude pursued by historical reenactment and other forms of popular history. The comparison to the Hemings–Jefferson case is apt in highlighting the postmodernity of the supposed "folk knowledge" surrounding African American quilting patterns. That new evidence performed a democratic application of elite science, in this case the science of DNA, employing the "genetic code" as a historical cipher that objective science has only recently read. This type of discovery is part of what Benjamin was interested in when he used the related metaphor of a historical photographic negative to explain what he meant by a "dialectical image":

> If one looks upon history as a text, then one can say of it what a recent author has said of literary texts—namely, that the past has left in them images comparable to those registered by a light-sensitive plate. "The future alone possesses developers strong enough to reveal the image in all its details."[35]

It is this perspective upon the past that is affirmed by the popular interest in a quilting code: that the past is unfinished and unfinalizable; that the future possesses "developers" that will reveal and redeem something in the past now obscured, overlooked, and forgotten. This conviction of memory as an almost mechanic or machinic process of recording also accords with Lacan's insights into the agency of the letter in the symbolic chain of the unconscious. The letter here morphs into a code, a drunkard's path, a migrating goose, or the North Star. The point of these myths is not to perpetrate a hoax in the present but to stand in for what remains equally unrepresentable in both mass cultural and academic narrations of the past.

Getting Justice Done by Mistake

I further my point regarding the dialectical image of the past by returning to the antebellum and considering a corpus of historical material, much of which would now be disqualified by the historical profession on grounds comparable to those with which the quilting code was rejected. These early black protohistorians were often self-educated, and their labors were conducted before history had professionalized in its modern form. And yet, as John Ernest argues in his study of this early black historical writing,

> Writing in the racial state and under the terms of the racial contract, African American historians were and are inevitably metahistorical—for the nature and condition of their subject makes the attempt to

write history inevitably a task of questioning the terms of history and the politics of historical writing.[36]

The inevitable metamessage of early black historical writing, Ernest argues, renders it "a performative historiographical mode" and one that retains the potential to inspire us:

> Returning to early African American historians, in short, might well be a way of returning African American history to its liberationist roots, approaches to history determined by shifting theaters of oppression and devoted to the world beyond the authorized stage.[37]

As I have been arguing throughout, the performance of history is not only a metaphor but an index of an empirical range of practices of history-making: historiographies, choreographies, and phonographies as well as palimpsests, surrogates, installations, proclamations, and reenactments. What makes nineteenth-century black intellectuals our contemporaries is not the superiority of their scholarship or politics, not their greater proximity to the vanishing point of our liberationist roots, but the repetition of the dilemma staged in their time and ours.

If the emergence of black history writing was an inextricable component of a comprehensive political response to slavery and white supremacy, then its performativity was linked to its contemporaneity, to an address to its historical present. That historical present was characterized by the exclusion of black people from freedom, progress, history, and full humanity, and thus the black address to the past was a metonymy of a broader strategy of response to exclusion.

Prime among those responses, as intellectual historian Mia Bay has noted, was sarcasm. "Parody, sarcasm, and anger abound in this black commentary on the dominant race. In discussing white people, nineteenth-century African-Americans often met the insults of white racism with insults of their own."[38] The use of sarcasm as a metamessage or way of inflecting ideas, rather than the ideas themselves, indexes the *contemporaneity* of these antebellum discourses. Antebellum black activists used sarcasm to distance themselves from their present condition, not only in relation to an ostensibly glorious past in Africa but also in relation to an ambiguous future in which racial justice might indeed be secured. William Cooper Nell, along with Charles Remond and Wendell Phillips, petitioned and testified before the Massachusetts legislature for a memorial to Crispus Attucks and the Boston Massacre in 1851. When they were turned down, the grounds provided—that Attucks had not been the first to die because a white boy had been killed in a previous altercation with the British garrison—prompted Nell's famously acid axiom that "a Colored man never gets Justice done him in the United States, except by mistake."[39]

In his sarcastic image of justice achieved by mistake, Nell apprehends with remarkable point the complex social relations of exclusion through which blackness was historically produced. Underscoring the connection between such a judgment and its possible future redress, William Wells Brown opined that only "when negro slavery shall be abolished in our land, then we may hope to see a monument raised to commemorate the heroism of Crispus Attucks."[40] Thus linking power to knowledge, Wells Brown apprehended that the past would not be a finished story but a terrain of struggle until the slave had been freed and racial equality attained.

Events indeed proved Brown correct. And yet that monument, when erected, did not redress the history it strove to represent. Indeed, when invited to attend the dedication of the Attucks memorial, the elderly Frederick Douglass begged off in a letter that politely noticed that the statue was not, as was claimed, the very first to be dedicated to a black man. That honor, the cosmopolitan Douglass slyly noted, instead went to the writer Alexander Dumas, who had already received the honor of a granite edifice in France:

> Looking upon the magnificent monument erected in the city of Paris to the memory of Alexander Dumas, one of the most brilliant literary men of the whole constellation of French writers, I could not but credit Frenchmen with a higher degree of justice and impartiality to colored men than had yet been attained by my own countrymen.[41]

This sentence stands out in an otherwise honeyed and ingratiating letter as a subtle jab at American vanity. Justice in America, Douglass implied, is done a black person, if not by mistake exactly, then only when some other prompting than the merits of the case goads action, such as the shame of seeing a more civilized Europe value a race toward which white Americans remained hostile. History-making in public was always to be understood as a cipher or stand-in for some other process, occurring behind the scenes. Black abolitionist political culture instilled a discipline that demanded that one always look behind the curtain to see what was actually going on.

Black abolitionists were aware of their penchant for sarcasm and humor and encouraged it as an effective strategy for distancing the self from the omnipresent saturation of racism and the crippling self-doubt that racism could produce:

> O! had I the ability and could reach the nation's ear, I would today, pour out a fiery stream of biting ridicule, blasting reproach, withering sarcasm, and stern rebuke. For it is not light that is needed, but fire; it is not the gentle shower, but thunder. We need the storm, the whirl-wind, and the earthquake.

In these lines from his famous speech, "What to the Slave Is the Fourth of July?" Douglass reproached a self-styled enlightened and Christian nation. Literalizing the metaphor of the "nation's ear," Douglass imagines "blasting" and "biting" into it, grasping and rebuking a social *flesh*. As his intellectual historian recounts, the power of Douglass's rhetoric was indeed experienced in such physical terms by many a stunned auditor, such as one who described it as "the vol-canic outbreak of human nature."[42] And Douglass was not alone in mastering this technique. In the 1850s, James McCune Smith looked back over the development of black politics since 1808, focusing in particular on the key years of the late 1820s and early 1830s, and noted the "wit and sarcasm" with which this countermimetic black politics had flourished.[43] Around the same time, in an oration on the progress and development of black rhetoric, William G. Allen simi-larly praised "a sarcasm which bites the heart to its very core."[44]

The comments of Douglass, Smith, and Allen all call attention to the etymological root of *sarcasmus:* a gnashing of teeth or tearing of flesh. Sarcasm, that is, was a bodily practice as much as a spoken reg-ister. The sarcastic assertion that in America racial justice came only by mistake might seem nihilistic, much as the powerful assertion that the commemoration of national independence deserves only "bit-ing ridicule" might seem similarly filled with despair. And yet such an antagonistic stance toward history and memory might usefully serve as a counterpedagogy of remembrance insofar as it insulated its wielder against the normalization of the past. The indirect route toward justice proposed in sarcastic improvisations upon historical memory speaks less, I think, to despair at the possibility of justice than to the need to place our hopes elsewhere than in the myth of steady progress. An antithetical and negative hope is thus contained in sarcastic commentary on commemoration and remembrance. It becomes an instance of carnivalizing time.

Sarcasm, we should note, is not so much a message as it is a linguistic and performative mood. "Any verbal act may be performed," so the linguistic philosopher John Haiman argues, "in a sarcastic tone of voice." That is to say, sarcasm is a metalinguistic message that has much in common with a grammatical mood such as the subjunctive. The particular manner in which sarcasm is inflected is manifold, but a recurrent outcome of a successful act of sarcasm is the metamessage "I don't mean this." The ability to say one thing while meaning another is central to all forms of irony, of which sarcasm is one. But what distinguishes sarcasm is the clarity and intentionality of the alienation of the speaker from his or her words. Sarcasm laminates language and performance with the metamessage "I don't mean this," thus delivering a mixed message responding to both the content of the message and, obliquely, to the cheapness or falsity of the form in which it is delivered.[45] It is, as Daphne Brooks suggests, an afro-alienation act.

Haiman suggests that all language potentially approaches the inconsequentiality that sarcasm self-consciously highlights. "Not only is talk cheap," he argues, "it is in the very process of 'cheapening' that actions become talk."[46] This notion of sarcasm as cheap language points to a possible affinity, however unexpected, with the predominant affective tone of the nineteenth century: sentimentality. If the sentimental can be defined as a cheapening of affect through ritualistic repetition, then sarcasm would become an important means to highlighting and thus interrupting that cheapening. Consider, in this light, the extremely sarcastic intertextual reference between the following passages, the first from Harriet Beecher Stowe's *Uncle Tom's Cabin* and the second from Martin Delany's *Blake,* written at least partly in rejoinder:

> "Hulloa, Jim Crow!" said Mr. Shelby, whistling, and snapping a bunch of raisins towards him, "pick that up, now!"
>
> The child scampered, with all his little strength, after the prize, while his master laughed.
>
> "Come here, Jim Crow," said he. The child came up, and the master patted the curly head, and chucked him under the chin.
>
> "Now, Jim, show this gentleman how you can dance and sing."
> The boy commenced one of those wild, grotesque songs common

among the negroes, in a rich, clear voice, accompanying his singing with many comic evolutions of the hands, feet, and whole body, all in perfect time to the music.[47] (Stowe, 1852)

Shortly there came forward, a small black boy about eleven years of age, thin visage, projecting upper teeth, rather ghastly consumptive look, and emaciated condition. The child trembled with fear as he approached the group.

"Now gentlemen," said Grason, "I'm going to show you a sight!" having in his hand a long whip, the cracking of which he commenced, as a ringmaster in the circus.

The child gave him a look never to be forgotten; a look beseeching mercy and compassion. But the decree was made, and though humanity quailed in dejected supplication before him, the command was imperative, with no living hand to stay the pending consequences. He must submit to his fate, and pass through the ordeal of training.

"Wat maus gwine do wid me now? I know wat maus gwine do," said this miserable child, "he gwine make me see sights!" when going down on his hands and feet, he commenced trotting around like an animal.

"Now gentlemen, look!" said Grason. "He'll whistle, sing songs, hymns, pray, swear like a trooper, laugh, and cry, all under the same state of feelings."

With a peculiar swing of the whip, bringing the lash down upon a certain spot on the exposed skin, the whole person being prepared for the purpose, the boy commenced to whistle almost like a thrush; another cut changed it to a song, another to a hymn, then a pitiful prayer, when he gave utterance to oaths which would make a Christian shudder, after which he laughed outright.[48] (Delany, 1861–62)

Stowe's depiction of Harry dancing for Mr. Shelby confirms her strategic acceptance of the romantic racialism that naturalized the minstrel image of blacks as comic, rhythmic, and high spirited. Dancing for raisins, Harry is introduced in a sympathetic, maternalistic scene that contrasts entirely with the savage ironies of Delany's version in which, rather than "jump, Jim Crow," Reuben is asked to perform a kind of one-man vaudeville of the emotions, switching from curses to laughter to tears at the switch of a whip. Unlike Harry, Reuben is offered a brief interiority, a voice Delany coarsens with dialect: "Wat maus gwine do wid me now?" This question speaks back to the romantic racialism of natural black performance, making the agency and culpability for his grotesque displays crystal clear. Not one to wield sarcasm with a light touch, a few paragraphs later Delany has Reuben die of wounds inflicted by his master's whip. This unexpected point of contact between the sarcastic and the sentimental provides a window into the abolitionist speech genres that, I argue, contemporary artists reiterate.

In "What to the Slave Is the Fourth of July?" Douglass also negotiates this contact zone between the sarcastic and the sentimental, in this case, between the extreme sentiment of patriotism surrounding national Independence Day and the scorching ironies of historical exclusion. Speaking as was customary on the fifth of July rather than on the fourth, Douglass asked his white audience, "Do you mean, citizens, to mock me, by asking me to speak to-day?":

> I am not included within the pale of this glorious anniversary! Your high independence only reveals the immeasurable distance between us. The blessings in which you, this day, rejoice, are not enjoyed in common. The rich inheritance of justice, liberty, prosperity and independence, bequeathed by your fathers, is shared by you, not by me. The sunlight that brought life and healing to you, has brought stripes and death to me. This Fourth [of] July is *yours,* not *mine. You* may rejoice, *I* must mourn. (2:189)

The sarcastic modality that colors this speech (such as in phrases like "the *pale* of this *glorious* anniversary") reflects the sarcasmus or tearing into the flesh, both the flesh of the speaker ("this day . . . has brought stripes and death to me") and to his auditors ("do you mean, citizens, to mock me, by asking me to speak to-day?"). Douglass's repeated reference to the day blurs the line between the fourth and fifth of July: "this Fourth [of] July" and "this day" are placed just slightly out of temporal joint, a gap that is then rhetorically elevated into an "immeasurable distance." History as an uncompleted project is placed insistently and uncomfortably into the hands of the present.

Sarcasm served as a fort-da game played with the past and its commemoration, the push against which sentimentality supplied the pull. Sarcasm displayed what Haiman describes as a "divided self," one that placed the sarcast in but not of the linguistic world in which what she or he spoke. As such a verbal representative of the divided self, sarcasm not only accords well with Du Bois's account of black

Figure 15. Sanford Biggers, *The Something Suite*. The Box, New York City, November 2007. Photograph copyright Paula Court. Courtesy of Performa.

double-consciousness, "this sense of always looking at one's self through the eyes of others," but is also a preferred mode for performing a negative heritage.[49] If heritage is the sentimental mode par excellence, sarcastic representations of the past push against heritage's pull with a negativity that draws force from the mixed message: "I don't mean this." It is in this way, I suggest, that it can be said to fashion a black representative space within memory that does justice to the antithetical coordinates of the racial past.

Such at least seemed to be the case during the *Something Suite* performance created by the artist Sanford Biggers in November 2007, which took its cue from the blackface tradition to proclaim a "post-minstrel cycle." Rather than deliberately restaging a minstrel show, as in Spike Lee's film satire *Bamboozled,* the *Something Suite* took shards and elements of sentimental, comic, and grotesque history—from plantation belles to gangsta rappers—and brought them together into experimental proximity. Intended to entertain rather than edify, the *Suite*'s Mr. Interlocutor cracked jokes ripped from the headlines but somehow managed, in inhabiting his dandified historical effigy, to be less minstrelized than many standup comics routinely seen on broadcast television. *Something Suite* managed, in other words, to draw from history an image that was antithetical to the profaned and travestied iconography of racial kitsch without excluding or excusing that history. For the duration of the performance, black representative space within memory came alive with "a past charged with now-time," as Benjamin puts it, "blasted out of the continuum of history."[50] And yet that space provides no stable perspective, just phantasmagoria. When Biggers's buffoons of history come out holding gilt-framed mirrors in front of their faces, the performative rupture with the pedagogic is literalized. Rather than teach us to remember, *Something Suite* confronts us with a disjunctive temporality, offering up no window into the past, only a reflecting back of a sly, mimetic effigy.

Black Representative Space in Memory

At the midpoint of his inquiry into "the development of black representational spaces tailored to the purposes of artistic representation," Darby English pauses to ask, "But what grounds this knowledge historically?"[51] His initially surprising answer, which grows in plausibility with a moment's reflection, is that the rhetorical conditions for the construction of this space "bears fairly clear signs of its having been customized for a biracial public." "Structurally speaking," he continues, "the idea of black culture in America was always integrationist."[52] Particularly through readings of W. E. B. Du Bois and Frantz Fanon, English explains clearly the specific ideological and rhetorical reasons why these two germinal thinkers have so simultaneously appealed to both essentialist and antiessentialist accounts of black culture. Du Boisian "double consciousness" may have spiritualized black oppression in white America, and the Fanonian "fact of blackness" may have literalized antiblack discrimination in a phenomenological datum, but both rhetorics, English persuasively argues, were, at least in a U.S. context, deployed specifically to open up cultural space within a white majority nation-state, to "integrate" even symbolically the precincts of a "biracial public" sphere.[53]

In this chapter, I have implicitly investigated black representative space within memory, now thinkable in terms of this dialectic between essentialist impulses and antiessentialist effects. Put another way, I have investigated the affective implications of a strategic black separatism within a broader historical unfolding of black integrationism and symbolic inclusion in the U.S. nation-state. I now make this implicit investigation explicit and ask exactly what it means to make black representative space in American memory, in particular, American memory of the early national and antebellum periods. To do so, I want to radicalize the implicitly postmodernist thrust of English's spatializing gesture by asking how thinking of the space, shape, and texture of memory comes to matter in and for black cultural politics. In this effort, Walter Benjamin's concept of the dialectical image, as it explodes within his still arresting notes on the philosophy of history, is a key resource to draw upon.

Among Benjamin's most persuasive arguments is that the urge to declare the past sovereign territory, one that must be seen with its own eyes and heard with its own ears, is the fundament of an ideology of empty, homogenous, and forward-moving progressive time. This is a time that in the end urges us to abandon both the past and the present in the name of an ever-receding, ever-illusive, pedagogic future. Nowhere is Benjamin clearer on this than in the following passage:

> The subject of historical knowledge is the struggling, oppressed class itself. . . . The Social Democrats preferred to cast the working class in the role of redeemer of *future* generations, in this way cutting the sinews of its greatest strength. This indoctrination made the working class forget both its hatred and its spirit of sacrifice, for both are nourished by the image of the enslaved ancestors rather than by the ideal of liberated grandchildren.[54]

If we extract the core of his message from its local referents (social democrats, fascism), we see that Benjamin is here striking a blow against "reproductive futurity" *avant la lettre*. Here I am evoking Lee Edelman's argument that heterosexuality in its modern form is always yoked to a vision of politics in which the *summum bonum* is indefinitely deferred through the figure of the child.[55] The pedagogic temporality of the nation-state, as embodied by the social democratic vision of a capture of state power by and for the working class, depends on the abandonment of a dialectical image, drawn from the past, of "enslaved ancestors." Benjamin was speaking of the European working class in these lines and thus intended that phrase at least partly metaphorically. But in the context of black cultural politics, and the construction of black representational space, we are entitled to take Benjamin quite literally as we ask whether or not black cultural politics are better served by the ideal of grandchildren liberated into a postracial future or by a spirit of sacrifice nourished by the hatred of racism and racial slavery. It is a dangerous question to ask in America today. I am not even entirely confident of my own personal answer to it. But I do believe that a consistent reading of Benjamin entitles one to ask it.

Specifying the enslaved ancestor as an "image," as Benjamin does here, bears much similarity with specifying that ancestor as a "sign" or "rememory," as I employed both Toni Morrison and Kathryn Bond Stockton to do at the opening of this chapter. These words are not meant to idealize the enslaved ancestor but to assist in her further materialization in the present. Contemporary art can serve the function of Benjamin's "developer," revealing a dialectical image of the past, or the agency of the letter in the unconscious, that is precisely not what was perceived or experienced or intended at the time and that can consequently not be assimilated to any model of retrospective agency or causality, such as is the almost universal intention of "experiential" modes of heritage pedagogy in the contemporary museum. Contemporary art has long been engaged in the project of institutional critique, and I do not mean to suggest that the performative interventions I cite here are merely concerned with the sort of limited criticism of elitist or exclusive institutions. Instead, I aver that their project to work through the tensions and contradictions of black representational space in memory, a project that English shows is necessarily hybrid, can also link up with certain salient strands in black popular memory as well. But in order for those strands to be identifiable, we must grasp how those modes of popular remembrance are much closer to the spirit of Benjamin's "hatred" than they are to the deferential dreams of a better future to come. I have called them "negative heritage" in precisely the same spirit as the placard declaring "Your heritage is my slavery!" that is, as a dialectical image revealing how, as Benjamin puts it, every document of civilization is at the same time a document of barbarism. Black popular memory of slavery is interested in this covert document of barbarism, but not exclusively. It does not abandon a hope of futurity, but that futurity is not the social democratic hope of gradual inclusion and improvement, but of the cataclysmic irruption, from within empty, homogenous time, of the messianic time with which Benjamin ends his meditations.

"Dominant discourses and practices of heritage," Jonathan Rutherford notes, "in their attempt to bring the past into present life, can end up achieving the opposite effect. Past and present are fused together and neither can be separated out nor understood."[56] I considered this fusion in terms of the performance effigy in chapter 1, in terms of the trope of racial mixture in chapter 2, in terms of the dream of a national popular in chapter 3, and now in terms of a pedagogy of historical remembrance. But the modality of negative heritage that Benjamin associates with the discipline of hatred (for the slavery of the past) and that I have discussed in terms of sarcasm (which cuts across the field of discourse in the present with an active disidentification) and the trope of mistake or glitch in memory bespeak a potential historical performativity. This performativity interrupts complacent dreams of presenting the past as it was and, by placing the past in a parallax view with the present, establishes a friction rather than a fusion, a clash rather than a harmonization. It results in a representational space that is both black and, in a specific sense, negative, in that it cannot spell out a set of instructions on how to conduct ourselves in the present, but can only instruct against the presumption that its stories lie at the ready to be told.

Conclusion: Mongrel Pasts, Hybrid Futures

> The pure products of America
> go crazy—
>
> —*William Carlos Williams*, To Elsie *(1923)*

In the late 1930s, toward the end of the Great Depression, a young school-girl from Pennsylvania was taken to meet her father for the first time. After experiencing the shock and discomfort of segregated transportation, her mother finally brought her to a law office in Edgefield, South Carolina, where, to her surprise, a "fair, handsome man" wearing a "light blue suit" swept into the room and asked the surprised girl, "What do you think of our beautiful city?" Moments later, he showed her something she took to be a "large coin":

> "This is our state seal. See the palmetto, growing out of that fallen oak. That represents our great victory, from a fort built of palmetto logs, over the British fleet built of oak. That Latin phrase there *Quis Separabit* . . . do you know what that means?"
>
> "No, sir."
>
> "Take a guess, Essie Mae."
>
> I looked helplessly at my mother, who couldn't suppress her laugh. "Your father used to be a schoolteacher," she explained.
>
> Mr. Thurmond, which was the only name I had for him then, put his hand on my shoulder. "It means 'Who Can Separate Us?'"[1]

The deep irony of this scene greatly impressed the illegitimate, mixed-race child of the staunch southern segregationist, Strom Thurmond,

Figure 16. Makeda Christodoulos (Essie Mae) and Hugh Sinclair (Strom Thurmond) in the Brick Theater production of Thomas Bradshaw's *Strom Thurmond Is Not a Racist*, February–March 2007. Scenic design by Ryan Elliot Kravetz. Courtesy of Thomas Bradshaw.

who recalled its details many decades later in a memoir. Having waited until his death to reveal their relationship, which Thurmond had long recognized in private, Essie Mae Washington-Williams claimed that she kept the secret of her paternity safe out of respect for her late father. Given the obvious historical parallel with the long-denied Sally Hemings–Thomas Jefferson relationship—not to mention the lesser known but equally instructive antebellum example of Richard Mentor Johnson and his two daughters by Julia Chinn—Washington-Williams's revelation made national headlines and had heads scratching at the plausible implausibility of a black woman from California who could have at any time ruined the career of one of the nation's staunchest racists, keeping the family peace.[2]

The relationship between Washington-Williams and Thurmond lived on not only in her 2005 memoir but also in a 2007 play by an enfant terrible of the black theater. Thomas Bradshaw's ironically named play, *Strom Thurmond Is Not a Racist,* received its premiere at the Brick Theater in Williamsburg, Brooklyn, that winter.

The intense melodrama of the ripped-from-the-headlines story was complemented by Bradshaw's trademark deadpan dialogue, in which characters mouth sentiments reeking with cliché and blunder badly through the minefield of American race relations, past and present, perpetually offending each other along with the audience (members of which have been known to flee the theater in disgust at some of Bradshaw's more memorable outrages). That is to say, whereas in his more fictionalized plots, such as *Cleansed,* the story of a biracial girl who decides to join a white supremacist gang, Bradshaw's provocations demand a requisite suspension of disbelief, *Strom Thurmond Is Not a Racist* lies firmly in the "truth is stranger than fiction" camp. This permits Bradshaw to be especially perceptive about the rote and mechanical nature of professions of sincerity. In one scene the youthful Strom and Essie Mae's pregnant mother, Carrie, a servant in the Thurmond household, contemplate their future:[3]

> STROM: *(He put his arms around her and looks into her eyes.)* I love you Carrie. I have never felt love the way I feel with you. You make my soul feel free. Like a shooting star lighting up the midnight sky!
>
> CARRIE: *(They kiss.)* Strom, I love you so much. I just wish things could be different. I wish that we could live in a world where we didn't have to hide our love for each other. A world where we could walk down the street hand in hand and not be thrown in prison. *(Pause.)* I want to raise a family with you Strom!
>
> STROM: And I with you. *(He kisses her belly.)* Nothing would make me happier.
>
> CARRIE: Do you think we ever really could Strom? Do you think things could ever really change?
>
> STROM: I hope so Carrie. I hope our dreams aren't in vain.
>
> CARRIE: *(Pause.)* I've made a decision.[4]

Carrie goes on to lay out a plan to send her child away, to Pennsylvania, to live with relatives. Later in the play, the now adult Essie Mae repeats her mother's gesture, turning down an anguished Strom's offer to divulge their relationship. In both scenes, the black women in his life are shown to be agents, but perversely so. Their agency protects and excuses a man who goes on to devoting most of his public life to persecuting other black people. On one level, then, *Strom Thurmond Is Not a Racist* is an antipsychological study in cognitive dissonance. On the other, it is an equally merciless exposé on enabling. The anticlimactic pathos of Essie Mae's final speech in the play, which so closely skirts the edges of Washington-Williams's own infinite forgiveness, does not so much complete the racial drama as bring it to a halt. "Death unites us all," claims the fictional Essie Mae.[5] But like the Latin phrase accompanying the palmetto on the South Carolina state emblem, that inseparable unity is itself internally fractured by race. *Strom Thurmond Is Not a Racist* leaves the viewer with the unsettling conclusion that Strom, Carrie, and Essie Mae could be as good as sincere in their determination to remain a family. Fidelity to one's blood, the play dramatizes, is itself no balm against the corrosions of racism, even or especially those that rise up from within the family's members.

Desiring Hybridity

That heterosexuality, marriage, and human reproduction should be recruited to the task of getting us beyond "race" is a primary historical irony to which the themes I address throughout *The Amalgamation Waltz* bring us. The temptation to see the private sphere as a respite from the public is an enduring one in American life and clearly captured both the real and the dramatized Strom Thurmond. Renee Romano, in her 2003 study of legal marriages across the color line since World War II, takes note of the claim that "love is the answer, not legislation."[6] Comparably, Rachel Moran argues that in the wake of *Loving v. Virginia* (the 1967 Supreme Court decision overturning antimiscegenation laws), "race has become submerged in romantic complexity."[7] Hollywood films as different as *Bulworth* (1998), *Monster's Ball* (2001), and *Something New* (2006) ultimately extol sex and intimacy as sites where racial divisions may be suspended or dissolved. And, in the wake of several decades of marriage freedom, the public visibility of children of mixed marriages—Tiger Woods, Mariah Carey, Halle Berry, Derek Jeter, and so on—is a source of frequent commentary.

If love, romance, and reproduction are the answer, however, what exactly is the question? Although seemingly benign and innocent, the recourse to romantic complexity as an answer to racism belies the manner in which heterosexuality, marriage, and human reproduction have all historically been recruited, with stunning effectiveness, to construct racial hierarchy and difference. And what is more, they are hardly unproblematic institutions in themselves, even considered apart from questions of racial justice. Queer theorists Lee Edelman and Lauren Berlant have argued that "reproductive futurity" has historically proven a pervasive strategy for limiting the range of what the future, and by extension, politics, may be allowed to mean.[8] As Bradshaw implies in cleverly suggesting that the same actor may play both Carrie and her daughter Essie Mae (as indeed was the case in the premiere production), the ability of the American racial order to indefinitely defer the arrival of the hybrid child who will retrospectively redeem the American misadventure of race is literalized in a rule of hypodescent in which each successive generation of mixed peoples are determined to be legally and socially black and held to the same discriminatory standard as everyone else of African descent. The rule of hypodescent is itself a ruse of reproductive futurity insofar as it manages the racial future by promising a fusion that never comes and, at the same time, lures the "mixed-race" subject with the gambit of a tactical disobedience in which one's own family history serves as grounds for dismissing the irrationality of the U.S. racial formation.

Studies that focus on the post–World War II, post-Loving history of marriage across the color line, multiracial individuals and families, and the recent debates over counting race in the national census, may not take a deep enough historical perspective to adequately expose the cultural work that heterosexuality, marriage, and human reproduction do in all of them. Rather than solutions, love, romance, and sexuality are problems, or at least part of a much more general problematic than is commonly supposed. This problematic is suggested in Moran's description of race being "submerged" in romantic complexity, a telling metaphor we might use to broach questions of the unconscious, memory, and history in ways that would trouble uncomplicated utopias of interracial intimacy. That which is forcibly submerged can come erupting back to the surface. It is much like, to switch metaphors, Benjamin's dialectical image, fusing past and present in one incongruous unity. The romantic complexity animating Strom and Carrie's tortured romance is also the "romantic racialism" of much antebellum antislavery fiction in which the different races were accorded distinct but complementary characteristics, ones explicitly modeled on gender, so that the fusion of American culture could be domesticated through tropes of one great national family.[9]

Heterosexuality has been a preeminent metaphor through which a heterogeneous, mongrel past is recuperated as both a stable racial binary in the present and a possible hybrid utopia in the future. Heterosexuality, marriage, and human reproduction are not the answer to "race" or racism. Indeed, they form part of its historical drama. We can see this inner affinity between racial romanticisms old and new in an exchange in the pages of *Douglass's Monthly,* between the black abolitionist and the American spiritualist Andrew Jackson Davis, who held the races to possess diametrically symmetrical essences. In answer to a reader's question "on the subject of Mongrels," the famous Seer of Poughkeepsie had argued in the pages of the *Herald of Progress* that

> there is a spiritual *geometry* in the forms of the constituents of blood. . . . The spermatozoa of the male and the female of any nation will not perfectly blend, unless *the shape* of the blood particles be consistent with the imperative requirements of the masculine and feminine principles . . . it will forever remain physiologically impossible to perfectly—i.e. harmoniously and conjugally—blend or hybridize the reproductive blood of extreme nationalities . . . *the best offspring are obtained from parents of exactly opposite temperaments, but of the same species or nationality.*[10]

On the one hand, this is garden variety hocus pocus. On the other, it spells out the interlocking logics of heterosexuality and racism in which the complementary opposites of the sexes coincide exactly with the noncomplementary opposites of the races. Race and gender, put another way, are analogized to explain why the former does not equate with the latter and to argue that a "spiritual geometry" of the blood ensures that, even with human reproduction across the color line, no harmonious or conjugal result is possible. "Amalgamation," Davis concluded, "cannot be practiced with impunity—The children of all incompatible blood-gobules will exhibit, both by disposition of character and habitual conduct, the *angular* particles which (unaffinitized) circulate in their veins and brain."[11] In one of the most ludicrously pseudoscientific excurses on the haughty mulatto, Davis here attributes a certain angularity of disposition, a certain refusal to fit equally into the racial framework, to "incompatible blood-gobules" coursing through the hybrid child's veins and brain.

Frederick Douglass, in his masterfully sarcastic response, targeted the specious discourse of halves and angles in Davis's quackery:

> As one of the subjects of this physical, metaphysical, spiritual and so-
> cial inquiry, we may be allowed at least a *half* word on one *half* the
> subject, leaving the other half to be disposed of by the *"whole"* men.[12]

Here Douglass tethers his response to a certain mobilization of complete manhood, although on balance his male chauvinism may be
more forgivable than Davis's sexist sex magic. Tactically inhabiting
the position of "half a man," Douglass disidentified with that ascrip-
tive identity long enough to enumerate all the physical, moral, and
mental ways in which "half" men compared with "whole" men. He
ultimately burlesqued the core idea of halfness underpinning Davis's
spiritual calculus and disavowed the specious "wholeness" of white
men unable to see the reality before their own eyes, so enchanted
were they with invisible geometries and racial temperaments such
as we still routinely encounter when confronting popular discourses
of race.

Following the work of Jennifer Brody, Naomi Zack, Jayne
Ifekwunigwe, and Caroline Streeter, and in dialogue with current and
forthcoming work by Naomi Pabst, Jared Sexton, Diana Paulin, and
Michelle Elam, I highlight here the performativity of mixed race as a
discourse that *makes* what it ostensibly *describes*. Davis's answer is a
good instance of this.[13] As critics have pointed out, however, efforts to
ridicule the fictiveness of race—by showing it to be contingent rather
than essential, constructed rather than a biological given—tend to
run up against the obscene remainder of racial terror and enjoyment
that seems always to survive race's theoretical demolishing. As one
critic puts it, while "there is no denying the fact that race is after all a
historical invention, and that like most inventions it veils the artifice
of its origin," this "in itself is not interesting" because "uncovering
'race's' genealogy is not to address racial practice."[14] Race's appeal
to the self-evidence of the senses—not just racial looking but also
hearing, smelling, touching, tasting—resists historicism through its
insistent appeal to racial inheritance. To confront these, we must, as
Douglass did, tactically inhabit the discourses of halfness to which
racial practice consigns us. But, like Douglass, we need not accept
those discourses unmodified.

What is our relation to the hybrid future, though, if we are not
to be its avatars? In this book, I have critiqued the claiming of a
mongrel past as national heritage. This act of historical reimagina-
tion, I argue, does not go far enough in its embrace of hybridity and

the mongrel, which are not proper objects of national fantasy but improper and uncanny figures located at the margins of culture or, in what amounts to much the same thing, its absent center. I have left the critique of the hybrid future to others, in part because that critique is more developed.[15] But this tactic might for some readers beg the question: How does the critique of the mongrel past matter, if at all, to the critique of the hybrid future? I turn to this final question in my conclusion. The antebellum dream of the hybrid future, I argued in my introduction, rested upon a biopolitical turn toward demography, a turn which allowed radicals to argue, for the first time, that a nation's racial character could and would transform of its own accord by its citizen's spontaneous pursuit of happiness. Human reproduction became a visible concern to statecraft insofar as its capacity to destabilize the distinction between citizen and denizen, people and multitude, became a legitimate public issue. While prior histories of antimiscegenation discourse have emphasized the deployment of racism in these biopolitical scenarios, particularly in the way in which they presented blackness as a contagion and sought to manage miscegenation by depicting it as a racial apocalypse, I have emphasized the underpinning shift that permitted both negative and positive scenarios alike to be conjured. The recourse to statistical and social scientific representation, with its built-in utopian and reformist dimensions, was as important over the long term as any particular antimiscegenation ideology.

With the defeat of those ideologies, at least at the state level, in the 1960s, that underlying utopian and reformist schema has, if anything, become more important and visible, as official discourse on both left and right has defaulted, as it were, to the original utopian perspective of abolitionists who thought that while nobody "*advocates* amalgamation . . . doubtless there are very many who believe that in time the two races *will* amalgamate."[16] The unread, uncanonical *Miscegenation* pamphlet has been unconsciously adopted as a national scripture, down to its claim that an admixture of black "blood" will make the white race more "comely."

Racial mixing and hybridity are neither problems for, nor solutions to, the long history of "race" and racism, but part of its genealogy. Racisms can emerge, thrive, and transform quite effectively without ever being undone by the magical, privatized powers we invest in interracial intimacy and reproduction.[17] The impossibly burdened figure of the biracial child cannot conceivably do the work of utopia that we repeatedly impose upon her.

Hybridity has been repeatedly enlisted in envisioning utopian and dystopian scenarios. This persistent projection of hybridity into a temporal and spatial elsewhere is itself a mechanism for resisting an awareness of the actual and ongoing mongrel past, a history which is neither a moral scandal nor a transcendental panacea, but an uneasy terrain of ordinary and difficult antagonism and conviviality. These mongrel pasts rarely figure in our ideological projections of hybrid futures, because they cannot support the exaggerated claims we might seek to make of them. Thus, the late Earl Woods notoriously held up his son Tiger Woods as "the chosen one," an idea endorsed both by GQ—which anointed Tiger a "messiah" in a 1997 cover story—and in various semiserious Web sites like tigerwoodsisgod.com, which pointedly asks,

> In a world that still harbors remarkable racial divisions, wouldn't it make sense for the Messiah to come in the form of someone who is one-quarter black, one-quarter Chinese, one-quarter Thai, one-eighth American Indian, and one-eighth white?[18]

If the world harbored such remarkable and enduring racial divisions, one wonders, then how did such an intricate compound of quarters and eighths appear suddenly on December 30, 1975? Wouldn't that suppose, at a minimum, several generations of intermingling? The mongrel, transnational pasts of Earl and Kutilda Woods—brought together by the geopolitics of the Vietnam War and the biopolitics of black overrepresentation in the U.S. military—are effaced in this futuristic embrace of their "Cablinasian" son, who steps onto the playing green ab ovo. The angular geometries of the fractional racial subject, whether abjured as in Davis's spiritualism or embraced in recent pop messianism, are equally specious.

What the language of fractions and intermixings affords, however, is a deployment of sexual difference through which the seeming transgression of race mixing is resolved, first into the "romantic complexity" of courtship and marriage, and then into the reproductive futurity of the "mixed-race" child, the "fruits of amalgamation."[19] It is startling to me how little the voluminous literature on interracial parenting, adoption, and identity seriously reflects upon the omnipresence of heterosexuality as its normalizing ballast. Within modern

Figure 17. E. W. Clay, *The Fruits of Amalgamation,* 1839. Courtesy of American Antiquarian Society.

heterosexuality, a child needs two parents (one father, one mother) to properly develop and locate his or her own gender identity. Little girls need fathers; little boys need mothers. And yet, this is a norm that is not one, as feminist and queer historians have shown. Godfathers, aunts and uncles, queer parents or more than two parents, uncanny pseudo-parents like wet nurses and au pairs and catholic priests ("fathers"), all dot the perimeter of this promised land of heterosexual nucleation, atavistic relics or futuristic neologisms that aid and abet human reproduction, but for their troubles are variously scorned, exploited, and scapegoated. Modern marriage, heterosexuality, and reproduction succeeds in presenting itself as a transhistorical norm only by abjecting and discounting the messy, premodern, and postmodern permutations that scholars ranging from Stephanie Coontz to Lisa Duggan point out have always been the actual norm.[20] The mixed-race child as harbinger of a transracial future is emplotted within the straight time of heterosexuality, wedded to progress. And yet in our everyday performances of intimacy and obligation, we continuously and unself-consciously deviate from that plot, enmeshing ourselves in other, queerer temporalities.[21] Since this is the case, is it not possible to unyoke racial hybridity from its association with progressive, heterosexual time? Into what alternate temporalities might it then fall?

From Amalgamation to "the Agalma" and Back Again

That the normative family should be so reliably called upon to do the political work of reconciling the races, but that this work should be seen as nowhere possible without queer, nonreproductive lines of affiliation, forms a central irony in the history I would like to unburden from the mirage of a hybrid future. The manner in which we escort the "invisible proscenium" of marriage and childbearing (as Eve Sedgwick so wittily puts it) with our queer, avuncular, and godmotherly investitures, suggests something unspoken or hard to speak about the peculiar performativity of the transracial future.[22] By aligning itself with the heterosexual norm, racial hybridity seeks to cast off its own history of stigma. This is part of the reason that hybrid futures remain so unstable, so prone to indefinite, intergenerational postponement and disappointment. This is part of the reason the mixed-race child, as effigy, is so recurrently a scapegoat, held responsible for an event whose truth she or he can neither speak nor pass over in silence.

This felt disconnect between mixed realities and dichotomizing discourses is naturally growing in America, as what some call an Obama generation of Americans increasingly emerge into visibility. Many, like the president himself, try to disavow the burden of racial reconciliation that some would thrust upon them, by virtue of their biracial parentage. As he recalled in his 1995 memoir:

> Some people have a hard time taking me at face value. When people who don't know me well, black or white, discover my background (and it is usually a discovery, for I ceased to advertise my mother's race at the age of twelve or thirteen, when I began to suspect that by doing so I was ingratiating myself to whites), I see the split-second adjustments they have to make, the searching of my eyes for some telltale sign.[23]

What are these people looking for? Lacan called it *objet a,* the invisible, inextricable irritant that disturbs our otherwise seamless experience of the symbolic order, the trace we strive constantly to retrace in order to get back to what we imagine to be the real. And a close analog of *objet a,* in Lacan's ornate lexicon, is the *agalma,* another theoretical object that occupies a similar position in his system, except that it is particularly associated with the positive good and with beneficent transference. Let me close this study with a brief excursus on this surprisingly revelatory concept.[24]

Lacan derives his account of the *agalma* from his reading of Plato, and in particular, the scene in the *Symposium* when Alcibiades, who has arrived late at the feast, proceeds to recount with drunken exuberance his fidelity and devotion to the crafty teacher Socrates. So great and steadfast is Socrates, Alcibiades claims, that he even turned down the latter's highly generous offer of sexual favors. That is to say, Alcibiades recognizes that Socrates is aroused by his youth and great beauty. Although Alcibiades is willing to grant Socrates favors because of his great admiration for his intellect, and even goes so far as to try to seduce the learned Socrates (whom he does not actually desire), Socrates retains his dignity in the face of the younger man's cockteasing.[25]

This is, as Lacan recognizes, a story of transference, one familiar to analysts and teachers alike. What he takes particular note of, however, is the word Alcibiades uses to describe the "divine images" hidden in Socrates' mind that he hopes to unlock by successfully becoming Socrates' lover.[26] That hidden treasure, or *agalma,* is precisely what Socrates, in a gesture Lacan recognizes as masterful, disavows. Instead, he accuses Alcibiades of praising him so effusively merely out of misplaced possessiveness. "You think that I ought to love you and no one else," Socrates tells Alcibiades, implicitly disavowing the great hidden *agalma* Alcibiades would claim as his own. The only hidden wisdom Socrates has, he infers, is the truth that he had *no* such hidden wisdom to offer and that Alcibiades would need to look within himself to find the source of the desires he so persistently and aggressively projects onto Socrates.[27]

The hybrid child is faced with a comparable transference, this time from the culture at large. The product of amalgamation, when she is not scorned as a mongrel bastard, is held to somehow contain a secret *agalma* that holds some mysterious power to redeem a fallen province of racism and racial awareness. Just as Socrates disavowed the treasures Alcibiades claimed were hidden within him, without disavowing Alcibiades' quest for truth and redemption, so must the hybrid child disavow the faulty expectation that she, in herself, holds some kind of passport to a future transcendence of race. This refusal, which is also another instance of what I have been calling a practice of negative heritage, does not wholly refuse the desires for fusion, reconciliation, or transcendence. But it does rebuff the attempt to make of the mongrel an *agalma* for the nation, the secret treasure that redeems a fallen nature.

Who can separate us? Who can bring us together? Let's leave the "fruits of amalgamation" out of our answers to these questions.

Acknowledgments

"It's okay to read," my late grandfather Hesbon Nyong'o once told me, noticing that my nose was always in a book, "just not all the time." I can't say I've mastered that balance yet, but this particular book is the result of a lot more than just reading. My intellectual path was instigated in the classes of Steven Gregory, Brian Fay, Donald Moon, Alex Dupuy, David Parker, Malika Mehdid, Gargi Bhattacharya, Alan Trachtenberg, Michael Denning, Hazel Carby, Nancy Cott, and Christopher Miller. It was furthered in heated discussions with Keith Donoghue, Amy Hundley, Ben Foss, Nicholas Salvato, Brian Herrera, Dalton Anthony, Noelle Morrissette, Robin Bernstein, Andrea Becksvoort, Seth Silberman, Ferentz Lafargue, Jayna Brown, Kandia Crazy Horse, Diana Williams, Camara Holloway, Daphne Brooks, Cheryl Finley, and Ann Murphy (go Aristocrats!). The Black Mods—Saidiya Hartman, Tina Campt, Phillip Brian Harper, Robert Reid-Pharr, Jennifer Morgan, Kim F. Hall, Alondra Nelson, and Herman Bennett—came along at the perfect time to put wind back in my sails. Friends on the Social Text Collective, including Brent Edwards, Randy Martin, Livia Tenzer, and Patrick Deer, generously welcomed me into one of the most exciting academic conversations in the city. At New York University, colleagues and comrades who have similarly welcomed and mentored me, and generally made this project possible, include José Esteban Muñoz, Anna McCarthy, Lisa Duggan, Timothy Mitchell, and particularly Barbara Browning, who generously read the entire manuscript. In the broader academic firmament, I owe admiring thanks and gratitude to Fred Moten, Karen Tongson, Judith Halberstam, John Stauffer, and Lauren Berlant.

LeAnn Fields generously spared precious conference time to help me clarify and sharpen my ideas. Rod Ferguson saw more in this manuscript than was perhaps really there, and I remain in his debt for shepherding it into Richard Morrison's excellent care at the University of Minnesota Press.

Henry Abelove has been a great friend and mentor whose influence is evident in every page I write. *The Amalgamation Waltz* began life as a dissertation directed by the incomparable duo of Paul Gilroy and Joseph Roach, whose combined mentorship gave new meaning to the expression "an embarrassment of riches." Shante "Paradigm" Smalls, Frank Léon Roberts, and Michelle Lindenblatt set the bar very high for subsequent research assistants, and Joshua Chambers-Letson took time out from his travels in Thailand for a last-minute proofreading of the manuscript. With all this help, any errors in fact or interpretation are truly my fault.

Marc Mayer has been more than a companion to me and is no doubt as grateful as I am that this book is finally done. I thank him with all my love and humility. Nico Icon kept me company and kept me sane during long hours at the computer. My siblings Kwame, Omo, and Isis have good-naturedly tolerated my use of our hybrid, postcolonial lives as grist for my theoretical mill. My late father Aggrey Omondi Nyong'o early on recognized and approved of my philosophical bent as in some ways a mirror of his own. To his memory and in tribute to my mother, Verna Jean Turkish, without whose faith and imagination I would be nothing, I dedicate this book.

Notes

Introduction

1. Erkkila, *Mixed Bloods and Other Crosses*, 44.

2. Obama, *The Audacity of Hope*, 231.

3. Stanley Crouch, "What Obama Isn't: Black Like Me," *Daily News*, November 2, 2006; Debra Dickerson, "Colorblind: Barack Obama Would Be the Great Black Hope in the Next Presidential Race—If He Were Actually Black," Salon.com, January 22, 2007.

4. Dickerson made this comment on the February 8, 2007, broadcast of Comedy Central's current events show *The Colbert Report*.

5. Crouch, "What Obama Isn't."

6. Žižek, *Tarrying with the Negative*, 201; Walcott, "Beyond the 'Nation Thing.'"

7. Subsequent genealogical discoveries linking his family to that of the white Republican vice president Dick Cheney added to a growing public fascination with subterranean familial linkages across color lines.

8. Rachel L. Swarns, "Obama Had Slaveowning Kin," *New York Times*, March 3, 2007.

9. On marriage as "a kind of fourth wall or invisible proscenium arch that moves through the world . . . continually reorienting around itself the surrounding relations of visibility and spectatorship," see Eve Kosofsky Sedgwick, "Around the Performative: Periperformative Vicinities in Nineteenth-Century Narrative," in Sedgwick, *Touching, Feeling*, 72.

10. Fields, "Of Rogues and Geldings," 1397.

11. Brody, "Memory's Movements," 744.

12. Edelman, *No Future*, 4.

13. Dening, *Performances*, xiv.

14. Foucault, "Nietzsche, Genealogy, History."

15. Harris, "From Abolitionist Amalgamation to 'Rulers of the Five Points'"; Rael, *Black Identity and Black Protest in the Antebellum North*.

16. I am not arguing that time is a social construct, only that our sense of time, its "progress" or "passage," is shaped by discourses such as heritage and race, among others.

17. On the history of the idea of race in the United States, see Bay, *The White Image in the Black Mind*; Fredrickson, *The Black Image in the White Mind*; Jordan, *White over Black*; Dain, *A Hideous Monster of the Mind*.

18. Perez-Torres, *Mestizaje*, 9.

19. On racial whiteness and white supremacy, see Saxton, *The Rise and Fall of the White Republic*; Allen, *The Invention of the White Race*; Hannaford, *Race*; Horsman, *Race and Manifest Destiny*; Morrison and Stewart, *Race and the Early Republic*.

20. Hall, "Whose Heritage?" 25.

21. Kinney, *Go Down, Moses: The Miscegenation of Time*.

22. Anderson, *Imagined Communities*; Bhabha, *The Location of Culture*; Benjamin, "On the Concept of History," 395.

23. Huddart, *Homi K. Bhabha*, 149–69.

24. Bhabha, *The Location of Culture*, 227.

25. Ibid., 209, 277.

26. Sexton, "The Consequences of Race Mixture," 260–61.

27. Austin, *How to Do Things with Words*; Derrida, *Limited Inc*; Butler, *Excitable Speech*; Felman, *The Scandal of the Speaking Body*; Parker and Sedgwick, *Performativity and Performance*.

28. Halbwachs, *On Collective Memory*, 38.

29. Schechner, *Between Theater and Anthropology*.

30. Obama's breakthrough into national politics—one launched with a televised exercise in eloquence—was recognizably a feat of political performance, one situated within (while at the same time innovating upon) a micropolitics of race coded in gesture, dress, and accent. The showbiz metaphors surrounding his rapid ascent—from the constant references to the crowds that gathered to hear him, to his media-designated "rock star" status, to the echo of the British Invasion that the phrase "Obama-mania" evoked—were bemused but rarely dismissive admissions of this political theatricality. Furthermore, Obama's self-conscious "audacity" and "hope-mongering" drew upon the performative in Bhabha's sense of the term, at least initially asserting his relative newness and inexperience as assets rather than liabilities. Against the pedagogic temporality of the national security state, with its dominant affect of fearful preparedness and the insistent imperative to trust the experienced father figures in the administration, Obama-mania evoked an exuberant new beginning of national enjoyment, embodied in the intense charisma of the "skinny guy with a funny name." See also Nyong'o, "Passing as Politics."

31. Marx, "The Eighteenth Brumaire of Louis Bonaparte," 32.

32. Dening, *Performances;* Roach, *Cities of the Dead.*

33. Freud, *Inhibitions, Symptoms and Anxiety.*

34. Lemire, *"Miscegenation"*; Weierman, *One Nation, One Blood;* Saks, "Representing Miscegenation Law."

35. Bolokitten, *A Sojourn in the City of Amalgamation.*

36. Holgate, *American Genealogy.* On Holgate's authorship, see Elise Virginia Lemire, "Making Miscegenation: Discourses of Interracial Sex and Marriage in the United States, 1790–1865" (PhD thesis, Rutgers, State University of New Jersey, 1996), 47–106.

37. "An archaic, specifically Victorian meaning of the term pure is 'excrement,' which was used to purify leather." Brody, *Impossible Purities,* 12. Thanks to Robin Bernstein for calling my attention to this passage. Aside from interests in genealogy and Swiftian racism, Holgate appears also to have been a textbook anal retentive, recording his decades-long struggles with constipation in excremental detail. Lemire, "Making Miscegenation," 91–92.

38. Werbner and Modood, *Debating Cultural Hybridity,* 4.

39. Jameson, *The Political Unconscious.*

40. Bakhtin, *The Dialogic Imagination.* See also Werbner, "The Limits of Cultural Hybridity."

41. Palumbo-Liu, "Theory and the Subject of Asian American Studies."

42. Santa Ana, "Affect-Identity," 25.

43. Nealon, *Foundlings;* Carolyn Dinshaw et al., "Theorizing Queer Temporalities," "Time Binds."

44. Foucault, "Nietzsche, Genealogy, History," 385.

45. Hall, "Whose Heritage?" 26.

46. Foucault, "Nietzsche, Genealogy, History," 386.

47. Foucault, *The Order of Things,* 341.

48. Sedgwick and Frank, "Shame in the Cybernetic Fold."

49. I borrow the expression "circum-Atlantic" from the work of Joseph Roach.

50. On infrahumanity, see Gilroy, *Between Camps,* 54–96. On the burdened subject of freedom, see Hartman, *Scenes of Subjection,* 115–24.

51. Ira Berlin, *Many Thousands Gone,* and "Time, Space, and the Evolution of Afro-American Society on British Mainland North America."

52. Rael, *Black Identity and Black Protest,* 14–21.

53. Easton, *To Heal the Scourge of Prejudice,* 89.

54. Ibid. Unless otherwise indicated, all emphases are in the original.

55. Ibid., 105–6.

56. Smith, *The Works of James McCune Smith,* 53.

57. Dain, *A Hideous Monster of the Mind,* 247.

58. *Frederick Douglass' Paper,* January 8, 1852.

59. Fredrickson, *The Black Image in the White Mind.*

60. Hartman, *Scenes of Subjection,* 12.

61. Erkkila, *Mixed Bloods and Other Crosses;* Lemire, *"Miscegenation."*

62. Sollors, *Neither Black nor White and Yet Both,* 396.

63. *Weekly Anglo-African,* March 5, 1864.

64. Hollinger, "Amalgamation and Hypodescent."

65. See, for instance, Samuels, "Miscegenated America."

66. Samuel S. Cox, *Miscegenation or Amalgamation. Fate of the Freedman. Speech of Hon. Samuel S. Cox, of Ohio, Delivered in the House of Representatives, February 17, 1864.* (Washington, D.C.: Constitutional Union, 1864). See also Kaplan, "The Miscegenation Issue in the Election of 1864."

67. *Weekly Anglo-African,* January 23, 1864.

68. Ibid.

69. See the February 6, 13, and 20; March 5 and 12; and April 2, 1864, issues of the *Weekly Anglo-African.* After some readers objected to the message of the pamphlet, on grounds that it was counter to black racial pride or, as one put it, brought up at a "very unseasonable time," the paper quietly dropped the advertisement it had been running.

70. Stewart, *Ordinary Affects,* 4.

71. "Our New York Correspondence," *Philadelphia Inquirer,* January 13, 1864.

72. Cited in Bloch, *Miscegenation, Melaleukation, and Mr. Lincoln's Dog,* 10.

73. Serena Mayeri, "Answering the 'Amalgamation Trumpeters': The Campaign to Repeal Interracial Marriage Laws in Massachusetts, 1831–1843" (paper presented at the Race Scholarship Forum, Yale Law School, December 1998).

74. Cott, *Public Vows.* On marriage and the decentering of race, see Romano, *Race Mixing.* On marriage and the decentering of gender, see Freeman, *The Wedding Complex.*

75. Leach, *True Love and Perfect Union.*

76. Nor would Richard Mentor Johnson have been elected vice president in the 1830s, the height, we have been led to believe, of antimiscegenation hysteria. See Brown, "The Miscegenation of Richard Mentor Johnson as an Issue in the National Election Campaign of 1835–1836."

77. "Miscegenation," *Anthropological Review* 2, no. 5 (1864): 116–17.

78. Ibid., 120–21.

79. Bloch, *Miscegenation, Melaleukation, and Mr. Lincoln's Dog.* I thank Diana Paulin for bringing this odd work to my attention. Bloch does not, as I have, track the reception of the pamphlet in the black press.

80. Croly and Wakeman, *Miscegenation.* Evidence of this can be found in the copy held in the Beinecke Library at Yale University, and previously

owned by the apologist for slavery U. B. Phillips. In the margins of this copy, possibly in Phillips's hand, are scribbled virulently racist reactions against its proposals demonstrating that however aware this reader was of its parodic intent (which was exposed shortly after its original publication), he or she could not constrain him- or herself from reacting in the heat of the moment to its incendiary proposals.

81. Bloch, *Miscegenation, Melaleukation, and Mr. Lincoln's Dog,* 47.

82. Lemire, *"Miscegenation,"* 87–114. See also Harris, "From Abolitionist Amalgamation to 'Rulers of the Five Points'"; Kerber, "Abolitionists and Amalgamators: The New York City Race Riots of 1834"; and Richards, *Gentlemen of Property and Standing.*

83. Bhabha, *The Location of Culture,* 95.

84. Horowitz, *Rereading Sex,* 214–17.

85. On the obscene center of ideology, see Žižek, *The Sublime Object of Ideology.*

86. This is true up to and including a defense, in raciological terms, of the pamphlet's underlying thesis of hybrid vigor. See, for example, Ziv, *Breeding between the Lines.*

87. *Weekly Anglo-African,* February 13, 1864.

88. Here we might reference to Paul Gilroy's concern with the rising emergence of "proteophobic" racism, based on fear of the unknown and unclassifiable, replacing the "simpler hatreds" of an earlier moment. Gilroy, *Postcolonial Melancholia,* 37. See also Sexton, *Amalgamation Schemes.*

89. Brooks, *Bodies in Dissent.*

90. Strausbaugh, *Black Like You,* 34.

1. The Mirror of Liberty

1. Discussed in the Introduction to this book.

2. See Arnold, *Doctor Death.* I thank Franny Nudelman for bringing this book to my attention.

3. Foucault, "Nietzsche, Genealogy, History," 376.

4. Bhabha, *The Location of Culture,* 145–74.

5. See also Browne, "Remembering Crispus Attucks."

6. Baucom, *Specters of the Atlantic.*

7. See also Young, "The Black Body as Souvenir in American Lynching"; and Goldsby, *A Spectacular Secret.*

8. Sappol, *A Traffic of Dead Bodies,* 306, 312.

9. The hybrid object thus differs from fetishism, which, he argues, fixes "on an object *prior to the perception of difference,*" an object that can therefore "look like anything (or nothing!)" so long as it "fulfils the fetishistic ritual." Bhabha, *The Location of Culture,* 164.

10. Seshadri-Crooks, *Desiring Whiteness;* Moten, *In the Break;* Fanon, *Black Skin, White Masks.*

11. Debord, *The Society of the Spectacle,* 9.

12. Brooks, *Bodies in Dissent,* 121–23.

13. Ernest, *Liberation Historiography.*

14. Marx, "The Eighteenth Brumaire of Louis Bonaparte."

15. The notable exception, Hannah Arendt's *On Revolution* (1962), seems to prove this rule. See also Antonio Negri's discussion in *Insurgencies,* 141–92.

16. Negri, *Insurgencies,* 23–24. On constituent power as "hybrid," 1.

17. Waldstreicher, *In the Midst of Perpetual Fetes.*

18. Fliegelman, *Declaring Independence,* 3, 192.

19. Ibid., 189–95, Waldstreicher, *In the Midst of Perpetual Fetes,* 294–352.

20. McNamara, *Day of Jubilee.*

21. Rediker, "The Revenge of Crispus Attucks," 43.

22. Linebaugh and Rediker, *The Many-Headed Hydra,* 353; Baucom, *Specters of the Atlantic,* 276–82.

23. Rediker, "Revenge of Crispus Attucks," 45.

24. Ibid., 36.

25. Ibid., 37.

26. This print exists in various states. For convenience, I refer to here the version reproduced as plate 14 in Brigham's authoritative monograph, *Paul Revere's Engravings,* 52–78.

27. Nell, *The Colored Patriots of the American Revolution.*

28. In response to a query, William Cooper Nell, Attucks's earliest historian, noted that "to my knowledge there are none but fancy [fanciful] sketches of him." Wesley and Uzelac, *William Cooper Nell, Nineteenth-Century African American Abolitionist, Historian, Integrationist,* 662.

29. Lacey, "Visual Images of Blacks in Early American Imprints," 166.

30. Agamben, *Homo Sacer,* 25.

31. *Boston Gazette,* October 2, 1750.

32. City Council, Boston, *A Memorial of Crispus Attucks, Samuel Maverick, James Caldwell, Samuel Gray and Patrick Carr from the City of Boston,* 83.

33. His "Indian heritage," one scholar speculates, may mean that he was a descendant of John Auttuck, a praying Indian who was hanged by the English colonists in 1676 for his alleged role in King Phillip's War. Belton, "The Indian Heritage of Crispus Attucks."

34. Linebaugh and Rediker, *Many-Headed Hydra,* 237.

35. Wroth and Zobel, *Legal Papers of John Adams,* 3: 266, 268.

36. On violence as the performance of waste, see Roach, *Cities of the Dead,* 41.

37. Wroth and Zobel, *Legal Papers of John Adams,* 3: 269.

38. The distinction between "people" and "multitude" is explored in Hardt and Negri, *Empire.* See also Virno, *A Grammar of the Multitude.*

39. Carlo Botta, *History of the War of the Independence of the United States of America*, (New Haven: N. Whiting, 1838), and the *Boston Transcript*, March 7, 1851. Both cited in Nell, *The Colored Patriots of the American Revolution*, 15.

40. Nelson, *National Manhood*.

41. Moten, *In the Break*, 1.

42. Foucault, *The History of Sexuality*, 43. Buttressing my claim of the erotic speciation of the mulatto was an article in the prominent *Atlantic Monthly* that compared the identity crisis of the biracial child to that of the protogay child. See Andrew Sullivan, "Why Obama Matters," *Atlantic Monthly*, December 2007.

43. Melish shows how gradual emancipation in New England was accompanied by the intensified regulation of a variety of racially subordinate peoples and discusses such acts as the 1784 Connecticut "Act concerning Indian, Molatto, and Negro Servants and Slaves," which effected gradual emancipation. The act was designed to pragmatically extend the regulation of subordinate populations, whether technically free or enslaved, black or otherwise. Melish, *Disowning Slavery*, 70.

44. Agamben, *The Coming Community*.

45. Kawash, *Dislocating the Color Line*, 196, 214.

46. Nyong'o, "'The Black First.'"

47. Benjamin, "On the Concept of History," 392.

48. Agamben, *State of Exception*, 59.

49. A photo of this march and banner can be found in the unpaginated illustrations to Lewis, *W. E. B. Du Bois*.

50. Much of what we know of Nell is the result of the assiduous labors of the pioneering scholar, Dorothy Porter Wesley. See Smith, "William Cooper Nell"; Wesley and Uzelac, *William Cooper Nell*; Wesley, "Integration versus Separatism."

51. Garnet, *The Past and the Present Condition*; Lewis, *Light and Truth*; and Pennington, *A Text Book of the Origin and History, &C. &C. Of the Colored People*. See also Ernest, *Liberation Historiography*; Sweet, *Black Images of America*.

52. Murphy, "Socrates in the Slums"; Jackson, *Lines of Activity*.

53. Wesley and Uzelac, *William Cooper Nell*, 47. Nell did not marry until age 53, and contrary to the clichéd association between wedlock and longevity, he died soon thereafter.

54. Wesley, "Integration versus Separatism," 214.

55. Ibid., 209–10.

56. Wesley and Uzelac, *William Cooper Nell*, 4.

57. But in 1866, Nell cosigned a petition complaining that Boston theaters were still excluding blacks. Wesley, "Integration Versus Separatism," 216–18.

58. Wesley and Uzelac, *William Cooper Nell*, 92.

59. Levine, *Martin Delany, Frederick Douglass, and the Politics of Representative Identity.*

60. Levine, *Martin R. Delany,* 3. Levine notes this precise wording may be apocryphal but that it accurately reflects the sentiment some of Delany's comrades felt toward what they took to be his excessive race pride.

61. Browne, "'To Defend Mr. Garrison,'" 415. See also Horton and Horton, "The Affirmation of Manhood."

62. Smith, "William Cooper Nell," 191.

63. Welke has argued that the gender logic of discriminatory treatment on common carriers was more successfully contested by black women than by black men, because they could more credibly appeal to their right to be treated like ladies. Welke, "When All the Women Were White, and All the Blacks Were Men."

64. Carby, *Race Men.*

65. Ross, *Manning the Race.*

66. Nell, *Services of Colored Americans in the Wars of 1776 and 1812,* 3–4.

67. Remond, *The Negroes & Anglo-Africans as Freedmen and Soldiers;* Nell, *Property Qualification or No Property Qualification.*

68. William Cooper Nell (Boston, April 15, 1845) to Wendell Phillips (London). Wendell Phillips Papers, Houghton Library, Harvard University. BMS Am 1953(924).

69. Ernest, *Liberation Historiography,* 135.

70. Nell, *The Colored Patriots of the American Revolution,* 18.

71. Badiou, *Being and Event,* 29.

72. "Faneuil Hall Commemorative Festival, March 5th, 1858. Protest against the Dred Scott "Decision." "Boston Massacre. March 5th, 1770." Broadside dated January 25, 1858. American Antiquarian Society.

73. Benjamin, "On the Concept of History," 391.

74. Wood, *Blind Memory,* 250, 251.

75. Kachun, *Festivals of Freedom;* White and White, *Stylin'.*

76. Higginbotham, *In the Matter of Color,* 371–89.

77. William Cooper Nell (Boston, August 21, 1839) to Wendell Phillips (London). Wendell Phillips Paper, Houghton Library, Harvard University. BMS Am 1953(924).

78. Easton, *To Heal the Scourge of Prejudice.*

79. "Boston Massacre, March 5th, 1770: The Day Which History Selects as the Dawn of the American Revolution. Commemorative Festival at Faneuil Hall, Friday, March 5, 1858. Protest against the Dred Scott Decision." March 5, 1858. American Antiquarian Society.

80. "Martyrdom of Crispus Attucks! March 5th, 1770, the Day Which History Selects as the Dawn of the American Revolution!" March 5, 1862. American Antiquarian Society.

81. "Crispus Attucks's Patriotic Leadership and Martyrdom, in State

Street, Boston, March 5, 1770—the Day Which History Selects as the Dawn of the American Revolution." March 5, 1864. American Antiquarian Society.

82. Reid-Pharr, *Conjugal Union*.

83. For a revisionist take on black radicalism, see Sinha, "Coming of Age."

84. Brooks, *Bodies in Dissent*, 83–102.

85. Wood, *Blind Memory*; Fisch, *American Slaves in Victorian England*; Blackett, *Building an Antislavery Wall*.

86. Messer-Kruse, *The Yankee International*.

87. Falk, "Black Abolitionist Doctors and Healers, 1810–1885."

88. Young, "The Political Economy of Black Abolitionists."

89. Kerr-Ritchie, "Rehearsal for War."

90. Moten, *In the Break*, 6.

91. Seshadri-Crooks, *Desiring Whiteness*, 31.

92. Ibid., 38.

2. In Night's Eye

1. Ruggles, *The "Extinguisher" Extinguished*, 45.

2. Ibid.

3. Ibid., 46.

4. For Rawls's account of the "veil of ignorance," see Rawls, *A Theory of Justice*.

5. In a letter to *The Colored American* (August 25, 1838), Ruggles complained of being "egregiously defrauded and lynched" en route to Providence, when the conductor forced him "into what they call the pauper (or jim crow car)" after Ruggles declined to bribe him. This is one of the earliest references I have found to a black activist referring to racial discrimination as "Jim Crow."

6. David Ruggles, "Caste among Quakers," *Mirror of Liberty*, August 1838, 8.

7. *The Mirror of Liberty*, January 1839, 34.

8. Lemire, *"Miscegenation."*

9. Richards, *Gentlemen of Property and Standing*, 16.

10. Ibid., 43.

11. Cohen, *Folk Devils and Moral Panics*.

12. Walters, "The Erotic South," and *The Antislavery Appeal*.

13. Richards, *Gentlemen of Property and Standing*, 45.

14. This pamphlet, signed "A Puritan," is usually credited to Ruggles's authorship. Ruggles published and sold and likely also wrote it, although it is also possible that George Bourne authored it. See Christie and Dumond, *George Bourne and The Book and Slavery Irreconcilable*.

15. [A Puritan], *The Abrogation of the Seventh Commandment, by the American Churches* (New York: David Ruggles, 1835), 5.

16. Volosinov, *Marxism and the Philosophy of Language,* 23.

17. Ibid. Hall, "For Allon White"; Stallybrass and White, *The Politics and Poetics of Transgression.*

18. Case, *Performing Science and the Virtual,* 23, 26.

19. In addition to the OED, see Lane, *An Arabic-English Lexicon,* 455; Wehr and Cowan, *A Dictionary of Modern Written Arabic,* 134. Devic confirms that "Ce mot nous est venu par les alchimistes avec le sens de mélange intime, combinaison, spécialment en ce qui regarde le mercure." Regarding a sexual metaphor, Devic's view is that "l'analogie est parfaite, car les alchimistes aiment à comparer la combinaison du mercure avec les métaux à l'union de l'époux avec l'épouse." Devic, *Dictionnaire etymologique des mots francais d'origine orientale: arabe, persan, turc, hebreu, malais,* 29–30. For a similar account of the word's use in Spanish, see Corominas and Pascual, *Diccionario crítico etimilógico castellano e hispánico,* 230–31.

20. See Stauffer, *The Black Hearts of Men.*

21. Hollinger, "Amalgamation and Hypodescent," 1387.

22. We see such a "racial frontier" posited elsewhere, for instance, in Stephens, *On Racial Frontiers.*

23. Kazanjian, *The Colonizing Trick,* 89–138.

24. Halttunen, *Confidence Men and Painted Women.*

25. Walker, *Moral Choices;* Abzug, *Cosmos Crumbling;* Boyer, *Urban Masses and Moral Order in America, 1820–1920.*

26. Nancy Reynolds Davison, "E. W. Clay: American Political Caricaturist" (PhD diss., University of Michigan, 1980), 90.

27. McAllister, *White People Do Not Know How to Behave,* 116–18.

28. Young, "The Subterranean World of Play [1971]."

29. Dart, "'Flash Style,'" 181.

30. Davison, "E. W. Clay," 85.

31. Lhamon, *Jump Jim Crow,* 22.

32. Anbinder, *Five Points,* 172.

33. Egan, *Life in London,* 227.

34. McAllister, *White People Do Not Know How to Behave,* 118.

35. Browning, *Infectious Rhythm.*

36. McAllister, *White People Do Not Know How to Behave,* 119.

37. Ibid., 118–19.

38. Elizabeth Claire, "Women, Waltzing and Warfare: The Social Choreography of Revolution at the End of the Long 18th Century" (PhD diss., New York University, 2004).

39. Katz, "The Egalitarian Waltz." Diana Williams (personal communication) points out the similarities between these images and those circulating around the quasi-mythic quadroon balls held in New Orleans (except that the latter exclusively represent white men with women of color). See Kmen, *Music in New Orleans.*

40. Foucault, *The History of Sexuality,* 126.

41. Ibid., 126–27.

42. Hinks, *To Awaken My Afflicted Brethren,* 178.

43. Kazanjian, *The Colonizing Trick,* 121.

44. Quoted in ibid., 116.

45. On colonization and emigration, see Kinshasa, *Emigration vs. Assimilation;* Miller, *The Search for a Black Nationality;* Fox, *The American Colonization Society, 1817–1840;* Smith, *The American Colonization Society and Emigration.*

46. Jefferson, *Notes on the State of Virginia,* 145.

47. Preston, *Young Frederick Douglass,* 13.

48. Erkkila, *Mixed Bloods and Other Crosses,* 212.

49. Stallybrass and White, *The Politics and Poetics of Transgression.* See also Bakhtin, *Rabelais and His World.*

50. The principle natural historical discourse of the *Notes,* as is well known, is devoted to defending the vitality of New World life forms against the imputations of Old World philosophes.

51. Sedgwick, *Touching, Feeling,* 38.

52. Ibid., 61.

53. Ferguson, *Aberrations in Black.*

54. It might be useful to distinguish my approach here from that of Judith Butler and others who have emphasized the use of injurious speech to constitute the subjects that are offended and thus interpolated by it. I am not seeking to develop an historical account of hate speech. The economy of affect I focus on here is not one in which a pre-established identity group insults another, thus founding a "wounded subjectivity." Butler, *Excitable Speech;* Brown, *States of Injury.*

55. I take this idea of black eavesdropping from Paul Gilroy, *The Black Atlantic,* 39.

56. Walker, *Walker's Appeal,* 17–18.

57. Ibid., 12.

58. Hartman, *Scenes of Subjection,* 115.

59. On violence in abolitionism, see McKivigan and Harrold, *Antislavery Violence.*

60. Stewart, *Productions of Mrs. Maria W. Stewart,* 69.

61. While Stauffer considers the awareness of the newspaper's black editor, Willis Hodges, of Brown's true identity evidence that Hodges "endorsed" Brown's "authentic" mask, my reading of the transformations of shame suggests a slightly different implication. Stauffer, *The Black Hearts of Men,* 122, 173.

62. Ibid., 173.

63. Villard, *John Brown,* 659–60.

64. Lhamon, *Jump Jim Crow*, 22–23.

65. Unknown, *The Kidnapped Clergyman, or Experience the Best Teacher* (Boston: Dow and Jackson, 1839), 21.

66. Ibid., 32–33.

67. Ibid., 53–54.

68. Ibid., 109.

69. See also Foreman, "'This Promiscuous Housekeeping.'"

70. Reid-Pharr, *Conjugal Union*, 73, 72.

71. Ibid., 79.

72. Ibid., 77.

73. Walker, *Appeal*, 10–11.

74. Stockton, *Beautiful Bottom, Beautiful Shame*, 24.

75. I was introduced to Sewally's story by Jonathan Ned Katz, *Love Stories*, 77–90. An earlier account was published in Gilfoyle, *City of Eros*, 136–37. Lacking knowledge of Sewally's preferred gender identity, I have opted to preserve the male gender identity ascribed by the courts and press, in order to highlight their sense of transgression.

76. Sewally returned to New York City, and to women's clothes, after doing his time upstate, and suffered repeated arrests in the 1840s and early 1850s. The *New York Daily Times*, May 16, 1853, reports an arrest in that year and notes prior time served at Rikers Island. He was often referred to as Beefsteak Pete in the news reports of these later arrests.

77. *New York World*, June 17, 1836.

78. O'Malley, "Specie and Species."

79. Chauncey, "Building Gay Neighborhood Enclaves."

80. Karen Haltunnen, "Humanitarianism and the Pornography of Pain in Anglo-American Culture."

3. Minstrel Trouble

1. Werbner and Modood, *Debating Cultural Hybridity*, 4.

2. Nell, *The Colored Patriots of the American Revolution*, 18. Variations of this phrase became a commonplace of Boston abolitionist rhetoric in the 1850s. Anson Burlingame, Theodore Parker, and Charles Remond Parker all used it in speeches.

3. Foner, *Free Soil, Free Labor, Free Men*.

4. Lincoln himself repeatedly disavowed any intention of ending slavery or fostering racial equality until the exigencies of war provided an opening for him to do so in the name of preserving the union. Lincoln's preference for conducting war under the sign of the national Thing rather than the cause of the slave itself bespeaks the circuitous causations of imagined community.

5. Stevens, *Anthony Burns*, 135–36.

6. Is it a further irony, or an indication that the cycle of reaccentuation never stops, that a black songwriter, James Bland, would compose a new version of the tune in 1878 and that it would then be adopted as the state song of Virginia? Hullfish, "James A. Bland."

7. Roach, *Cities of the Dead,* 239–281.

8. Sellers, *The Market Revolution.*

9. Lott, *Love and Theft,* 45.

10. Yates, *The Life and Correspondence of Charles Mathews,* 289–90.

11. Christgau, "In Search of Jim Crow."

12. Lott, *Love and Theft,* 106.

13. Browning, *Infectious Rhythm.*

14. The carnivalesque, to be clear, is not the same thing as carnival. And aside from the important exception of Louisiana and the Gulf Coast, carnival did not possess a place in a nation for which even the conventional theater could be morally suspect, and which during the postfamine, post-1848 years increasingly associated alcoholic revelry with the abominable customs of immigrant Irish Catholics and German Lutherans streaming in from the Old World, polluting the New Eden.

15. Lipsitz, *The Possessive Investment in Whiteness.*

16. Roediger, *The Wages of Whiteness,* 95.

17. *London Times,* June 10, 1851.

18. Here I am indebted to Smith-Rosenberg's pathbreaking work on Davy Crockett as American political trickster. See Carroll Smith-Rosenberg, *Disorderly Conduct.*

19. Lhamon, *Raising Cain,* 22–55.

20. "Love and theft" is at heart a showbiz phrase, as Brian Herrera notes (personal communication). "I love it . . . and I'll steal it!" The brilliance of this formulation reached an apotheosis when no less a figure than Bob Dylan chose it for the title of a new album, a move that ushered "love and theft" into an elite canon of American key phrases, enacting its principle in the process of reiterating its form. Brian Herrera, personal conversation.

21. Marx's break with Proudhon came with the publication of *The Poverty of Philosophy* in 1847.

22. Robinson, *An Anthropology of Marxism.*

23. Yellin, *Women and Sisters,* 122.

24. *Philadelphia Woman's Advocate,* as reprinted in the *Provincial Freeman* (Toronto), May 12, 1855. On Webb, see Clark, "Solo Black Performance before the Civil War"; Gardner, "Stowe Takes the Stage" and "'A Nobler End.'"

25. Gilmore, *The Genuine Article.*

26. Ibid., 39.

27. We are familiar with Quentin Tarantino's argument, made less palatable in the wake of Michael Richards's recent meltdown, that the word

"nigger" is simply part of the American vernacular. And the incendiary standup comics of the 1960s and 1970, from Lenny Bruce to Richard Pryor, all took their stand against the bourgeois standards of decency upheld by that recent defector from their ranks, Bill Cosby.

28. Agnew, *Worlds Apart.*

29. Blackett, *Building an Antislavery Wall,* 104.

30. Gaines, *Uplifting the Race,* 67–99.

31. Cockrell, *Demons of Disorder,* 141–42.

32. Lhamon, *Jump Jim Crow,* 21.

33. Bank, *Theatre Culture in America, 1825–1860,* 138.

34. An early guide to New York's brothels described itself as a "moral reform directory."

35. Welke, "When All the Women Were White" and *Recasting American Liberty.*

36. *Pacific Appeal,* May 24, 1862.

37. Ibid. Linking the political rights of men to the presence or absence of blackface became a commonplace rhetorical strategy, used by Douglass himself during an 1859 trip to England. The growing popularity of minstrelsy among the British public, he then claimed, had increased prejudice against black people.

38. Wallace, *Constructing the Black Masculine.*

39. *The Colored American,* March 6, 1841.

40. Ibid., December 9, 1837.

41. *Baltimore Sun,* November 18, 1837. Microfilm New York Public Library.

42. The *Sun* appended a note, "We have not attempted to give the precise words of Mr. C. The above, however, is the substance of his address, which created, as may be inferred, a manifest sensation." It is conceivable the speech was misreported or invented, but there is little internal evidence to suggest that this is a hoax. Rice, who performed in Baltimore for at least several more days, moving to the Front Street Theatre, never wrote in to rebut the claim.

43. Brooks, *Bodies in Dissent,* 4–6.

44. *North Star,* October 27, 1848.

45. O'Malley, "Specie and Species"; Gilmore, *The Genuine Article,* 42.

46. O'Malley, "Specie and Species," 370.

47. See, for example, *Frederick Douglass' Paper,* May 20, 1852. Popular generally among abolitionists, it became part of the antislavery songbook.

48. While I do not claim that Douglass anticipated Marx's critique of commodity fetishism, in inverting the conventional valence of blackness in the discourse of the period, he was exposing the contradiction the essentialisms of race and money entail for each other. While his 1848 statement was clearly animated by an outrage and contempt for what he saw in min-

strelsy, and while it clearly represented a kind of antithesis to the respectable masculinity he sought to achieve (whether that antithesis was presented as urban or rural, uncouth or overly sophisticated), his "strategic essentialism" in taking offense at the theft of blackness was clearly meant to register an ironical awareness of the richness of black fun. Money was articulated with manhood and could serve as a telos of self-making. But as an object and objective, it was never simple. As we saw in "Sambo's Mistakes," money could also be pursued for the sake of display and consumption, degrading the subject even as it enabled a new panoply of pleasures. This is what Douglass meant when he accused minstrels of pandering.

49. Blassingame, *The Frederick Douglass Papers,* 2: 345.

50. Meer, *Uncle Tom Mania,* 71.

51. *Frederick Douglass' Paper,* March 23, 1855.

52. Lott, *Love and Theft,* 78–79, 89.

53. To the contrary, when pushed, he could only resort to mealy-mouthed reiterations of "white republic" bromides.

54. Stauffer, *The Black Hearts of Men,* 45–56.

55. *London Times,* June 10, 1850.

56. Fisch, "'Exhibiting Uncle Tom in Some Shape or Other.'"

57. *London Times,* June 11, 1850.

58. "Prejudice Against Color," *North Star,* June 13, 1850. Reprinted in Foner, *The Life and Writings of Frederick Douglass,* 2: 128–29.

59. *London Times,* July 18, 1850. Reprinted in Foner, *The Life and Writings of Frederick Douglass,* 2: 131–32.

60. Douglas, "Speech Delivered at Bloomington, Ill., by Senator S.A. Douglas, July 16, 1858," 93.

61. Holzer, *The Lincoln-Douglas Debates,* 110.

62. Douglas, "Speech Delivered at Bloomington," 93–94.

63. "The Unholy Alliance of Negro Hate and Antislavery," *Frederick Douglass' Paper,* April 5, 1856. Reprinted in Foner, *The Life and Writings of Frederick Douglass,* 2: 387.

64. Lawrence Thomas Lesick, "The Lane Rebels: Evangelicalism and Antislavery in Antebellum America" (PhD diss., Vanderbilt University, 1979), 97.

65. Holzer, *The Lincoln-Douglas Debates,* 143, 144.

66. Bingham, *The Columbian Orator,* xiii–xxvii.

67. Douglass, *Autobiographies,* 41–42.

68. See Baepler, *White Slaves, African Masters.*

69. Bingham, *The Columbian Orator,* 88–103.

70. Scots and English, languages that share an origin in Anglo-Saxon, were nevertheless distinct languages in a complicated relationship of dominance in the nineteenth century. One scholar notes that in the era of Burns: "In effect the Age of Enlightenment and Philosophy and the beginnings of the Industrial Revolution were being superimposed on the old feudal and

rural culture of Scotland, and in speech terms this corresponds roughly to the functional demarcation line between English as the language of abstract and formal thought and Scots as the language of immediacy and intimacy at a lower intellectual pitch." Murison, "The Language of Burns," 67–68.

71. Pettinger, "Send Back the Money," 43, 44.

72. Muñoz, *Disidentifications,* 168.

73. Burns, *Burns: Poems and Songs,* 515.

74. Levine, *Martin Delany, Frederick Douglass, and the Politics of Representative Identity,* 11.

75. *North Star,* June 29, 1849.

4. Carnivalizing Time

1. Žižek, *The Parallax View.*

2. Baucom, *Specters of the Atlantic,* 27. Arrighi, *The Long Twentieth Century.*

3. Darby English, *How to See a Work of Art in Total Darkness.*

4. Foucault, "Nietzsche, Genealogy, History," 386.

5. Benjamin, "On the Concept of History," 389–400.

6. Betty B. Chandler, "Carrying the Cause of Unity across the South," *Valley Beautiful Beacon,* January 11, 2007.

7. According to one news report, Edgerton envisions his mission in comparable terms to the artist John Sims as one of "constantly teaching values and attempting to reunite our nation from a period in our history of so long ago." Abby Slutsky, "Thirty Protest Art Exhibit in G'burg," *Evening Sun,* September 3, 2004; Chandler, "Carrying the Cause of Unity across the South."

8. Actually, the Internet reveals a small industry of performers reenacting the famous life of Henry "Box" Brown. For more on who he was, see Brooks, *Bodies in Dissent,* 66–130; and Ruggles, *The Unboxing of Henry Brown.*

9. Stockton, *Beautiful Bottom, Beautiful Shame,* 180.

10. Ibid., 194.

11. Gill, *The Cambridge Companion to Wordsworth,* 109.

12. Harper, "Controversy Disrupts Gettysburg Exhibition." The artist's film in progress documents the controversy detailed below as well as other exhibits and events related to the project. The full scope of his multimedia activities are publicized at http://www.johnsimsprojects.com. Widely referred to as "the Confederate Flag," the Battle Flag was not in fact the official flag of the Confederate States of America, which was the much less well known "Stars and Bars." See Coski, *The Confederate Battle Flag.*

13. Wills, *Lincoln at Gettysburg.*

14. Connerton, *How Societies Remember.*

15. Brooklyn-based musician Marc Anthony Thompson, aka Chocolate Genius, Inc., employed a version of the recolored Battle Flag for the cover of his *Black Yankee Rock* LP (2005).

16. See, for example, the skeptical popular history, Bennett, *Forced into Glory*. Recently, some white commentators have begun to take into account the contradictions of Lincoln's racial attitudes and political actions as well; for example, Michael Lind, *What Lincoln Believed*.

17. Roach, "The Great Hole of History"; Brown-Guillory, "Reconfiguring History"; Elam and Rayner, "Echoes from the Black (W)Hole."

18. "And if one wants to call this inscription in naked flesh 'writing,'" they continue, "then it must be said that speech in fact presupposes writing." Deleuze and Guattari, *Anti-Oedipus*, 145.

19. Hungerford, "Memorizing Memory."

20. "Gettysburg College to Move Controversial Exhibit Indoors; Artist Threats to Quit," Associated Press, August 31, 2004.

21. English, *How to See a Work of Art*.

22. Sims, Hulser, and Copeland, *Legacies*.

23. Berger, *Fred Wilson*.

24. Corrin, *Mining the Museum*, 11.

25. Boime, *The Art of Exclusion*.

26. Nyong'o, "Racial Kitsch and Black Performance."

27. A third exhibit, *New York Divided*, followed, which reverted to a more traditional if still exemplary mode of historical display.

28. Benjamin, *Selected Writings*, 208.

29. For more on the racial affinities of phantasmagoria, see Brooks, *Bodies in Dissent*, 14–65.

30. Ibid., 15.

31. See also Yellin, *Harriet Jacobs*.

32. Noam Cohen, "In Douglass Tribute, Slave Folklore and Fact Collide," *New York Times*, January 23, 2007.

33. Derrida, *Archive Fever*, 17–18.

34. A cottage industry of books and television specials have taken up the claims of *The Da Vinci Code*, the most illuminating of which was a special on the History Channel in which the announcer's script rebutted every purported art historical discovery made by the novel, while the "historical re-enactments" that accompanied that script acted out those self-same hoaxes. As it so often does, the History Channel had its cake and ate it, professing a pious adherence to the historical method with a wink and a nod, all the while infusing its visuals with the *desired* past without which it would have no viewers.

35. Benjamin, *Selected Writings*, 405.

36. Ernest, *Liberation Historiography*, 4.

37. Ibid., 9, 37.

38. Bay, *The White Image in the Black Mind,* 77.

39. Nell, *Services of Colored Americans,* 7.

40. Brown, *The Black Man, His Antecedents,* 110.

41. City Council, Boston, *A Memorial of Crispus Attucks,* 94–95.

42. Foner, *The Life and Writings of Frederick Douglass,* 2:192. Further citations in text. Quoted in Martin, *The Mind of Frederick Douglass,* 24.

43. Communipaw [James McCune Smith], "From Our New York Correspondent," *Frederick Douglass' Paper,* February 16, 1855.

44. Calloway-Thomas, "William G. Allen," 332.

45. While an obvious parallel suggests itself to Henry Louis Gates's concept of "signifyin(g)," the black use of sarcasm does not appear to draw particularly on the vernacular tradition and can even, as in the responses to minstrelsy I considered in chapter 3, rudely interrupt and contest the reduction of black expressivity to vernacular or oral forms. More importantly, if signifyin(g) works best as a weapon of the weak that passes barely detected in the hidden transcripts of power, then it actually fits poorly as a model onto overt acts of black sarcasm, whose meanings are explicitly aggressive and confrontational. If anything, sarcasm in the mode Smith and Allen valorize bespeaks an elite more than a popular lineage, a point Haiman alludes to in identifying a difference between sarcasm and suppositiously plain or common modes of speech (even as he calls attention to the growing omnipresence of the sarcastive that is making plain speech an increasing oddity). Identifying sarcasm with rhetoric reflects this tension between ordinary and practiced language and affords a concrete view of how the social location of sarcasm might differ from that of signifyin(g). Its use was valorized in relation to the select public contexts in which individual black men and women were afforded an opportunity to chastise all white people within earshot, to imagine themselves pouring rebuke in the nation's ear, not the everyday micropolitics of resistance that are (deservedly) celebrated in the signifyin(g) literature.

46. Haiman, *Talk Is Cheap,* 28, 10.

47. Stowe, *Uncle Tom's Cabin,* 3.

48. Delany, *Blake,* 67.

49. Du Bois, *The Souls of Black Folk,* 3.

50. Benjamin, "On the Concept of History," 395.

51. English, *How to See a Work of Art,* 44, 45.

52. Ibid., 57, 47.

53. The anticolonial uses of Fanon, of course, require an altogether different argumentative path than that taken here.

54. Benjamin, "On the Concept of History," 394.

55. Edelman, *No Future.*

56. Littler and Naidoo, *The Politics of Heritage,* 85.

Conclusion

1. Washington-Williams and Stadiem, *Dear Senator,* 36–37.

2. Brown, "The Miscegenation of Richard Mentor Johnson."

3. In what follows, I refer to the fictional characters in Bradshaw's play by their first names and the real-life figures on which they are based by their last names.

4. Thomas Bradshaw, *"Strom Thurmond Is Not a Racist" and "Cleansed,"* 17–18.

5. Ibid., 39.

6. Romano, *Race Mixing,* 287.

7. Moran, *Interracial Intimacy,* 116.

8. Berlant, *The Queen of America Goes to Washington City;* Edelman, *No Future.* Other queer theorists have contested Edelman's account in particular, in terms of the racial politics it elides. See, for example, Muñoz, "Cruising the Toilet."

9. On romantic racialism, see Fredrickson, *The Black Image in the White Mind.*

10. As reprinted in *Douglass' Monthly,* December 1860. I have slightly reordered the quote for emphasis, as indicated by my ellipsis, but otherwise preserved the language verbatim.

11. Ibid.

12. Ibid.

13. Elam, *Mixed Race in the New Millennium;* Paulin, "Representing Forbidden Desire" and "Acting out Miscegenation"; Sexton, "The Consequences of Race Mixture" and "There Is No Interracial Sexual Relationship"; Pabst, "Blackness/Mixedness"; Ifekwunigwe, *Scattered Belongings;* Zack, *Race and Mixed Race;* Brody, *Impossible Purities;* Streeter, "Ambiguous Bodies."

14. Seshadri-Crooks, *Desiring Whiteness,* 20.

15. See Gordon, "Race, Biraciality, and Mixed Race"; and Spencer, *The New Colored People.* See also Nyong'o, "No Halvsies!"

16. Cited in Bloch, *Miscegenation, Melaleukation, and Mr. Lincoln's Dog,* 10.

17. I am on this point in agreement with the arguments made in Romano, *Race Mixing,* and Moran, *Interracial Intimacy.*

18. And as if in counterpoint, blackathlete.com complains bitterly of Tiger Woods's "anti-Black persona" and the irony of his frequent evocation of his late father, a "pure African American" we are assured, when Woods himself so insistently distances himself from black people, not least in—what else?—his interracial marriage. Both Web sites accessed August 8, 2006.

19. My thinking on the future of the mixed-race has been shaped by Gubar, *Racechanges,* 203–39.

20. Coontz, *The Way We Never Were*; Duggan, *The Twilight of Equality?*

21. Halberstam, *In a Queer Time & Place.*

22. Sedgwick, *Touching, Feeling*, 72.

23. Obama, *Dreams from My Father*, xv.

24. Lacan, *Ecrits*, 309–11.

25. The translation of Plato's *Symposium* I prefer is Shelley's, begun in 1818 and rarely published since. A modern edition is Plato, *The Banquet.*

26. Ibid., 85. "Divine images" is Shelley's translation of the Greek word *agalma.* Bruce Fink's translation of Lacan's French rendering is "inestimable treasure." Lacan, *Ecrits*, 309.

27. Plato, *The Banquet*, 79–93.

Bibliography

Abzug, Robert H. *Cosmos Crumbling: American Reform and the Religious Imagination.* New York: Oxford University Press, 1994.

Agamben, Giorgio. *The Coming Community.* Minneapolis: University of Minnesota Press, 1993.

———. *Homo Sacer: Sovereign Power and Bare Life.* Stanford, Calif.: Stanford University Press, 1998.

———. *State of Exception.* Chicago: University of Chicago Press, 2005.

Agnew, Jean-Christophe. *Worlds Apart: The Market and the Theater in Anglo-American Thought, 1550–1750.* Cambridge: Cambridge University Press, 1986.

Allen, Theodore W. *The Invention of the White Race: Racial Oppression and Social Control.* Vol. One. London: Verso, 1994.

Anbinder, Tyler. *Five Points: The 19th-Century New York City Neighborhood That Invented Tap Dance, Stole Elections, and Became the World's Most Notorious Slum.* New York: Free Press, 2001.

Anderson, Benedict. *Imagined Communities: Reflections on the Origin and Spread of Nationalism.* Revised ed. London: Verso, 1991.

Arnold, Ken. *Doctor Death: Medicine at the End of Life; An Exhibition at the Wellcome Institute for the History of Medicine.* London: Wellcome Trust, 1997.

Arrighi, Giovanni. *The Long Twentieth Century.* London: Verso, 1994.

Austin, J. L. *How to Do Things with Words.* Cambridge, Mass.: Harvard University Press, 1997.

Badiou, Alain. *Being and Event.* London: Continuum, 2005.

Baepler, Paul, ed. *White Slaves, African Masters: An Anthology of American Barbary Captivity Narratives.* Chicago: University of Chicago Press, 1999.

Bakhtin, Mikhail. *The Dialogic Imagination.* Translated by Caryl Emerson and Michael Holquist. Edited by Michael Holquist. Austin: University of Texas Press, 1981.

———. *Rabelais and His World.* Bloomington: Indiana University Press, 1984.

Bank, Rosemarie K. *Theatre Culture in America, 1825–1860.* Cambridge: Cambridge University Press, 1997.

Baucom, Ian. *Specters of the Atlantic: Finance Capital, Slavery, and the Philosophy of History.* Durham, N.C.: Duke University Press, 2005.

Bay, Mia. *The White Image in the Black Mind: African-American Ideas about White People, 1830–1925.* New York: Oxford University Press, 2000.

Bill Belton. "The Indian Heritage of Crispus Attucks." *Negro History Bulletin,* no. 35 (1972): 149–52.

Benjamin, Walter. "On the Concept of History." In *Walter Benjamin: Selected Writings,* vol. 4, *1938–1940,* edited by Howard Eiland and Michael W. Jennings, 389–400. Cambridge, Mass.: Harvard University Press, 2003.

Bennett, Lerone. *Forced into Glory: Abraham Lincoln's White Dream.* Chicago: Johnson, 2000.

Berger, Maurice, ed. *Fred Wilson: Objects and Installations, 1979–2000.* Baltimore: University of Maryland Baltimore County, 2001.

Berlant, Lauren. *The Queen of America Goes to Washington City: Essays on Sex and Citizenship.* Durham, N.C.: Duke University Press, 1997.

Berlin, Ira. *Many Thousands Gone: The First Two Centuries of Slavery in North America.* Cambridge, Mass.: Harvard University Press, 1998.

———. "Time, Space, and the Evolution of Afro-American Society on British Mainland North America." *American Historical Review* 85, no. 1 (1980): 44–78.

Bhabha, Homi. *The Location of Culture.* Routledge Classics ed. London: Routledge, 2005.

Bingham, Caleb. *The Columbian Orator.* Edited by David W. Blight. New York: New York University Press, 1998.

Blackett, R. J. M. *Building an Antislavery Wall: Black Americans in the Atlantic Abolitionist Movement, 1830–1860.* Baton Rouge: Louisiana State University Press, 1983.

Blassingame, John W., ed. *The Frederick Douglass Papers,* Vol. 2, 1847–1854. Series One: Speeches, Debates and Interviews. New Haven: Yale University Press, 1982.

Bloch, J. M. *Miscegenation, Melaleukation, and Mr. Lincoln's Dog.* New York: Schaum, 1958.

Boime, Albert. *The Art of Exclusion: Representing Blacks in the Nineteenth Century.* Washington: Smithsonian Institution Press, 1990.

Bolokitten, Oliver. *A Sojourn in the City of Amalgamation: In the Year of Our Lord 19—*. New York: Bolokitten, 1835.

Boyer, Paul S. *Urban Masses and Moral Order in America, 1820–1920.* Cambridge, Mass.: Harvard University Press, 1978.

Bradshaw, Thomas. *"Strom Thurmond Is Not a Racist" and "Cleansed."* New York: Samuel French, 2007.

Brigham, Clarence. *Paul Revere's Engravings.* New York: Atheneum, 1969.

Brody, Jennifer DeVere. *Impossible Purities: Blackness, Femininity and Victorian Culture.* Durham, N.C.: Duke University Press, 1998.

———. "Memory's Movements: Minstrelsy, Miscegenation, and American Race Studies." *American Literary History* 11, no. 4 (1999): 744.

Brooks, Daphne. *Bodies in Dissent: Spectacular Performances of Race and Freedom, 1850–1910.* Durham, N.C.: Duke University Press, 2006.

Brown, Thomas. "The Miscegenation of Richard Mentor Johnson as an Issue in the National Election Campaign of 1835–1836." *Civil War History* 39, no. 1 (1993): 5–30.

Brown, Wendy. *States of Injury: Power and Freedom in Late Modernity.* Princeton, N.J.: Princeton University Press, 1995.

Brown, William Wells. *The Black Man, His Antecedents, His Genius, and His Achievements,* 2nd, rev. and enl. edition. New York: T. Hamilton, 1863.

Brown-Guillory, Elizabeth. "Reconfiguring History: Migration, Memory, and (Re) Membering in Suzan-Lori Parks's Plays." In *Southern Women Playwrights: New Essays in Literary History and Criticism,* edited by Robert L. McDonald and Linda Rohrer Paige, 183–97. Tuscaloosa: University of Alabama Press, 2002.

Browne, Patrick T. J. " 'To Defend Mr. Garrison': William Cooper Nell and the Personal Politics of Antislavery." *New England Quarterly* 70, no. 3 (1997): 415–42.

Browne, Stephen H. "Remembering Crispus Attucks: Race, Rhetoric, and the Politics of Commemoration." *Quarterly Journal of Speech* 85, no. 2 (1999): 169–87.

Browning, Barbara. *Infectious Rhythm: Metaphors of Contagion and the Spread of African Culture.* New York: Routledge, 1998.

Burns, Robert. *Burns: Poems and Songs.* Edited by James Kinsley. London: Oxford University Press, 1969.

Butler, Judith. *Excitable Speech: A Politics of the Performative.* New York: Routledge, 1997.

Calloway-Thomas, Carolyn. "William G. Allen: On 'Orators and Oratory.' " *Journal of Black Studies* 18, no. 3 (1988): 313–36.

Carby, Hazel V. *Race Men.* Cambridge, Mass.: Harvard University Press, 1998.

Case, Sue-Ellen. *Performing Science and the Virtual*. New York: Routledge, 2006.

Chauncey, George. "Building Gay Neighborhood Enclaves: The Village and Harlem." In *Gay New York: Gender, Urban Culture, and the Making of the Gay Male World, 1890–1940*. New York: Basic Books, 1994.

Christgau, Robert. "In Search of Jim Crow: Why Postmodern Minstrelsy Studies Matter." *Believer,* February 2004.

Christie, John W., and Dwight Lowell Dumond. *George Bourne and The Book and Slavery Irreconcilable*. Wilmington: Historical Society of Delaware, 1969.

City Council, Boston. *A Memorial of Crispus Attucks, Samuel Maverick, James Caldwell, Samuel Gray and Patrick Carr from the City of Boston*. Boston, 1889. Reprint, Miami, Fla.: Mnemosyne, 1969.

Clark, Susan F. "Solo Black Performance before the Civil War: Mrs. Stowe, Mrs. Webb, and 'The Christian Slave.'" *New Theatre Quarterly* 13, no. 52 (1997): 339–48.

Cockrell, Dale. *Demons of Disorder: Early Blackface Minstrels and Their World*. Cambridge: Cambridge University Press, 1997.

Cohen, Stanley. *Folk Devils and Moral Panics: The Creation of the Mods and Rockers*. 3rd ed. London: Routledge, 2002.

Connerton, Paul. *How Societies Remember*. Cambridge: Cambridge University Press, 1989.

Coontz, Stephanie. *The Way We Never Were: American Families and the Nostalgia Trap*. New York: Basic Books, 1992.

Corominas, Joan, and José A. Pascual, eds. *Diccionario crítico etimilógico castellano e hispánico*. Madrid: Editorial Gredos, 1980.

Corrin, Lisa G, ed. *Mining the Museum: An Installation by Fred Wilson*. New York: New Press, 1994.

Coski, John M. *The Confederate Battle Flag: America's Most Embattled Emblem*. Cambridge, Mass.: Harvard University Press, 2005.

Cott, Nancy F. *Public Vows: A History of Marriage and the Nation*. Cambridge, Mass: Harvard University Press, 2000.

Croly, David Goodman, and George Wakeman. *Miscegenation: The Theory of the Blending of the Races, Applied to the American White Man and Negro*. New York: H. Dexter, Hamilton & Co., 1864.

Dain, Bruce. *A Hideous Monster of the Mind: American Race Theory in the Early Republic*. Cambridge, Mass.: Harvard University Press, 2003.

Dart, Gregory. "'Flash Style': Pierce Egan and Literary London, 1820–28." *History Workshop Journal,* no. 51 (2001): 180–205.

Debord, Guy. *The Society of the Spectacle*. Translated by Ken Knabb. London: Rebel Press, 2006.

Delany, Martin Robinson. *Blake, or The Huts of America, a Novel*. Boston: Beacon, 1970.

Deleuze, Gilles, and Félix Guattari. *Anti-Oedipus: Capitalism and Schizo-phrenia.* Translated by Robert Hurley, Mark Seem, and Helen R. Lane. Minneapolis: University of Minnesota Press, 1983.

Dening, Greg. *Performances.* Melbourne: Melbourne University Press, 1996.

Derrida, Jacques. *Archive Fever: A Freudian Impression.* Translated by Eric Prenowitz. Chicago: University of Chicago Press, 1996.

———. *Limited Inc.* Evanston, Ill.: Northwestern University Press, 1988.

Devic, L. Marcel. *Dictionnaire etymologique des mots francais d'origine orientale: Arabe, persan, turc, hebreu, malais.* Paris: Imprimerie Nationale, 1876.

Dinshaw, Carolyn, Lee Edelman, Roderick A. Ferguson, Carla Freccero, Elizabeth Freeman, Judith Halberstam, Annamarie Jagose, Christopher Nealon, and Nguyen Tan Hoang. "Theorizing Queer Temporalities: A Roundtable Discussion," *GLQ: A Journal of Lesbian and Gay Studies* 13, no. 2–3 (2007): 177–95.

Douglas, Stephen. "Speech Delivered at Bloomington, Ill., by Senator S. A. Douglas, July 16, 1858." In *The Complete Works of Abraham Lincoln,* edited by John G. Nicolay and John Hay. New York: Tandy, 1894.

Douglass, Frederick. *Autobiographies.* New York: Library of America, 1994.

Du Bois, W. E. B. *The Souls of Black Folk: Essays and Sketches.* Chicago: McClurgt, 1903.

Duggan, Lisa. *The Twilight of Equality? Neoliberalism, Cultural Politics, and the Attack on Democracy.* New York: Beacon Press, 2003.

Easton, Hosea. *To Heal the Scourge of Prejudice: The Life and Writings of Hosea Easton.* Edited by George R. Price and James Brewer Stewart. Amherst: University of Massachusetts Press, 1999.

Edelman, Lee. *No Future: Queer Theory and the Death Drive.* Durham, N.C.: Duke University Press, 2004.

Egan, Pierce. *Life in London, or The Day and Night Scenes of Jerry Hawthorn, Esq. and His Elegant Friend Corinthian Tom, Accompanied by Bob Logic, the Oxonian, in Their Rambles and Sprees through the Metropolis.* London: Sherwood, 1821. Reprint, New York: Appleton, 1904.

Elam, Harry, and Alice Rayner. "Echoes from the Black (W)Hole: An Examination of the America Play by Suzan-Lori Parks." In *Performing America: Cultural Nationalism in American Theater,* edited by Jeffrey D. Mason and J. Ellen Gainor, 178–92. Ann Arbor: University of Michigan Press, 1999.

Elam, Michele. *Mixed Race in the New Millennium.* Stanford, Calif.: Stanford University Press, forthcoming.

English, Darby. *How to See a Work of Art in Total Darkness.* Cambridge, Mass.: MIT Press, 2007.

Erkkila, Betsy. *Mixed Bloods and Other Crosses: Rethinking American Literature from the Revolution to the Culture Wars.* Philadelphia: University of Pennsylvania Press, 2004.

Ernest, John. *Liberation Historiography: African American Writers and the Challenge of History, 1794–1861.* Chapel Hill: University of North Carolina Press, 2004.

Falk, Leslie A. "Black Abolitionist Doctors and Healers, 1810–1885." *Bulletin of the History of Medicine* 54, no. 2 (1980): 258–72.

Fanon, Frantz. *Black Skin, White Masks.* Translated by Charles Markmann. New York: Grove, 1967.

Felman, Shoshana. *The Scandal of the Speaking Body: Don Juan with J. L. Austin, or Seduction in Two Languages.* Stanford, Calif.: Stanford University Press, 2003.

Ferguson, Roderick A. *Aberrations in Black: Toward a Queer of Color Critique.* Minneapolis: University of Minnesota Press, 2004.

Fields, Barbara J. "Of Rogues and Geldings." *American Historical Review* 108, no. 5 (2003): 1397–1405.

Fisch, Audrey A. *American Slaves in Victorian England: Abolitionist Politics in Popular Literature and Culture.* Cambridge: Cambridge University Press, 2000.

———. "'Exhibiting Uncle Tom in Some Shape or Other': The Commodification and Reception of *Uncle Tom's Cabin* in England." *Nineteenth-Century Contexts* 17, no. 2 (1993): 145–58.

Fliegelman, Jay. *Declaring Independence: Jefferson, Natural Language and the Culture of Performance.* Stanford, Calif.: Stanford University Press, 1993.

Foner, Eric. *Free Soil, Free Labor, Free Men: The Ideology of the Republican Party before the Civil War.* Oxford: Oxford University Press, 1995.

Foner, Philip S., ed. *The Life and Writings of Frederick Douglass.* 5 vols. New York: International, 1950, 1971.

Foreman, P. Gabrielle. "'This Promiscuous Housekeeping'": Death, Transgression, and Homoeroticism in *Uncle Tom's Cabin.*" *Representations,* no. 43 (1993): 51–72.

Foucault, Michel. *The History of Sexuality,* Vol. One, *An Introduction.* Translated by Robert Hurley. New York: Vintage, 1978.

———. "Nietzsche, Genealogy, History." In *Aesthetics, Method, and Epistemology: Essential Works of Foucault, 1954–1984,* edited by Paul Rabinow, 369–91. New York: New Press, 1998.

———. *The Order of Things: An Archaeology of the Human Sciences.* New York: Vintage, 1970.

Fox, Early Lee. *The American Colonization Society, 1817–1840.* Baltimore: Johns Hopkins Press, 1919.

Fredrickson, George M. *The Black Image in the White Mind: The Debate* on *Afro-American Character and Destiny, 1817–1914*. New York: Harper & Row, 1972.

Freeman, Elizabeth. "Time Binds, or Erotohistoriography." *Social Text*, no. 84/85 (2005): 57–68.

———. *The Wedding Complex: Forms of Belonging in Modern American Culture*. Durham, N.C.: Duke University Press, 2002.

Freud, Sigmund. *Inhibitions, Symptoms and Anxiety*. New York: Norton, 1997.

Gaines, Kevin. *Uplifting the Race: Black Leadership, Politics and Culture in the Twentieth Century*. Chapel Hill: University of North Carolina Press, 1996.

Gardner, Eric. "Stowe Takes the Stage: Harriet Beecher Stowe's the Christian Slave." *Legacy: A Journal of American Women Writers* 15, no. 1 (1998): 78–84.

———. "'A Nobler End': Mary Webb and the Victorian Platform." *Nineteenth-Century Prose* 29, no. 1 (2002): 103–16.

Garnet, Henry Highland. *The Past and the Present Condition, and the Destiny, of the Colored Race a Discourse Delivered at the 15th Anniversary of the Female Benevolent Society of Troy, Feb. 14, 1848*. Troy, 1848.

Gilfoyle, Timothy J. *City of Eros: New York City, Prostitution, and the Commercialization of Sex, 1820–1920*. New York: Norton, 1992.

Gill, Stephen Charles, ed., *The Cambridge Companion to Wordsworth*. Cambridge: Cambridge University Press, 2003.

Gilmore, Paul. *The Genuine Article: Race, Mass Culture, and American Literary Manhood*. Durham, N.C.: Duke University Press, 2001.

Gilroy, Paul. *Between Camps: Nations, Cultures, and the Allure of Race*. London: Routledge, 2004.

———. *The Black Atlantic: Modernity and Double Consciousness*. Cambridge, Mass.: Harvard University Press, 1993.

———. *Postcolonial Melancholia*. New York: Columbia University Press, 2005.

Goldsby, Jacqueline. *A Spectacular Secret: Lynching in American Life and Literature*. Chicago: University of Chicago Press, 2006.

Gordon, Lewis R. "Race, Biraciality, and Mixed Race." In *"Mixed Race" Studies: A Reader*, edited by Jayne O. Ifekwunigwe, 158–65. New York: Routledge, 2004.

Gubar, Susan. *Racechanges: White Skin, Black Face in American Culture*. New York: Oxford University Press, 1997.

Haiman, John. *Talk Is Cheap: Sarcasm, Alienation, and the Evolution of Language*. New York: Oxford University Press, 1998.

Halberstam, Judith. *In a Queer Time & Place: Transgender Bodies, Subcultural Lives*. New York: New York University Press, 2005.

Halbwachs, Maurice. *On Collective Memory.* Translated by Lewis A. Coser. Chicago: University of Chicago Press, 1992.

Hall, Stuart. "For Allon White: Metaphors of Transformation." In *Stuart Hall: Critical Dialogues in Cultural Studies,* edited by David Morley and Kuan-Hsing Chen, 287–305. New York: Routledge, 1996.

———. "Whose Heritage? Un-Settling 'the Heritage,' Re-Imagining the Post-Nation." In *The Politics of Heritage: The Legacies of "Race,"* edited by Jo Littler and Roshi Naidoo, 23–35. London: Routledge, 2005.

Halttunen, Karen. *Confidence Men and Painted Women: A Study of Middle-Class Culture in America, 1830–1870.* New Haven, Conn.: Yale University Press, 1982.

———. "Humanitarianism and the Pornography of Pain in Anglo-American Culture." *American Historical Review* 100, no. 2 (1995): 303–34.

Hannaford, Ivan. *Race: The History of an Idea in the West.* Washington, D.C.: Woodrow Wilson Press, 1996.

Hardt, Michael, and Antonio Negri. *Empire.* Cambridge, Mass.: Harvard University Press, 2000.

Harper, Glenn. "Controversy Disrupts Gettysburg Exhibition." *Sculpture* 23, no. 9 (2004).

Harris, Leslie M. "From Abolitionist Amalgamation to 'Rulers of the Five Points': The Discourse of Interracial Sex and Reform in Antebellum New York City." In *Sex, Love, Race: Crossing Boundaries in North American History,* edited by Martha Hodes, 191–212. New York: New York University Press, 1999.

Hartman, Saidiya V. *Scenes of Subjection: Terror, Slavery, and Self-Making in Nineteenth-Century America.* New York: Oxford University Press, 1997.

Higginbotham, A. Leon. *In the Matter of Color: Race and the American Legal Process: The Colonial Period.* New York: Oxford University Press, 1978.

Hinks, Peter P. *To Awaken My Afflicted Brethren: David Walker and the Problem of Antebellum Slave Resistance.* University Park: Pennsylvania State University Press, 1997.

Holgate, Jerome B. *American Genealogy, Being a History of Some of the Early Settlers of North America and Their Descendants, from Their First Emigration to the Present Time.* Albany, N.Y., 1848.

Hollinger, David. "Amalgamation and Hypodescent: The Question of Ethnoracial Mixture in the History of the United States." *American Historical Review* 108, no. 5 (2003): 1363–90.

Holzer, Harold, ed. *The Lincoln-Douglas Debates: The First Complete, Unexpurgated Text.* New York: HarperCollins, 1993.

Horowitz, Helen Lefkowitz. *Rereading Sex: Battles over Sexual Knowl-*

edge and Suppression in Nineteenth-Century America. New York: Knopf, 2002.

Horsman, Reginald. *Race and Manifest Destiny: The Origins of American Racial Anglo-Saxonism*. Cambridge, Mass.: Harvard University Press, 1981.

Horton, James Oliver, and Lois E. Horton. "The Affirmation of Manhood: Black Garrisonians in Antebellum Boston." In *Courage and Conscience: Black & White Abolitionists in Boston*, edited by Donald M. Jacobs, 127–53. Bloomington: Indiana University Press, 1993.

Huddart, David. *Homi K. Bhabha*. Routledge Critical Thinkers. London: Routledge, 2005.

Hullfish, W. R. "James A. Bland: Pioneer Black Songwriter." *Black Music Research Journal* 7 (1987): 1–33.

Hungerford, Amy. "Memorizing Memory." *Yale Journal of Criticism* 14, no. 1 (2001): 67–92.

Ifekwunigwe, Jayne O. *Scattered Belongings: Cultural Paradoxes of "Race," Nation and Gender*. London: Routledge, 1999.

Jackson, Shannon. *Lines of Activity: Performance, Historiography, Hull-House Domesticity*. Ann Arbor: University of Michigan Press, 2000.

Jameson, Fredric. *The Political Unconscious: Narrative as a Socially Symbolic Act*. Ithaca, N.Y.: Cornell University Press, 1981.

Jefferson, Thomas. *Notes on the State of Virginia, 1785*. Reprint, New York: Penguin, 1999.

Jordan, Winthrop. *White over Black: American Attitudes toward the Negro, 1550–1812*. Baltimore: Penguin Books, 1969.

Kachun, Mitchell. *Festivals of Freedom: Memory and Meaning in African American Emancipation Celebrations, 1808–1915*. Amherst: University of Massachusetts Press, 2003.

Kaplan, Sidney. "The Miscegenation Issue in the Election of 1864." *Journal of Negro History* 34, no. 3 (1949): 274–343.

Katz, Jonathan Ned. *Love Stories: Sex between Men before Homosexuality*. Chicago: University of Chicago Press, 2001.

Katz, Ruth. "The Egalitarian Waltz." *Comparative Studies in Society and History* 15, no. 3 (1973): 368–77.

Kawash, Samira. *Dislocating the Color Line: Identity, Hybridity, and Singularity in African-American Narrative*. Stanford, Calif.: Stanford University Press, 1997.

Kazanjian, David. *The Colonizing Trick: National Culture and Imperial Citizenship in Early America*. Minneapolis: University of Minnesota Press, 2003.

Kerber, Linda K. "Abolitionists and Amalgamators: The New York City Race Riots of 1834." *New York History* 48, no. 1 (1967): 28–39.

Kerr-Ritchie, Jeffrey. "Rehearsal for War: Black Militias in the Atlantic World." *Slavery and Abolition* 26, no. 1 (2005): 1–34.

Kinney, Arthur F. *Go Down, Moses: The Miscegenation of Time.* New York: Twayne, 1996.

Kinshasa, Kwando M. *Emigration vs. Assimilation: The Debate in the African American Press, 1827–1861.* Jefferson, N.C.: McFarland, 1988.

Kmen, Henry A. *Music in New Orleans: The Formative Years, 1791–1841.* Baton Rouge: Louisiana State University Press, 1966.

Lacan, Jacques. *Ecrits: A Selection.* Translated by Bruce Fink. New York: Norton, 2002.

Lacey, Barbara E. "Visual Images of Blacks in Early American Imprints." *William and Mary Quarterly* 53, no. 1 (1996): 137–80.

Lane, Edward William. *An Arabic-English Lexicon, Derived from the Best and the Most Copious Eastern Sources.* London: Williams and Norgate, 1863, 455.

Leach, William. *True Love and Perfect Union: The Feminist Reform of Sex and Society.* New York: Basic Books, 1980.

Lemire, Elise Virginia. *"Miscegenation": Making Race in America.* Philadelphia: University of Pennsylvania Press, 2002.

Levine, Robert S. *Martin Delany, Frederick Douglass, and the Politics of Representative Identity.* Chapel Hill: University of North Carolina Press, 1997.

———, ed. *Martin R. Delany: A Documentary Reader.* Chapel Hill: University of North Carolina Press, 2003.

Lewis, David Levering. *W. E. B. Du Bois: Biography of a Race, 1868–1909.* New York: Holt, 1993.

Lewis, Robert Benjamin. *Light and Truth: Collected from the Bible and Ancient and Modern History, Containing the Universal History of the Colored and the Indian Race, from the Creation of the World to the Present Time.* Boston: Committee of Colored Gentlemen, 1844.

Lhamon, W. T. *Jump Jim Crow: Lost Plays, Lyrics, and Street Prose of the First Atlantic Popular Culture.* Cambridge, Mass.: Harvard University Press, 2003.

———. *Raising Cain: Blackface Performance from Jim Crow to Hip Hop.* Cambridge: Harvard University Press, 1998.

Lind, Michael. *What Lincoln Believed: The Values and Convictions of America's Greatest President.* New York: Doubleday, 2005.

Linebaugh, Peter, and Marcus Rediker. *The Many-Headed Hydra: Sailors, Slaves, Commoners, and the Hidden History of the Revolutionary Atlantic.* Boston: Beacon, 2000.

Lipsitz, George. *The Possessive Investment in Whiteness: How White People Profit from Identity Politics.* Revised and expanded edition. Philadelphia: Temple University Press, 2006.

Littler, Jo, and Roshi Naidoo, eds. *The Politics of Heritage: The Legacies of "Race."* London: Routledge, 2005.

Lott, Eric. *Love and Theft: Blackface Minstrelsy and the American Working Class.* New York: Oxford University Press, 1993.

Martin, Waldo E. *The Mind of Frederick Douglass.* Chapel Hill: University of North Carolina Press, 1984.

Marx, Karl. "The Eighteenth Brumaire of Louis Bonaparte." In *Marx: Later Political Writings,* edited by Terrell Carver, 31–127. Cambridge: Cambridge University Press, 1996.

McAllister, Marvin Edward. *White People Do Not Know How to Behave at Entertainments Designed for Ladies & Gentlemen of Colour: William Brown's African & American Theater.* Chapel Hill: University of North Carolina Press, 2003.

McKivigan, John R., and Stanley Harrold, eds. *Antislavery Violence: Sectional, Racial, and Cultural Conflict in Antebellum America.* Knoxville: University of Tennessee Press, 1999.

McNamara, Brooks. *Day of Jubilee: The Great Age of Public Celebrations in New York, 1788–1909: Illustrated from the Collections of the Museum of the City of New York.* New Brunswick, N.J.: Rutgers University Press, 1997.

Meer, Sarah. *Uncle Tom Mania: Slavery, Minstrelsy, and Transatlantic Culture in the 1850s.* Athens: University of Georgia Press, 2005.

Melish, Joanne Pope. *Disowning Slavery: Gradual Emancipation and "Race" in New England, 1780–1860.* Ithaca, N.Y.: Cornell University Press, 1998.

Messer-Kruse, Timothy. *The Yankee International: Marxism and the American Reform Tradition, 1848–1876.* Chapel Hill: University of North Carolina Press, 1998.

Miller, Floyd John. *The Search for a Black Nationality: Black Emigration and Colonization, 1787–1863.* Urbana: University of Illinois Press, 1975.

Moran, Rachel F. *Interracial Intimacy: The Regulation of Race & Romance.* Chicago: University of Chicago Press, 2001.

Morrison, Michael A., and James Brewer Stewart, eds. *Race and the Early Republic: Racial Consciousness and Nation-Building in the Early Republic.* Lanham, Md.: Rowman, 2002.

Moten, Fred. *In the Break: The Aesthetics of the Black Radical Tradition.* Minneapolis: University of Minnesota Press, 2003.

Muñoz, José Esteban. "Cruising the Toilet: Leroi Jones/Amiri Baraka, Radical Black Traditions, and Queer Futurity." *GLQ: A Journal of Lesbian and Gay Studies* 13, no. 2–3 (2007): 353–67.

———. *Disidentifications: Queers of Color and the Performance of Politics.* Minneapolis: University of Minnesota Press, 1999.

Murison, David. "The Language of Burns." In *Critical Essays on Robert Burns,* edited by Donald A. Low, 54–70. London: Routledge, 1975.

Murphy, Kevin P. "Socrates in the Slums: Homoerotics, Gender, and Settlement House Reform." In *A Shared Experience: Men, Women, and the History of Gender,* edited by Laura McCall and Donald Yacovone, 273–96. New York: New York University Press, 1998.

Nealon, Christopher S. *Foundlings: Lesbian and Gay Historical Emotion before Stonewall.* Durham, N.C.: Duke University Press, 2001.

Negri, Antonio. *Insurgencies: Constituent Power and the Modern State.* Translated by Maurizia Boscagli. Minneapolis: University of Minnesota Press, 1999.

Nell, William Cooper. *The Colored Patriots of the American Revolution.* Boston: Wallicut, 1855. Reprint, New York: Arno, 1968.

———. *Property Qualification or No Property Qualification: A Few Facts from the Record of Patriotic Services of the Colored Men of New York During the Wars of 1776 and 1812, with a Compendium of Their Present Business and Property Statistics.* New York: Thomas Hamilton, 1860.

———. *Services of Colored Americans in the Wars of 1776 and 1812.* Boston: Prentiss, 1851.

Nelson, Dana. *National Manhood: Capitalist Citizenship and the Imagined Fraternity of White Men.* Durham, N.C.: Duke University Press, 1998.

Nyong'o, Tavia. "'The Black First': Crispus Attucks and William Cooper Nell." *Dublin Seminar for New England Folklife Annual Proceedings* (2003): 141–52.

———. "No Halvsies!" *American Quarterly* 59, no. 2 (2007): 459–66.

———. "Passing as Politics: Framing Black Political Performance." *Women and Performance,* no. 29 (2005): 53–78.

———. "Racial Kitsch and Black Performance." *Yale Journal of Criticism* 15, no. 2 (2002): 371–91.

Obama, Barack. *The Audacity of Hope: Thoughts on Reclaiming the American Dream.* New York: Crown, 2006.

———. *Dreams from My Father: A Story of Race and Inheritance.* New York: Times Books, 1995.

Oliver Bolokitten, pseud. *A Sojourn in the City of Amalgamation: In the Year of Our Lord 19—.* New York, 1835.

O'Malley, Michael. "Specie and Species: Race and the Money Question in Nineteenth-Century America." *American Historical Review* 99, no. 2 (1994): 369–95.

Pabst, Naomi. "Blackness/Mixedness: Contestations over Crossing Signs." *Cultural Critique,* no. 54 (2003): 178–212.

Palumbo-Liu, David. "Theory and the Subject of Asian American Studies." *Amerasia Journal* 21, no. 1–2 (1995): 58–59.

Parker, Andrew, and Eve Kosofsky Sedgwick, eds. *Performativity and Performance.* New York: Routledge, 1995.

Paulin, Diana. "Acting Out Miscegenation." In *African American Performance and Theater History: A Critical Reader,* edited by Harry J. Elam and David Krasner, 251–70. Oxford: Oxford University Press, 2001.

———. "Representing Forbidden Desire: Interracial Unions, Surrogacy, and Performance." *Theatre Journal* 49, no. 4 (1997): 417–39.

Pellegrini, Ann. *Performance Anxieties: Staging Psychoanalysis, Staging Race.* New York: Routledge, 1996.

Pennington, James W. C. *A Text Book of the Origin and History, &C. &C. Of the Colored People.* Hartford: Skinner, 1841.

Perez-Torres, Rafael. *Mestizaje: Critical Uses of Race in Chicano Culture.* Minneapolis: University of Minnesota Press, 2006.

Pettinger, Alasdair. "Send Back the Money: Douglass and the Free Church of Scotland." In *Liberating Sojourn: Frederick Douglass and Transatlantic Reform,* edited by Alan J. Rice and Martin Crawford, 31–55. Athens: University of Georgia Press, 1999.

Plato. *The Banquet.* Translated by Percy Bysshe Shelley. Provincetown, Mass.: Pagan, 2001.

Preston, Dickson J. *Young Frederick Douglass: The Maryland Years.* Baltimore: Johns Hopkins University Press, 1980.

Rael, Patrick. *Black Identity and Black Protest in the Antebellum North.* Chapel Hill: University of North Carolina Press, 2002.

Rawls, John. *A Theory of Justice.* Cambridge, Mass.: Harvard University Press, 1971.

Rediker, Marcus. "The Revenge of Crispus Attucks, or The Atlantic Challenge to American Labor History." *Labor* 1, no. 4 (2004): 35–44.

Reid-Pharr, Robert F. *Conjugal Union: The Body, the House, and the Black American.* New York: Oxford University Press, 1999.

Remond, Sarah Parker. *The Negroes & Anglo-Africans as Freedmen and Soldiers.* London: Emily Faithfull, 1864.

Richards, Leonard L. *Gentlemen of Property and Standing: Anti-Abolition Mobs in Jacksonian America.* London: Oxford University Press, 1971.

Roach, Joseph. *Cities of the Dead: Circum-Atlantic Performance.* New York: Columbia University Press, 1996.

———. "The Great Hole of History: Liturgical Silence in Beckett, Osofisan, and Parks." *South Atlantic Quarterly* 100, no. 1 (2001): 307–17.

Robinson, Cedric J. *An Anthropology of Marxism.* Aldershot, U.K.: Ashgate, 2001.

Roediger, David R. *The Wages of Whiteness: Race and the Making of the American Working Class.* London: Verso, 1991.

Romano, Renee Christine. *Race Mixing: Black-White Marriage in Postwar America*. Cambridge, Mass.: Harvard University Press, 2003.

Ross, Marlon Bryan. *Manning the Race: Reforming Black Men in the Jim Crow Era*. New York: New York University Press, 2004.

Ruggles, David. *The "Extinguisher" Extinguished*. New York: David Ruggles, 1834.

Ruggles, Jeffrey. *The Unboxing of Henry Brown*. Richmond: Library of Virginia, 2003.

Saks, Eva. "Representing Miscegenation Law." *Raritan* 8, no. 2 (1988): 39–69.

Samuels, Shirley. "Miscegenated America: The Civil War." *American Literary History* 9, no. 3 (1997): 482–501.

Santa Ana, Jeffrey. "Affect-Identity: The Emotions of Assimilation, Multiraciality, and Asian American Subjectivity." In *Asian North American Identities: Beyond the Hyphen,* edited by Eleanor Ty and Donald C. Goellnicht, 15–42. Bloomington: Indiana University Press, 2004.

Sappol, Michael. *A Traffic of Dead Bodies: Anatomy and Embodied Social Identity in Nineteenth-Century America*. Princeton, N.J.: Princeton University Press, 2002.

Saxton, Alexander. *The Rise and Fall of the White Republic: Class Politics and Mass Culture in Nineteenth-Century America*. London: Verso, 2003.

Schechner, Richard. *Between Theater and Anthropology*. Philadelphia: University of Pennsylvania Press, 1985.

Sedgwick, Eve Kosofsky. *Touching, Feeling: Affect, Pedagogy, Performativity*. Durham, N.C.: Duke University Press, 2003.

Sedgwick, Eve Kosofsky, and Adam Frank. "Shame in the Cybernetic Fold: Reading Silvan Tomkins." In *Touching, Feeling: Affect, Pedagogy, Performativity,* edited by Eve Kosofsky Sedgwick, 93–121. Durham, N.C.: Duke University Press, 2003.

Sellers, Charles Grier. *The Market Revolution: Jacksonian America, 1815–1846*. New York: Oxford University Press, 1991.

Seshadri-Crooks, Kalpana. *Desiring Whiteness: A Lacanian Analysis of Race*. London: Routledge, 2000.

Sexton, Jared. *Amalgamation Schemes: Antiblackness and the Critique of Multiracialism*. Minneapolis: University of Minnesota Press, 2008.

———. "The Consequences of Race Mixture: Racialised Barriers and the Politics of Desire." *Social Identities* 9, no. 2 (2003): 241–75.

———. "There Is No Interracial Sexual Relationship: Race, Love, and Sexuality in the Multiracial Movement." In *The Problems of Resistance: Studies in Alternate Political Cultures,* edited by Steve Martinot and Joy James, 135–54. Amherst, N.Y.: Humanity, 2001.

Sims, Lowery Stokes, Kathleen Hulser, and Cynthia R. Copeland. *Lega-*

cies: Contemporary Artists Reflect on Slavery. New York: New-York Historical Society, 2006.

Sinha, Manisha. "Coming of Age: The Historiography of Black Abolitionism." In *Prophets of Protest: Reconsidering the History of American Abolitionism,* edited by Timothy McCarthy and John Stauffer, 23–38. New York: New Press, 2006.

Smith, James McCune. *The Works of James McCune Smith: Black Intellectual and Abolitionist.* Edited by John Stauffer. New York: Oxford University Press, 2006.

Smith, John David, ed. *The American Colonization Society and Emigration: Solutions to "The Negro Problem."* New York: Garland, 1993.

Smith, Robert P. "William Cooper Nell: Crusading Black Abolitionist." *Journal of Negro History* 55, no. 3 (1970): 182–99.

Smith-Rosenberg, Carroll. *Disorderly Conduct: Visions of Gender in Victorian America.* New York: Oxford University Press, 1985.

Sollors, Werner. *Neither Black nor White and Yet Both: Thematic Explorations of Interracial Literature.* New York: Oxford University Press, 1997.

Spencer, John Michael. *The New Colored People: The Mixed-Race Movement in America.* New York: New York University Press, 2000.

Stallybrass, Peter, and Allon White. *The Politics and Poetics of Transgression.* Ithaca, N.Y.: Cornell University Press, 1986.

Stauffer, John. *The Black Hearts of Men: Radical Abolitionists and the Transformation of Race.* Cambridge: Harvard University Press, 2001.

Stephens, Gregory. *On Racial Frontiers: The New Culture of Frederick Douglass, Ralph Ellison, and Bob Marley.* Cambridge: Cambridge University Press, 1999.

Stevens, Charles Emery. *Anthony Burns: A History.* Boston: John P. Jewett, 1856.

Stewart, Kathleen. *Ordinary Affects.* Durham, N.C.: Duke University Press, 2007.

Stewart, Maria W. *Productions of Mrs. Maria W. Stewart, Presented to the First African Baptist Church & Society.* Boston, 1835.

Stockton, Kathryn Bond. *Beautiful Bottom, Beautiful Shame: Where "Black" Meets "Queer."* Durham, N.C.: Duke University Press, 2006.

Stowe, Harriet Beecher. *Uncle Tom's Cabin.* Edited by Elizabeth Ammons, Norton Critical Edition. New York: Norton, 1994.

Strausbaugh, John. *Black Like You: Blackface, Whiteface, Insult & Imitation in American Popular Culture.* New York: Penguin, 2006.

Streeter, Carolyn. "Ambiguous Bodies: Black/White Women in Cultural Representations." In *The Multiracial Experience: Racial Borders as the New Frontier,* edited by Maria P. Root, 305–20. London: Sage, 1996.

Sweet, Leonard I. *Black Images of America, 1784–1870.* New York: Norton, 1976.

Teed, Paul E. "Racial Nationalism and Its Challengers: Theodore Parker, John Rock, and the Antislavery Movement." *Civil War History* 41, no. 2 (1995): 142–60.

Thompson, Nato, ed. *Ahistoric Occasion: Artists Making History.* North Adams: Massachusetts Museum of Contemporary Art, 2006.

Villard, Oswald Garrison. *John Brown: A Biography, 1800–1859.* Garden City, N.Y.: Doubleday, 1929.

Virno, Paolo. *A Grammar of the Multitude: For an Analysis of Contemporary Forms of Life.* Cambridge, Mass.: Semiotext(e), 2003.

Volosinov, V. N. *Marxism and the Philosophy of Language.* Translated by Ladislav Matejka and I. E. Titunik. New York: Seminar, 1973.

Walcott, Rinaldo. "Beyond the 'Nation Thing': Black Studies, Cultural Studies and Diaspora Discourse (or the Post-Black Studies Moment)." In *Decolonizing the Academy: African Diaspora Studies,* edited by Carol Boyce Davis, Meredith Gadsby, Charles Peterson and Henrietta Williams, 107–24. Trenton, N.J.: African World Press, 2004.

Waldstreicher, David. *In the Midst of Perpetual Fetes: The Making of American Nationalism, 1776–1820.* Chapel Hill: University of North Carolina Press, 1997.

Walker, David. *Walker's Appeal, in Four Articles; Together with a Preamble, to the Coloured Citizens of the World, but in Particular, and Very Expressly, to Those of the United States of America, Written in Boston, State of Massachusetts, September 28, 1829.* Boston: David Walker, 1830.

Walker, Peter. *Moral Choices: Memory, Desire, and Imagination in Nineteenth-Century American Abolition.* Baton Rouge: Louisiana State University Press, 1978.

Wallace, Maurice O. *Constructing the Black Masculine: Identity and Ideality in African American Men's Literature and Culture, 1775–1995.* Durham, N.C.: Duke University Press, 2002.

Walters, Ronald G. *The Antislavery Appeal: American Abolitionism after 1830.* New York: Norton, 1984.

———. "The Erotic South: Civilization and Sexuality in American Abolitionism." *American Quarterly* 25, no. 2 (1973): 177–201.

Washington-Williams, Essie Mae, and William Stadiem. *Dear Senator: A Memoir by the Daughter of Strom Thurmond.* New York: Regan, 2005.

Wehr, Hans, and J. Milton Cowan. *A Dictionary of Modern Written Arabic.* Ithaca, N.Y.: Cornell University Press, 1961.

Weierman, Karen Woods. *One Nation, One Blood: Interracial Marriage in American Fiction, Scandal, and Law, 1820–1870.* Amherst: University of Massachusetts Press, 2005.

Welke, Barbara. *Recasting American Liberty: Gender, Race, Law, and the Railroad Revolution, 1865–1920*. New York: Cambridge University Press, 2001.

———. "When All the Women Were White, and All the Blacks Were Men: Gender, Class, Race, and the Road to Plessy, 1855–1914." *Law and History Review* 13, no. 2 (1995): 261–316.

Werbner, Pnina. "The Limits of Cultural Hybridity: On Ritual Monsters, Poetic Licence and Contested Postcolonial Purifications." *Journal of the Royal Anthropological Institute* 7, no. 1 (2001): 133–52.

Werbner, Pnina, and Tariq Modood, eds. *Debating Cultural Hybridity: Multi-Cultural Identities and the Politics of Anti-Racism*. London: Zed Books, 1997.

Wesley, Dorothy Porter. "Integration versus Separatism: William Cooper Nell's Role in the Struggle for Equality." In *Courage and Conscience: Black and White Abolitionists in Boston*, edited by Donald M. Jacobs, 207–24. Bloomington: Indiana University Press, 1993.

Wesley, Dorothy Porter, and Constance Porter Uzelac, eds. *William Cooper Nell, Nineteenth-Century African American Abolitionist, Historian, Integrationist: Selected Writings from 1832–1874*. Baltimore: Black Classic Press, 2002.

White, Shane, and Graham White. *Stylin': African-American Expressive Culture from Its Beginnings to the Zoot Suit*. Ithaca, N.Y.: Cornell University Press, 1999.

Wills, Garry. *Lincoln at Gettysburg: The Words That Remade America*. New York: Simon & Schuster, 1992.

Wood, Marcus. *Blind Memory: Visual Representations of Slavery in England and America, 1780–1865*. New York: Routledge, 2000.

Wroth, L. Kinvin, and Hiller B. Zobel. *Legal Papers of John Adams*. 3 vols. Cambridge, Mass.: Harvard University Press, 1965.

Yates, Edmund, ed. *The Life and Correspondence of Charles Mathews, the Elder, Comedian, by Mrs. Mathews*. London: Routledge, 1860.

Yellin, Jean Fagan. *Women and Sisters: The Antislavery Feminists in American Culture*. New Haven, Conn.: Yale University Press, 1989.

———. *Harriet Jacobs: A Life*. New York: Basic, 2003.

Young, Harvey. "The Black Body as Souvenir in American Lynching." *Theatre Journal* 57, no. 4 (2005): 639–57.

Young, Jock. "The Subterranean World of Play." In *The Subcultures Reader*, edited by Ken Gelder, 148–56. 1971. London: Routledge, 2005.

Young, R. J. "The Political Economy of Black Abolitionists." *Afro-Americans in New York Life and History* 18, no. 1 (1994): 47–71.

Zack, Naomi. *Race and Mixed Race*. Philadelphia: Temple University Press, 1993.

Ziv, Alon. *Breeding between the Lines: Why Interracial People Are Healthier and More Attractive*. Fort Lee, N.J.: Barricade Books, 2006.

Žižek, Slavoj. *The Parallax View*. Cambridge, Mass.: MIT Press, 2006.

———. *The Sublime Object of Ideology*. London: Verso, 1989.

———. *Tarrying with the Negative: Kant, Hegel, and the Critique of Ideology*. Durham, N.C.: Duke University Press, 1993.

Archives and Collections

Accessible Archives

American Antiquarian Society

American Memory, Library of Congress

Anti-Slavery Papers, Boston Public Library

British Library

Black Abolitionist Papers

Frederick Douglass Papers, Library of Congress

Glasgow University Library

Harvard Theatre Collection

Wendell Phillips Paper, Houghton Library, Harvard University

Library Company of Philadelphia

Mitchell Library, Glasgow University

New York Central College Collection, Cortland County Historical Society

New-York Historical Society

Yale University, Beinecke Rare Book and Manuscript Library

Nineteenth-Century Newspapers and Magazines

Anglo-African Magazine

Anti-Slavery Reporter

Colored American

Emancipator and Journal of Public Morals

Frederick Douglass' Paper

Freedom's Journal

Harper's Weekly

Liberator

London Times

Mirror of Liberty

National Anti-Slavery Standard

New York Times

New York World

Weekly Anglo-African

Index

abolition, 14, 19, 24–26, 29, 43, 51–52, 54–74, 77–79, 81–82, 85, 90–94, 99–101, 104, 112–13, 122–26, 132, 156–57, 160, 172, 174, 196n47; and amalgamation, 74, 172, 174; black, 19, 54–74, 85, 90–92, 99–101, 104, 123–26, 132, 156–57, 160, 172; figurations of the mulatto in, 51–52, 61; and marriage across the color line, 26; minstrel response to, 122; moral panic as response to, 71–73, 122; performance culture of, 66, 92–94, 112–13, 126, 132, 196n47; satire/parody of, 14, 24–26, 29, 69–70, 77–78, 81–82, 90–92, 122

Abrogation of the Seventh Commandment, by the American Churches (Ruggles), 73

Ackerman, Rudolph, 79

Adams, John, 47, 49–50, 61

Adorno, Theodor, 149

affect: and amalgamation, 74; and history, 16–17, 137, 139–42, 149–50, 158–60; and hybridity, 15, 184n30; of parody, 28;
and racial governmentality, 76, 87–90, 92–93, 101, 119, 158–60; and reason, 30, 92–93. *See also* sentimentality; shame

Africa, 2–5, 69, 86, 90, 124, 131, 155

agalma, 177–79, 202n26

Agamben, Giorgio, 39, 47, 52–54

agency, hybrid. *See* hybridity

Agnew, Jean–Christophe, 115

Allen, William G., 157, 200n45

amalgamation: and democracy, 83; derivation of, 74, 192n19; as metaphor, 74–75, 83–85, 124; and metallurgy, 74, 124; miscegenation, contrast with, 22–26, 31, 74–75, 84; practical, 14, 29, 74, 98–99; and racial governmentality, 75–76, waltz, 81–83. *See also* miscegenation

ambivalence, 29, 131, 141. *See also* hybridity

Anderson, Benedict, 11, 37

animality, 87

anomaly, 51–54

anthropodermic bibliopegy, 34–35

anxiety, 14, 30

archive, the, 7–9, 16, 19, 24, 30,

Tavia Nyong'o is a cultural historian in the Department of Performance Studies, New York University. His research interests include black performance, visual culture, and gender and sexuality studies. His writing has appeared in the *Yale Journal of Criticism, Radical History Review, Social Text,* and the *Nation.* He can be reached at http://www.tavianyongo.com.